Dancing the
DREAM

ALSO BY JAMIE SAMS

Medicine Cards™ (with David Carson)

Sacred Path Cards™

The Sacred Path Workbook

Other Council Fires Were Here Before Ours (with Twylah Nitsch)

The Thirteen Original Clan Mothers

Earth Medicine

JAMIE SAMS

Dancing the
DREAM

THE SEVEN SACRED PATHS
OF HUMAN TRANSFORMATION

HarperOne
An Imprint of HarperCollins*Publishers*

HarperOne

HarperCollins books may be purchased for educational, business, or sales promo-
tional use. For information, please e-mail the Special Markets Department at
SPsales@harpercollins.com.

HarperCollins Web site: http://www.harpercollins.com

HarperCollins®, 📚®, and HarperOne™ are trademarks of HarperCollins Publishers.

FIRST HARPERCOLLINS PAPERBACK EDITION PUBLISHED IN 1999

Library of Congress Cataloging-in-Publication Data

Sams, Jamie
     Dancing the dream : the seven sacred paths of human transformation / Jamie
Sams. — 1st ed.
     Includes index.
     ISBN: 978–0–06–251514–8
     1. Spiritual life. 2. Dreams. 3. Self-realization—Religious aspects—
Miscellanea. 4. Indians of North America—Religion—Miscellanea. 5. Medicine
wheels. 6. Conduct of life. 7. Success. I. Title.
BL624.S226   1998
299'.74—dc21   97–52607

23 24 25 26 27 LBC 45 44 43 42 41

Contents

Acknowledgments

I WOULD like to thank my agent, Katinka Matson, who during my personal rites of passage on these paths cared enough to listen to me with her heart. Words cannot express how much your support means to me.

I would also like to thank my Cherokee tribal sisters; Rita Coolidge, Priscilla Coolidge, and Pauline Satterfield for filling my life with the music of your *Walela* album. Your songs took me home and re-instilled my spirit with our Cherokee pride, giving me the strength to let my heart sing once more.

I would also like to thank all the readers who have supported my work and all the human beings who are discovering that they are vessels of Great Mystery's creative force and infinite love.

Thank you for being!

Author's Note

THE ancient Native American wisdom of the Crystal Skull and White Buffalo Dreaming Societies, both of which I have been a part of, has been held in secret for centuries. These two Dreaming Societies are comprised of Dreamers, Seers, and healers from many of the tribes from Mexico and a few members from southern tribes in the United States. Our teachings are sacred, and due to the prophecy we have held for centuries, we knew that the information regarding the seven paths of initiation and transformation was not to be revealed until the nine hells on the Mayan calendar had ended. Since the late 1500s, with the coming of the conquistadores, practicing the spirituality of our ancestors was punishable by death. Native Americans north and south of the border between the United States and Mexico were forced to keep spiritual ceremonies secret and our ancient wisdom out of the hands of those who would misuse that information. In the United States, the ceremonies of Native Americans were officially banned for over one hundred years. In Mexico, the torture rendered by church officials and political regimes was present until 1989 when the first intertribal Native American ceremony was allowed to be held in public. Finally, the nine hells ended in January of 1997; now it is time to share the wisdom that my teachers taught me.

The information contained in this book is a marriage of the secret initiations that I experienced and my observations in the personal journey that evolved from those rites of passage. I have not divulged the details of any ceremonies held sacred by the Dreaming Societies because they apply only to certain people from the tradition of the Southern

Seers. I have endeavored to draw the map of consciousness that applies to every person on every path. I was never told how the gates of consciousness that were opened in my initiations would manifest in my life, and I have encountered far more than I expected along the way. I am deeply grateful for the strict instruction I received, which enabled me to remember each facet of the journey and to offer the wisdom of my teachers and my observations to each of you.

I would also like to offer a gentle reminder for readers and friends who have missed huge amounts of information in my previous books because they did not read the introductions. These loving but impatient friends have told me that they skipped my introductions in order to get to "all the good stuff." This book will not have an introduction, as I have put all the needed material in the chapters, creating a step-by-step foundation. If you want to understand the whole enchilada, please don't sabotage yourselves, unless you happen to want to learn the hard way, like I did!

—Jamie
The Resident Trickster

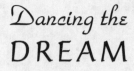

Dancing the
DREAM

CHAPTER 1
▼▼▼▼▼▼▼▼▼▼▼▼▼▼▼▼▼▼▼▼▼▼▼▼▼▼

The silver threads of the Dream Weave are fed by imagination and inspiration. They form the paths that take us safely to the heart of the invisible wonders that are ever-present in physical life.

—Berta Broken Bow

▲▲
DANCING THE DREAM

Where are the dances of Oneness,
That I knew before my birth?
Did I surrender my wholeness
In order to walk the Earth?

Did I choose forgetting
In order to make life real?
Did I inhabit a human body
So I could learn how to feel?

I am here to dance the dream
In my sacred human form.
To celebrate my uniqueness
And ask no other to conform.

Dancing through life's lessons,
I will learn to move with grace,
While I dream of remembering
The potential of the human race.

—Jamie Sams

Each Life Is a Sacred Path

EVERY human being who walks the Earth Mother has an individual sacred path through life. That sacred path is created by the weaving of many tangible and intangible threads, which connect all of our emotions, dreams, thoughts, and experiences. The spirit's invisible thread of life force unfurls at birth and carries us through the twists and turns of growing up and learning about life on planet Earth. Our lives will change directions many times as experiences urge us to grow. Every decision we make and every shift in our perceptions can alter the course of our path through life and bring new experiences or expanded horizons. Every time we alter our priorities, we change our path. Every time we allow ourselves to use our imagination, we change our view of reality. Every time we decide to change direction, we design and redesign our lifestyles, habits, priorities, personal needs, and goals.

If you are alive, you are on a sacred path. In your life you have followed a multitude of paths with different directions, and yet all those paths dovetail, creating the one life path that represents your unique journey through the physical world. Becoming aware that each of us also travels an intangible or spiritual path is the beginning of the awakening processes found on the seven sacred paths of human initiation and transformation.

Some people go through life believing that there is no scheme, no rhyme or reason, to the workings of the universe. They see no connections between themselves, other life forms, and the Creator—until some life event forces them to go beyond that unconscious condition. How and when life beckons us to change is different for every individual.

Many people grow and mature, endure heartache, experience personal breakthroughs, and still do not consciously embrace the paths of transformation.

BEGINNING THE SEVEN SACRED PATHS OF HUMAN TRANSFORMATION

The seven paths of transformation are never forced upon us; they present themselves as opportunities. We may feel that we are at the mercy of life's events, but even amid tragedy, fears, or loss, we are given choices and the opportunity to wake up. We can deny the existence of these alternate paths of understanding and remain safely unaware of them, or we can risk looking deeper. When the light goes on and we embrace the awakening process, we start to remember the things that our spirits have always known. As we become more conscious, we become aware of the divine significance or spiritual purpose that we carry within us. Doors begin to open, and we start to perceive the spirit or life force that animates our universe. Only then do we awaken and realize exactly how our lives are intricately woven within the whole.

The awakening process allows us to become aware of a bigger picture. Each part of the seven sacred paths of human transformation allows us to expand beyond our former tunnel vision. There are no lesser or greater paths through life. We have free will and are allowed either to look beyond the accepted horizons or to remain on a life path that suits our views of reality. The seen and unseen realms are of equal importance. Becoming aware of the intangible forces that shape the human experience adds innumerable possibilities to our life experiences. If we choose to explore the intangible realms of consciousness, what my teachers call the Dream Weave, we discover new layers of the life force found in spirit, thought, emotion, dreams, feelings, aspirations, creativity, and intent. Our budding awareness of the intangible aspects of human life adds new dimensions of understanding and wisdom, allowing us to see how divine consciousness intertwines with every aspect of physical life.

If you choose to embrace these paths, you will remember that before your birth your spirit, your spark of life, was exhaled from the Creator, the Great Mystery, God. That spark of life came from the Creator's Fire of Creation and was attached to an invisible thread of spiritual energy that sent you forth into the universe and animated the physical body you inhabit with life force. Embracing these paths, you will remember your purpose for being, your role in life, and how to transform any part of your human experience that keeps you from becoming your potential. The challenges that you face during the awakening process and transformation are your personal initiations, marking your passage of change.

On the first path, the East Direction on the Medicine Wheel, we become illuminated and begin to see clearly that there is a purpose for our lives. We embrace a new form of clarity, which takes us beyond our former "What is life offering me?" perspective. On the second path, the South Direction, we learn how to rise above childish human reactions, compulsions, and unhealthy emotions. The third path, the West Direction, teaches us how to heal our pasts, our bodies, and our self-esteem. On the fourth path, the North Direction, we learn how to share the wisdom we have gained as well as how to live with compassionate, nonjudgmental, open hearts. The fifth path is the Above Direction, where we embrace the unseen worlds of spirit, the heavenly realms, the unknown parts of the universe, and the intangible forces in Creation. The sixth path is the Below Direction, where we learn how to perceive the unseen forces in the natural world and the connections to spirit existing in all living things, and we learn how to bring our own spirits fully into our human bodies. On the seventh path, the Within or NOW Direction, we learn how to gain access to all life in our universe within our own human body and to walk through life in a state of full spiritual awareness, without any separation or judgment.

UNIVERSAL TRUTHS APPLY TO ALL OF US

Other cultures and philosophies have outlined these same seven paths of human initiation. The map I was taught is from one Native American perspective called the tradition of the Southern Seers, but all cultures and religions have reflected many of the same truths from their individual perspectives.

In the Catholic tradition, seven sacred sacraments are used to embody the faith and to develop the attributes and compassion of Christlike understanding. In the Hindu and Buddhist traditions, seven energy centers called chakras within the human body allow the life force and spiritual energy to travel through a person, bringing enlightened states of awareness. The Hindu and Buddhist traditions contain different practices and spiritual disciplines, but both acknowledge the personal spiritual journey that allows a person to attain a sense of wholeness.

In the Muslim tradition, Hagar, concubine of Abraham, was cast out into the desert with her son, Ishmael, when Abraham's wife, Sarah, became jealous of her. Hagar had accepted Jehovah, the God of Abraham, while living with the tribes of Israel. When she ran out of water in the desert and Ishmael was near death, Hagar called upon Jehovah. God appeared to her and told her to have faith and that she and the child would be saved. God commanded Hagar to run between two hills in the desert seven times in order to show her faith in the one God. At the end of the seventh path, a spring came bubbling up from the desert between the legs of her son, where he lay in the sand, creating an oasis. Hagar lived there with her son and taught the people in passing caravans who came for water about her miracle of faith. The story of Hagar's seven paths of faith formed the beginning foundations of the Islamic religion and gave an overview of the seven paths Muslims follow to know Allah or God.

In the Jewish tradition, the number seven is very important. In Hebrew, seven is shivah. Jehovah or God created the world in six days, and on the seventh day he rested. The seventh day is the Jewish Sabbath or Shabbat, which has its root in the word *seven*. Shabbat begins at sunset on Friday night, which is considered to be the beginning of Saturday by the Jewish people. During that sundown, the feminine aspect of God descends upon the people. From then until the following sunset the people worship, pray, and rest, doing nothing that would keep them from being receptive to the feminine aspect of God, which they consider to be spirit. When a person dies, there are seven days of grieving, called sitting shivah, which also stems from the word *seven*. These end with the family going to the cemetery to release the loved one's spirit. The first harvest of any type of fruit or vegetable is marked with a holiday called Shabuoth, which is the plural of the Hebrew word for a week composed of seven days. The sacred holiday of Passover always falls in the seventh month of the Jewish calendar.

In the Seneca and Cherokee spiritual traditions, the seven sacred directions on the Medicine Wheel represent the seven paths of human initiation. The first six directions are represented by the East path, the

South path, the West path, the North path, the Above path, and the Below path. In the Seneca spiritual tradition the seventh path is called the Within path; in the Cherokee tradition it is called the NOW. Each of the seven paths contains particular focal points and life lessons. The human maturity process is not linear, because life is a circle or wheel, reminding us that wherever we go and whatever we experience, the self is still present when we arrive, bringing us home to ourselves and all that we have become during our learning process.

These various interpretations of the circle of life and its spiritual sacredness offer humankind many ways of understanding the map of human growth and spiritual potential. Metaphorically, we are given seven paths to fully discover all parts of this beautifully diverse Creation and our human places within the whole. Because people respond to spirituality in different ways depending upon their Sacred Points of View, each spiritual tradition has different ways of marking the seven stages of growth and discovery, which are the human rites of passage.

SIMULTANEOUS PATHS OF CHANGE

The seven paths of human transformation are wheels of experience reflecting the manner in which human beings learn how to use life force. These paths coexist simultaneously. They are not linear, and each individual embraces lessons on several paths at the same time.

Imagine a person sitting at a desk, trying to balance a checkbook, answer the phone with three lines blinking, write down notes from those calls, and find a file needed by a co-worker who is hovering over the desk: you have the picture of how human beings operate on many levels at once. We use certain percentages of our attention and our life force to accomplish many tasks at once. Yes, we can learn how to do many things at once when we embrace life's initiations. We can be actively involved with our family lives, our jobs, our dreams, and our growth processes at the same time. We can use our life force to accomplish the rigors of daily routines, explore and heal our personal issues, and make a relationship work, and at the same time we can be experiencing fleeting moments of unexplainable insights or paranormal phenomena.

More life force is freed up as we conquer life's challenges and heal our past issues. This additional life force gives us energy to explore new areas, and life becomes an adventure. This is not to say that the adventure is not harrowing at times; life can be nerve-racking as well as unbelievably fulfilling. How we learn to use the life force that we have available determines how many separate paths of initiation we can embrace simultaneously. Spiritual evolution is an individual growth process.

The natural progression of human development usually requires that we learn one skill and then focus on the next skill we will need to embrace in order to become expert in any given area. If we do not have food to eat, we don't give a hoot about what our dreams mean. If we are trying to heal the wounds of sexual or physical abuse, we must apply much determination, focus, and energy, and we might not have enough extra life force available to explore life beyond our need to survive. On these paths of initiation, we still follow this natural process as we develop our skills; however, the way we need to experience our personal lessons determines which lessons or skills we embrace simultaneously.

There is one exception to this multiple-path scenario. It is possible to gain access to certain parts of the fifth through seventh paths while most of our attention is still focused on developing the skills of the first through fourth paths, but we cannot fully complete those latter paths until we can command enough energy to consciously explore the unseen worlds of the Dream Weave. For that kind of spiritual expertise to be possible, certain physiological changes must take place within the human body. For the most part, those changes do not occur until we have fully developed the skills of the first through third paths and most of the skills of the fourth path. Many of the experiences on the fifth through seventh paths are not usually available to us until we have the life force needed to approach those levels of awareness.

ARE ALL SEVEN PATHS FOR ME?

I want to stress that it is not necessary for everyone to complete all seven paths. Transformation is a personal journey that is directed by an individual's desire to explore the various paths. Not everyone has the desire to gain access to the unseen realms of awareness within the universe, and there is no reason that anyone should ever embrace a path that does not suit his or her personal needs. If you find your fulfillment in life on the first three paths of initiation, that too is perfect. Or if you choose to embrace the unseen worlds, developing the skills presented on all seven paths, that is perfect. In both cases, the life lessons embraced are suited to the divine intent held by your individual spirit or soul.

There are no greater or lesser human spirits. Every soul streams forth from the Creator, knowing what it has come to experience long before it animates a human body. It is only in the human birth process that the forgetting occurs. As we walk through our lives, we remember the soul's inner knowing and integrate that inner knowing inside our physical bodies. No human being can presume to know every purpose of another person's role in life or all of the lessons that another soul has come to learn by taking a human body. We can choose to remember for ourselves what we want to know about our soul's path through human existence. We will remember to the degree that we have the desire and the persistence needed to develop the skills required on any path that we choose to embrace.

If we choose not to embark on these paths, nothing is lost and nothing will remain unfinished. We will continue to learn about those invisible realms when our spirit departs our human form, when our physical body dies. The wheel of life force and the cycles of transformation are eternal. The human spirit cannot be destroyed, because it is a part of the Great Mystery. Our souls or spirits are pure energy. We can change the forms that energy takes, but energy itself cannot be destroyed. Every soul will eventually experience all seven paths of initiation, but *how* and *when* those paths are experienced is always determined by the individual spirit.

One of my teachers once said to me, "If you choose to embrace these paths, know that you will never be the same again." I would like to say to every reader, if you choose to pick up the gauntlet that was placed within your reach, you will be awakened to the fact that human life is the ultimate initiation and that by healing separation, humans discover their places within the infinite wholeness that the Great Mystery embodies in our universe. Embracing the journey of these seven sacred paths is the quest of a courageous spiritual warrior who seeks to understand the mysteries of the unknown, the unspoken languages of the animals, the healing qualities of the plants, the spiritual messages offered in the natural world, the interwoven patterns of the stars, the sweetness of the angelic realms, the aliveness of the universe, the touch of divine intervention, the inner peace of the spirit, and the infinite wholeness that comes from moving beyond the limiting human concepts of separation.

The gift of taking this warrior's journey is that we no longer fear death or separation or aloneness, and we realize that nothing in the universe is outside of us. We emerge from the seven paths in wholeness, and we continue to walk through our physical lives as fully awakened human beings. We come to understand the circular nature of life, transformation, death, and rebirth within the spiraling circle that is eternally unfolding. The spirit is infinite, and walking the seven paths instills that spiritual aliveness in our human bodies. We embrace every part of human life with the divine grace that we learn to accumulate as we come full circle, approaching life from the multiple viewpoints of wholeness that we have encountered during our transformation process.

THE DREAM WEAVE

Imagine a road map or blueprint of lines of energy connecting all things; you would be visualizing the Dream Weave. The colors and textures of the intersecting lines of energy differ according to the individual viewing them, because each person has a different perspective on life. For centuries, our adept Native American Dreamers and Seers have been aware of this energetic web connecting all matter, energy, space, and time. Physicists have called the elementary particles or the connecting energy between atoms *gluons*. The Southern Seers see these elementary particles as forming a web of energy connecting the seen and unseen worlds of our universe. Our ancient legends say that Grandmother Spider wove the web of the universe, connecting all creativity and life and instilling the Great Mystery's creative principle in all things. Native American Ancestors, who were Seers and Dreamers, perceived Grandmother Spider weaving the web of the universe to show us the interrelatedness of all things. The Southern Seers perceive the web of energy as made of Spirit or divine life force. We begin to see and feel the energy web of the universe when we heal our fears and release old wounds, lifting the veils of separation that were created by how we previously viewed the world.

The Dream Weave is made of divine streams of consciousness and life force as well as nonphysical things that humans create, such as feelings, thoughts, inspiration, opinions, judgments, imagination, dreams, aspirations, intentions, and pure creativity. All these elements contain energy, but we do not see them as physical objects. We can perceive these elements when we experience them in ourselves; then, they are real to us. Few of us, however, realize that the human-directed unseen energies have created mental, emotional, and spiritual webs of interactive life force influencing all that we know of the physical realms.

The Dream Weave is a web of our combined human creative energy interacting with the life force contained in every atom in Creation and encompassing everything in our universe. Before this energy web takes on physical characteristics or form, it is created by our feelings, thoughts, and viewpoints, which contain energy. Every time we act, or every time we react to something that occurs in our lives, a thought, feeling, viewpoint, or judgment is present. Those thoughts have a life force of their own and directly influence how we live. When we change what we think, how we feel, or what opinions we hold, our experience of life changes too. The Dream Weave responds to the changes we make in ourselves and offers us new opportunities every time we open our perceptions to new possibilities, changing the habits that could have kept us stuck in a rut.

Energy is needed to achieve any goal in life, but few people understand that they misuse energy every time they waste it on worry, negativity, or gossip. People have not been taught that they can move energy or gather the energy they need from the Earth Mother, the Creator, and the universe. Every physical object contains energy. Every unseen thought and feeling also contains energy in the form of emotion. We learn how to follow paths of transformation by acknowledging the energy we use or misuse through our personal behaviors. Refocusing that energy in a positive way takes us beyond our lackluster behaviors, which leak precious reserves of energy, and into new transformative levels of life's experiences. To discover and properly use that universal life force or energy, we must understand how the Dream Weave works.

Most people do not realize that they direct their thoughts and feelings into the world. The classic cartoon of a character walking around with a black cloud over his or her head shows why we tend to avoid a person who is emitting anger or negativity. That anger is felt by others, even though it is not a physical thing. The person carrying the black cloud may wonder why others are avoiding him or her. If that person is directing envy, jealousy, or anger toward others, the effect can be as

potent as slugging a person in the stomach. As seen in the Dream
Weave, the negative energy of those directed emotions implode on the
sender and penetrate the Sacred Space or energy field of the recipient.
The results are the same in the seen and unseen worlds. Just as images
from a news broadcast with scenes of disaster and stories of violence
can impinge on one's senses and diminish one's sense of well-being,
bad intent or ugly thoughts can make a person experience a loss in
vitality, energy, sense of purpose, or the ability to cope.

Although we are aware of what we think and feel about given subjects, usually we are not aware that our opinions create patterns that
surround us and have bearing on our life experiences. We carry invisible burden baskets, which contain our limitations, our negative
thoughts, and our emotional wounds. Sometimes through dreaming,
we can unravel our fear patterns or the threads of our limitations. Many
people feel that they cannot remember their dreams. These folks have
no memory of the subconscious creation or unraveling process, but the
process is occurring just the same. We work out many of our problems
during sleep.

The decisions we make in our lives are directly influenced by the
options we choose while sleeping and dreaming. Something that has
worried us the night before can seem easily fixed in the morning. After
a hard day, if we consciously choose to let go of having to have the last
word, in the morning we may find that we are able to meet others
halfway and don't need to continue arguing. Through our conscious decision, we have altered the Dream Weave by reweaving our intentions.

For example, if people have never traveled far beyond the area
where they were born, they might carry hidden fears or judgments
about anyone who thinks differently or practices a different religion or
customs. If those fears are not healed, in time the prejudices mount
and become hard opinions, limiting people's ability to embrace new
horizons. When we heal our fears of unfamiliar traditions or foreign
lands, we can see the beauty in diverse cultural practices. Over time, by
experiencing new things, we embrace a type of human sharing that
gives us a panoramic view of our humanity and allows us to see ourselves as universal, planetary citizens.

Every time we eliminate a fixed idea that was created by our fear of
the unfamiliar, we break through a ridge of stuck energy. Our false,
preconceived notions and our resistance to change are then released.
When we go beyond any self-imposed limitation, we experience a

profound sense of relief, accompanied by a flood of new life force. If we resist feeling our emotions, we are required to use enormous amounts of energy to constrict the flow of life force, creating another type of dam that disallows potential growth. Because feelings and thoughts are intangible, they exist in the Dream Weave, beyond our normal vision. We may not see the false concepts disappearing when we eliminate them, but we feel the results of the life force floodgates opening when energy begins to flow through our bodies once more.

Until life gives us a wake-up call, we are usually unconscious of the patterns we weave in the unseen worlds or the states of consciousness that we encounter when we are dreaming. Most of us don't see the connection between our personal thoughts and behavior and how others respond to us. The fact is that human beings are an energetic sum of everything that we dream, imagine, think, perceive, and feel at any given moment. Our internal picture of *who we think we are* directly affects and determines how we perceive the world and our personal experiences. In my tradition, that perception of life, which is totally individual, is called the "Sacred Point of View." Reality is created and recreated when we shift our Sacred Points of View to include new possibilities and expanded ideas.

We have the ability to change our behaviors and to shift our perspectives on how we see things, what we feel about life, and which opinions we adopt. That ability comes not only from personal choice and free will but also from seeing all life experiences as initiations that lead us to becoming whole human beings. We all grow and change at individual rates and in our own rhythms. Everyone is unique; consequently, the paths that we embrace during our lives are determined by our unique levels of understanding. From our personal vantage points, we mentally assemble our view of life by adding one piece of data at a time. Personal reality is constructed through those mental beliefs, and life responds by showing us the positive or negative attitudes that we included in our construction process.

In the beginning we may have the perspective of a tiny field mouse, who sees small blades of grass as a giant forest that must be foraged through. Over time we can perceive our surroundings in a different manner, like the deer whose gaze reaches across the meadow to the horizon, where stony bluffs rise from rolling hills. After embracing our transformative experiences, we earn the right to see the overview, as does the eagle, scouting all that unfolds below us as we fly high. All of these perspectives are natural, and each holds many lessons about life. When we can see from Eagle's viewpoint, we must also maintain the scrutiny that allows Mouse to pay attention to small details. Every viewpoint is valid and necessary; none is greater or lesser than the others. As we grow, we learn to use every perspective we have encountered, adding new viewpoints without discounting any former skills. We adopt expanded, multilayered views of reality, which offer the benefits of countless new possibilities.

Until we begin our seven paths of initiation, our perceptions of reality and the overview of Creation are necessarily limited. Just how limited is determined by how many times we have shut down since we were born. We tend to shut down through traumas, emotional and psychological pain, physical abuse, or the lack of nurturing environments. These unpleasant events can create veils of separation, which include forgetting or denial. These veils of separation hide the spirit or energy surrounding all physical life forms, leaving us with only the solid view of what we think or believe is real.

If, for instance, we could see the energy connected to hurtful words as they tear through our own energy fields, and if we could watch the diminishing of our life force as the verbal blow is received, we would never scream at or taunt another person. Harsh or cruel words aimed at another can create the same damage that a weapon creates when used violently on the body. The hurt and rotten feelings we experience when others treat us this way should be enough to teach us, but many of us do not understand this truth. The human need for revenge is not usually healed until the end of the second or third paths of initiation. Prior to that time, we usually respond to an impulsive gut reaction, and the vicious cycle begins again.

WHAT ARE THE BENEFITS IF I GO THE DISTANCE?

The ultimate goals of all rites of passage or initiations in human life are: (a) learning to heal the past and all regret; (b) having no fear of the future; and (c) focusing on being aware and fully present at all times. Passing successfully through the first four paths of initiation, we can restore the sensitivity that we embodied as children, allowing us to expand our awareness and our perceptions. Through the latter three paths of initiation, we expand into universal consciousness and lift the layers of unawareness bit by bit, becoming aware of the vast levels of worlds within worlds that exist within nature, our planet, and our universe.

Ultimately, we come to realize that all life is interrelated and interdependent. No answer is outside of us; we contain the answers because we are connected to all truths through the weaving of our individual paths with the universal threads of energy found in the Dream Weave. When we no longer carry any victim consciousness, feeling that we are separate from the universe, we learn to join in the Dream Weave without fear. Some of the skills we learn to develop as we dance the dream are the skills of picking a path, focusing our intention, following through with commitment, claiming the wisdom found in the unseen web of the Dream Weave, and using that wisdom. When we walk these truths in our daily lives, we discover that we are dancing the dream.

My teacher Joaquin Muriel Espinosa expressed a deep understanding of the human condition and taught me why we benefit from our despair as well as our joys. He said, "When humanity can learn to thrive on joy, there will be no need for human despair. As it stands today, the hearts of humanity rarely embrace courage and compassion unless confronted with conflict, pain, or personal tragedy. One day, human beings will support one another and themselves in the absence of heartache."

Joaquin reminded me that general life lessons are common to every human path and are experienced by all of us, no matter what belief system, tradition, spiritual discipline, or religious persuasion. In our spiritual tradition, the Southern Seers, we have observed that we all experience heartaches, desires, trials, elation, and tribulations that strengthen our ability to endure and lead us to seek further understanding. These self-propelling events happen at different times for each of us. The life lessons that result are rites of passage marking the human maturation process. These passages into uncertainty or chaos give us unequaled opportunities to find our courage and strength. The world of duality disguises these events, making us feel that disaster is upon us, but these lessons are also blessings that insist that we stretch beyond our self-imposed limitations.

Since every person has a unique Sacred Point of View, each of us is going to embrace the lessons on the seven paths in our own way. When seen from an energetic or spiritual point of view, all lessons are equal and all human burdens are equal. No person can measure how much

joy and pain another experiences, nor can we compare our lessons to
someone else's. The need or desire to become more aware of the personal behaviors and thoughts that are directing our life experiences
varies from person to person.

It is a rare individual who completes the life lessons presented on
all seven paths in one lifetime. In fact, until our present time, most
people never went beyond the third path of initiation, which is the
healing path. At this time, near the end of this millennium, many doors
have opened in human consciousness. New paths through the Dream
Weave have been created by those with the willingness and determination to scout the unknown reaches of consciousness, making these
pathways safe for others to follow. Prior travelers on these paths may
have bogged down in various pools of quicksand in past centuries
when the paths were scantily mapped, but each of you reading this
book is being given a safe road map of consciousness and human spiritual evolution, complete with signposts that mark the quagmires to
help you to make your own choices.

Our personal progress is a matter of free will. How deep we are
willing to go to reach understanding depends ultimately upon our
desire to become explorers. We can see ourselves as victims being
tossed between bliss and despair, or we can look deeper and begin to
take responsibility for our thoughts, feelings, and actions. When we
choose to change, refusing to become victims, we have chosen to see
life from the eye of Eagle. The power of personal connection to the
Creator and to spirituality is found in the individual who is willing to
commit to life's paths of initiation. When we acknowledge that we are
spiritual beings who are willing to fight in the trenches of human self-
empowerment, insisting on personal integrity, we have chosen to test
ourselves by entering the paths of human initiation that lead to authentic wholeness.

OUR PATH APPEARS WHEN WE ACKNOWLEDGE THE DREAM WEAVE

Everyone can learn to tap into the Dream Weave. To perceive the weaving of energy that makes the Medicine Blanket, or solid reality, we must
become aware of our thoughts, ideas, opinions, and emotions. When
we become aware of these nonphysical elements within ourselves, we

marvel at the way our individual threads dance through the universe and change with every thought we have and every decision we make. When we notice the pattern of events that unfolds when we acknowledge the intangible, our paths suddenly appear. We must then find the courage to venture into territory that is unexplored, yet hauntingly familiar to our spiritual natures.

Some people tap into the Dream Weave while sleeping and dreaming, while others reach the same truths through meditation or Tiyoweh, "entering the silence." Yet other individuals find understanding through other spiritual disciplines or personal discovery. Whatever the method, the final outcome will be the same. We are evolving into a species that can recognize and use energy in its nonphysical form, and we are learning how the energy we personally put out into the universe affects the experiences we encounter in our lives.

We embrace the adventure by searching for our personal paths amid the patterns and divine designs of Creation. The initiations appear when we apply those truths by walking them in physical life. *How we use the wisdom we find is the process of human initiation.* The sharpness of our intentions and the acuteness of our awareness consciously create the foundations of our personal physical realities. How precisely accurate we become in attaining the outcomes we desire depends upon our willingness to go the distance. Every time we change our Sacred Point of View, life responds and our reality shifts. The nonphysical imprints that are made by our mental, emotional, and spiritual choices are the intangible aspects that form our path. We create and arrange the patterns of action we employ in life. Our daily experiences and interactions with others interweave, creating the fabric of our lives, the metaphorical Medicine Blanket that is our solid reality.

DARK NIGHTS OF THE SOUL

When we refuse to pay attention to the subtle signs that change is needed in our lives, four major passages into internal human chaos and despair will dramatically force the course of our lives to change. The Southern Seers' term, the "Spirit's Black Night," literally translates into the "Dark Nights of the Soul." In human life, we experience these four passages into darkness on the spiritual, emotional, psychological, and physical levels. At these times, we feel that the light in the window representing the safety of home has vanished, we think that there is no way out, or we feel that we have lost our connection to the Great Mystery, God, the Creator. We may feel abandoned or alone; we may think that no one understands our passage in life and that there are unseen forces working against us. Most people recognize the characteristics of the Dark Nights because they have undergone one or more of these passages into periods of pain, uncertainty, or loss.

In our Native American tradition, we see the Dark Nights of the Soul as rites of passage, initiations that call us to respond in ways that ultimately temper and strengthen the warrior nature contained in the human spirit. Any woman or man or child on the Earth can embrace that bravery within themselves, "counting coup" or experiencing a victory over the Dark Night of the Soul simply by surviving, knowing that they have done the best that they could at that time. Accepting these difficult rites of passage allows us to be brave, to take courage, and to acknowledge the warrior nature of our spiritual essences. The awakened human spirit walks the paths of human transformation with exacting grace and has been waiting for us to discover the power of the spiritual warrior existing inside us. If we act from our warrior nature, facing the issues at hand rather than shutting down during harrowing times, we will not have to repeat the difficult lessons that life uses to force us to confront unpleasant issues. Then we finally begin to understand the hidden strengths of our personal Medicines.

If we continue to deny what is happening and refuse to take responsibility in those situations, the Dark Night of the Soul may continue like a roller-coaster for years. For instance, addictions can destroy lives and create a Dark Night of the Soul for entire families. Long illnesses are another example, affecting both the patient and the caregivers. The loss of a home due to fire or disaster can affect everyone living there. If people do not have a way to rebuild, they may give up, adding another family to the roles of the homeless masses. In millions of ways, havoc can be wreaked in our lives; depending upon our attitude, either we choose to pick up the pieces and begin again, or we choose to give up. Every decision we make sets a new course of action, reweaving the patterns in our lives and in some way influencing all future events.

It is very hard to separate the four Dark Nights of the Soul. Because our physical, psychological, emotional, and spiritual natures are so successfully interwoven, we often cannot identify the type of Dark Night that we are experiencing. Some people experience the mental or psychologi-

cal Dark Night of the Soul during their teenage years or early twenties when they are trying to adopt ideas of their own and form an identity in terms of who they are, where they fit, and how they can be liked or admired by their peers. There are many hard lessons to be learned as young people find out, through trial and error, what does and does not work for them. The consequences of rash behavior can be lethal in our present world. For others, who seem to glide through the glory days of their youth, the psychological Dark Night of the Soul can come in their middle years, when they realize that life did not continue to produce the joy they expected. If at middle age they have no sense of self because they followed a plan based on what they thought everyone else expected of them, they may fall into the abyss of hopelessness and despair.

All Dark Nights of the Soul ultimately teach us how to let go of cowardice. To paraphrase Cormac McCarthy, author of *All the Pretty Horses*: It is the coward who abandons himself or herself first, and from that place of cowardice, all other betrayals come easy. Any person who has successfully gone through a Dark Night of the Soul has developed the ability to endure, to find inner strength, to learn from mistakes and be accountable for them, to pick up the pieces, and to carry on as a better person. When we acknowledge the bravery it takes to be human, we can see things in a different light. It is an act of courage to live in this world at this time, so we must honor ourselves and the valor required to embrace the human condition without abandoning our integrity and purpose for being.

An *emotional* Dark Night of the Soul can be brought on by the death of a loved one, having a marriage fall apart, betrayal, heartache over a child in trouble, and a variety of other situations. The deep pain or numbness that accompanies this emotional Dark Night may take years to heal. Emotional losses can shake us to the very core of our being and seemingly rob us of the will to carry on. It is during this Dark Night that we learn the value of our personal abilities of endurance and how to garner strength from the kindness offered by others as well as from the support we find in the faith that we can heal. This Dark Night can teach us to rediscover hope and to let go of our personal pain. We can learn how to spot the places where we deny our feelings or become victims to our emotions. We can learn how to trust that we are growing stronger each day. In time, we learn that all people who have suffered some misfortune and have survived develop a quality of courage and inner strength that those who have not suffered do not yet possess.

The *physical* Dark Night of the Soul is a rite of passage that keeps us from taking good health for granted. This wake-up call takes different forms in different people. When we get a report from a doctor that warns us of an irregularity or borderline condition, we are usually experiencing the result of our lack of attention to our body's needs. We can ignore it or begin to honor our health, changing habits that affect our physical well-being in negative ways. Illnesses can force us to pay attention to everything we have been doing that does not support the basic needs of our physical bodies.

If a fall or a car crash causes a loss of health or physical freedom, we are given a new set of challenges that can teach us lessons about our personal determination and how to use our abilities to overcome adversity. The results of our efforts vary from person to person, but the process of living through it all is the initiation. We can choose to give up or to use our lives to inspire others. We can choose to fight for our place in life and reclaim our joy, or we can wallow in the overwhelming challenges at hand.

Physical Dark Nights can teach us how to show support for one another. We also learn the unequaled lessons of endurance by confronting our fears of loss or pain. We learn how to deal with personal sacrifice and how to care for others. We learn a multitude of lessons that can shape our characters in a positive way, or we can allow our experiences to become another excuse for being too weak to endure.

Spiritual Dark Nights of the Soul can occur when we have put our faith in the wrong person instead of in the Creator. For example, a spiritual leader, who is very human, can fall off the pedestal that we created by giving that leader too large a role in our lives. Do we throw away all trust, abandoning our faith in all we once held sacred? Or do we accept this rite of passage as an opportunity to grow? In such cases, we are being given a chance to see that we have misunderstood our authentic spiritual source by placing it in human hands rather than trusting the Great Mystery or God. Expecting any human being to be godlike or perfect at all times is a crooked trail. When we trust our own direct connections to the Creator, Great Mystery, God, we gain access to our authentic source of life force and spiritual well-being.

Great losses, like the death of loved ones, can destroy our happiness and begin a spiritual Dark Night of the Soul. Because we cannot figure out how a loving Creator could "let this happen," we find ourselves raging against God. We often blame God for our losses in life, forcing the destruction of any former foundations of faith and trust. It takes an enormous amount of courage to accept that our experiences are something that we cannot figure out at the time they happen and that there is a divine plan that may or may not reveal itself. Time changes our views and we go on, but whether we continue to have faith and trust depends upon our ability to heal the need to blame God, life, others, or the self. Again, the choice is ours.

Staying connected to a personal faith is another choice we face as we go through any Dark Night of the Soul. The key to unlocking our stuck doors during our passage is found in prayer and in asking for guidance. The answer will not necessarily come in the form of a blinding vision or an angelic presence. Personal revelations can come as a whisper in the heart or a fleeting thought or feeling that we can choose to ignore, but the guidance or spiritual inspiration is there if we ask for assistance and remain open to it. Synchronistic events, like a word of kindness from a total stranger or a caring hand reaching out to touch us with compassion, can change our lives. We may find our answers from observing how another has survived a tragic event. Everything we experience in life can be the initiation, and every opinion we have about how we are to survive and grow can support or inhibit our process.

THE ROLE OF GRATITUDE

The power that is always available to us when we are in crisis can be found in the simple "attitude of gratitude." When life throws us a series of devastating curve balls, it can be unbelievably hard to find things to be grateful about. I learned the lesson of gratitude from my Granny Sams. She never let a day pass when she did not visit shut-ins or find some way to help others. One day I asked her about her daily practice, and she replied, "When your Aunt Mary was two, we discovered she had cerebral palsy, and I was confronted with my pain and my shame, thinking I had done something wrong when I gave her birth. I worked with her five hours a day, and I was often so frustrated and overwhelmed, I would sit and cry. Then I would pick myself up and go to the Crippled Children's Hospital and volunteer another three hours before coming home to fix dinner for the family. Volunteering taught me how grateful I needed to be for my blessings. There were opera-

tions that could help Mary, and her mind was very bright. When I
worked with all of those other children who were quadriplegic or permanently crippled by polio, I saw how many blessings I had that I had
not counted."

Finding our attitude of gratitude may be a difficult task, but the
more we learn to return thanks, the more space we make for new, unexpected blessings to appear in our lives. There is no substitute for finally acknowledging the blessings that we have taken for granted. In
this process, we rediscover the magic and wonder of the most simple
of gifts. Do we have to suffer from emphysema before we can have
gratitude for the precious breath of life? Do we have to lose our homes
before we can return thanks for having shelter? If we have taken for
granted all our blessings of health or a loving family, will we need to
be reminded to be grateful through near tragedy or actual loss?

Every time we show gratitude for the millions of ways we are
blessed daily, we send our energy into the unseen world of the Dream
Weave, and those threads of gratitude strengthen our spiritual connections. The resulting fabric of trust and faith is the safety net that catches
us when we go through a Dark Night of the Soul, protecting us against
the internal enemy of victim thinking. Opportunity is the last thing that
we normally think of when we are in crisis, but that is one gift that is
always being given. We are given the opportunity to grow, to learn how
strong we really are, to see the value of loving support, to become
more sensitive to the pain of others, to share our burdens with others
instead of thinking we are always alone, and to ultimately trust that we
will be better people on the other side of our present, darkened passage through life.

When people ask me if these Dark Nights of the Soul are necessary,
I give two answers. One is that people can choose to learn through joy
or through sorrow. The second answer is this: I personally have never
seen a human being who has grown into his or her potential without
confronting some Dark Night of the Soul. Those who seem to have
lived ideal lives probably stayed in denial. It has been my experience
that we find balance and authentic growth by counting both joy and
sorrow as blessings.

When we go through these rites of passage, we are given a choice
about how to relate to our experiences. We can choose to grow by
adopting the view that all things work together for our spiritual
growth and evolution. In that light, we learn to find our courage, and

we grieve and release our pasts. Then we learn that we can be fully present and begin again. Along the way, we find humor, laughing at our former fears, which can no longer strike terror in our hearts. We embrace new goals and dreams, we better our attitudes, we cleanse our thoughts and feelings, and we open to all that life offers in order to dance the dreams that have once again captured our hearts and minds.

Every Dark Night brings a multitude of wake-up calls, so our Dark Nights of the Soul may trigger a need to radically shift how we live. The challenging lessons of life never stop coming, but the manner in which we respond to those lessons will expand and change. Once we choose to look and to authentically see the truth of life's challenges, we find that the light at the end of the tunnel does exist. In fact, we can feed ourselves that light by altering the idea that it comes only from outside us. When we decide to see our passage through the tunnel of chaos and despair as an opportunity, we effectively invite our personal Spiritual Essence to light the way through the passage into and out of darkness. We are given miraculous moments of illumination, finding that the clarity we have received can change our perceptions and our lives forever.

First we must believe that we are indeed beautiful parts of the Great Mystery's universe. When we see ourselves instead as being at the mercy of life's mysteries, we forget spiritual connections. In all Native American traditions we honor the Spiritual Essence in all living things. We can see the Eternal Flame of Love that the Creator placed inside of every part of Creation: in rocks, plants, clouds, animals, and humans. We all carry that flame of light. When we deny our Spiritual Essences, we can become lost in Dark Nights of the Soul. Going through a Dark Night of the Soul, we can rediscover the inner light that was bestowed upon us, showing us how to find our way through any darkness on life's path.

CHAPTER 2

*When we reconstruct the fragments of our dreams, we bring
an aliveness to the spirit that allows the imagination to go
beyond basic human drives and the need to survive. Imagining
a better world allows us to actively participate in creating our
dreams, and when we take on that responsibility, we embrace
the Remembering.*

—Joaquin Muriel Espinosa

▲▲

DREAMING ONENESS

Take me gently into the dawn,
Where my dream becomes the light,
Uniting with the radiance of the sun,
Shedding the indigo of my spirit's flight.

Return me to the waking world,
With vivid images imprinting my heart,
Grasping the maps of newborn paths,
Allowing my life to become living art.

—Jamie Sams

Remembering Our Oneness

ACCORDING to the teachings of my Seneca Elders, Grandpa Moses Shongo and his granddaughter, Twylah Nitsch, we have experienced the Fourth World of Separation for the last sixty or seventy thousand years. Our world has seen holy wars, a multitude of religions, the atom bomb, racial hatred, and a host of other devastating events that have destroyed our sense of human oneness and our sense of being interrelated, at one with the natural world and all life. It is no wonder that we are so fragmented that we cannot reach our divine human potential or find our spirit's authentic purposes. The seven sacred paths offer us a variety of ways to reclaim those parts of our wholeness that have been annihilated by mistrust, fear, and humanity's inhumanity. To remember our oneness, we are asked to go beyond the veils created by generations of forgetting. As we explore the realms of the self and allow our dreams to reflect our spirit's purpose, we touch our potential wholeness time and again, allowing the spirit to awaken, and we begin consciously to remember. With each of the seven paths, the oneness, which we had forgotten, begins to take firm root in our daily lives.

PAYING ATTENTION TO OUR DREAMS

Any path of transformation begins with human experience—how we perceive life in general. The experiences that we have during our waking hours are packed full of sensations, perceptions, colors, and forms as well as our reactions to these elements. All this input is not readily digested, since a vast array of experiences is packed into a few waking hours. Because most of us are not fully present as we are going through our day, we sort out the sensory overload later while our body and mind are resting. Our usual hustle and bustle tend to keep our mind's internal dialogue constantly chattering. Thoughts of what to do next or what we should have done keep us in the past or future instead of fully present. Consequently, our brain and body must wait until the mind goes silent to process and digest all that our eyes have seen and all that we have felt, heard, and experienced.

As we enter each of the seven sacred paths of transformation, we develop new abilities or skills that open new levels of conscious awareness in our mind, body, emotions, and perceptions. With discipline, we are able to still the mind's internal dialogue and to open new levels of perceptions even during our waking hours so that we become more fully attentive and present. When we accomplish this, our dreams begin to change radically, and the dream content becomes a reflection of the growth we are achieving during our initiations.

In the early 1970s I lived in San Luis Potósi, Mexico, and studied with three Native American Elder teachers. Joaquin Muriel Espinosa, Cisi Laughing Crow, and Berta Broken Bow trained me to be a Seer and a Dreamer. A Seer is a person who can access the unseen worlds of spirit and energy while in waking states. A Seer can follow the lines of energy in those realms to receive information and can locate the areas where those energies manifest themselves in our physical world. A Dreamer is a person who can focus on his or her personal intent while sleeping. In their dreams, these people reach into the unseen worlds of energy to gather information, interpret the metaphors of those dreams, and apply the data found to physical life. The Seer and the Dreamer have equal access to the energetic worlds surrounding everything in our universe, worlds that are invisible to most human beings until they begin the fourth-path lessons.

As I have discussed, the Dream Weave is the name my teachers used to describe the unseen world of spirit, thought, emotion, and intangible energy that is a part of our physical reality. The common denominator that binds together these two worlds of physicality and intangible energies is a grid of energy lines operating like a radio wave or frequency, without visible form. To gain access to the invisible world of the Dream Weave we must enter Tiyoweh, the stillness, and go beyond the chatter of the human mind to the infinite, majestic silence. Just as we are able to tune the radio dial to our favorite stations, we must still our personal thoughts and feelings so that we can tune in to a serene frequency, matching the majestic, universal consciousness of Great Mystery. Only then can we receive the messages that are understood by our Spiritual Essences. The Spiritual Essence of any human is devoid of chaos, confusion, and fear, the main elements that create the constant chatter in the human mind.

If you are worried that you will not be able to find the connective tissue of the Dream Weave and gain access to the Universal, relax. Everyone—not just Seers and Dreamers—can learn to tap into the Dream Weave. Just as Dreamers put their bodies to sleep to reach this state of awareness, some people meditate, others follow a drumbeat and journey out of body, some fast and pray, and others use ceremonial dancing. Any spiritual discipline, followed faithfully, can allow a person to enter a serene state of stillness, and that practice is the key that opens the door. There is no single correct way to tap the universal consciousness. All paths and methods are valid, taking us to the same place: the serene centers of our Spiritual Essences.

The Southern Seers tradition teaches some of the ways that we can enter the stillness. Everyone sleeps, so all of us can learn to tap into the Dream Weave, because when the physical body is resting, the mind shuts off the chatter. Many people say, "What about me? I don't remember my dreams." There are many reasons why people don't remember their dreams, yet science has shown that we all dream. Without dreams or rapid eye movement sleep, we can become ill. One of the main reasons we forget our dreams is that our loud alarm clocks force us from dream state into waking state, slamming the dreaming body into the physical body with great force. Any loud noise or abrupt movement will shatter our dream images and create forgetting. When we feel like we have awakened on the wrong side of the bed, it is usually because we have been interrupted while in the middle of a dream where we were far into the process of working through problems or receiving needed information. The unfinished business creates an energetic rip in the dreaming body, destroying our sense of emotional well-being.

As a child, I was often ill. It was only when I studied with my teachers in Mexico at twenty-two that I realized why. It was my father's custom to wake me and my sister by yelling, "Good morning Mary Sunshine . . . Rise and shine!" Although my father's intent was good, the abrupt manner in which he woke me slammed my dreaming body into my physical body, and I was so sensitive that I became physically ill. The dreaming body can fragment and shatter if not treated with respect. When I was studying with Cisi, Berta, and Joaquin, the cardinal rule was to never wake me up until my body chose to awaken.

I learned that when the physical body sleeps, the dreaming body awakens. The dreaming body is an energetic duplicate of ourselves, the antenna of our Spiritual Essence. As a human being, you are an immortal, spiritual consciousness that happens to have a physical body. That Spiritual Essence reconnects daily to the unseen worlds, because all levels of consciousness within this universe are connected in the Dream Weave. This glowing, luminous part of you slips into other realities, the unseen worlds of thought and feeling, which are merely the energetic or nonphysical duplicate of everything you perceive as solid during the waking portion of your day.

When asleep, we begin to tap into the Dream Weave by investigating it through our personal experiences. This is something we do naturally; our dreams reflect all the thoughts, feelings, fears, aspirations, creative potential, unexpressed ideas, and life force energy that we embrace during daily life. With focused intent and developed skill, we can go beyond the personal and into the universal parts of the Dream Weave. As we explore each of the paths of initiation, we open ourselves to areas of the unseen worlds of spirit taking us beyond our tunnel-vision view of the self.

Some of the most challenging parts of exploring the Dream Weave are found on the fifth and sixth paths, where we learn to reach into the unseen worlds *at will*. We learn to maneuver in the different worlds of consciousness as easily as we walk down the street. We learn how to locate any level of awareness that we choose to explore, and we consciously use the life force we have appropriated and embodied at will. Some may find these abilities fantastic or unbelievable or frightening and undesirable, but no one is forced to follow any path of initiation. Even people who want to develop the abilities of the last three paths of initiation realize that the work along the way requires more energy and determination than most human beings are willing to give.

THE REMEMBERING

The Remembering is a term used by my teachers to refer to a re-membering or reconstitution of the fragments of human consciousness. The Re-membering creates authentic wholeness and an awakened spirit that is firmly housed inside the physical body. As we bring forgotten parts of our human potential back into ourselves and develop those gifts, talents, and abilities, we become stronger and wiser, and eventually we become fully conscious of the tangible and intangible worlds simultaneously. The process of remembering cannot be forced; it begins by being aware that we have chosen to grow and evolve. As we become more present, we develop a more accurate memory of daily events, and we have vivid recall of our dreams.

If you have made the choice to consciously tap into the Dream Weave, you may want to correct some simple things that can keep you from allowing yourself to dream and to remember. Change your alarm clock to one that wakes you with very soft music. Drink a large glass of water before sleeping, and if you need to get up during the night, write down key words or dream images on a notepad next to your bed. Make the conscious decision that you want to remember your dreams. Never yell when waking another, and respect that person's dreamspace. Respect your dreamspace as well, and honor it as the place where you are given metaphorical keys that allow you to further understand yourself and your potential. Commit to between a half hour and an hour of silence or meditation every day. Learn to quiet your mind so that its chatter won't keep you from receiving the images and messages that freely come when you are fully present. If you do these things devotedly, you will remember your dreams and the Dream Weave will reveal itself to you bit by bit, as you are ready for each further level of understanding.

THE SEVEN VEILS OF SEPARATION

We cannot see the intangible realms that influence our physical reality until we remove the false idea that the energetic world is not a part of the wholeness offered by the Creator to humankind. The veils of separation are created when we are born in human bodies and when we learn to respond to life through our senses, emotions, and thoughts. Our souls or spirits enter physical bodies, animating the flesh, bone, blood, and organs with divine life force. Prior to our birth, our soul or spirit is connected to God, the Creator, the Great Mystery, and has a clear awareness of the oneness of universal consciousness and life force. After we are born, every thought and emotion creates an energetic thread that combines with all others, weaving the intangible veils of separation that keep us from remembering authentic oneness, which contains no duality. This is as it should be: duality has a divine purpose and is necessary to the human growth process. The purpose of learning through opposites is one that we begin to see when we embrace the seven sacred paths of human transformation.

The veils of separation are the polarized energetic barriers that exist at every access point of the Dream Weave. Until we begin to remove the dualistic ideas within the veils, we cannot perceive the authentic truths pertaining to our physical world, the potential within our own natures, or the vastness of the Dream Weave. Brief glimpses of various truths are seen and accumulated over time as we eliminate the veils of separation.

Our understanding is limited by the tiny range of human perceptions offered through the use of human eyes, ears, noses, mouths, thoughts, and feelings. The veils are composed of the data we gather from our perceptions while we experience life and the assumptions, decisions, and determinations we make about how life works. They are like multiple layers of contact lenses made of thin membranelike material allowing us to distinguish light and dark forms but not clearly perceive the details of the whole picture.

These layers of cloudy illusions drop away as we undergo and successfully complete the life lessons and realizations found on the seven paths of transformation. The veils do not fall away instantaneously with one quick swoop of the hand; instead, each of the seven paths allows us to strip a few threads, until the veils of illusion are lifted gradually. We observe these changes when we begin to authentically perceive the many truths in our universe and to expand our awareness of what exists in Creation. There is no particular order or specific fashion in which the veils disappear. We have our breakthroughs in unique ways and in different time periods of our lives. When the final vestiges of the seventh veil begin to dissolve at the beginning of the sixth path of transformation, we rediscover the authentic identity of our Spiritual Essence and our body, the sacred vessel that holds this essence. Then we are able to begin gaining access to all levels of universal consciousness at will. The separation between us, all other life forms, and the Great Mystery is permanently removed, because we can perceive that everything has spiritual content and is alive with divine life force.

Each of the seven veils has its own qualities. The first veil keeps us from remembering the oneness of the universe. We forget that everything in Creation exists inside the Great Mystery or God. We forget

that everything in Creation contains life force and spirit and that everything is energetically connected by those universal elements. We forget
that every atom making up life and form in Creation contains the Eternal Flame of Love and that everything has a purpose. We forget that all
life is created in divine perfection and that we are a part of that perfect
plan. As we remember these truths, this veil is dissolved or lifted in
layers.

We create the second veil of separation by forgetting the authentic
identity of our Spiritual Essences and how we are connected to the Creator and the rest of Creation. When we forget our spiritual identities,
we also forget why we are here in physical bodies. When we forget
why we are here on the earth, we also forget our original purpose for
becoming human. Before we were born in this world, we all promised
ourselves that we would remember our divine identities and would accomplish certain tasks or missions while we experienced human life.
This veil is peeled away in layers every time we encounter another aspect of our Spiritual Essence, and we remember why we are here and
our original purpose within the divine plan.

The third veil of separation is created through the limitations of our
sensory perceptions. In developing our human perceptions we begin
by discovering life through the physical senses: taste, smell, touch,
hearing, and sight. During early childhood we are open to other perceptions, but those begin to disappear as we are taught not to use any
extra senses. We are taught to perceive only the solid objects that adults
consider to be "real." Everything else is considered to be either a fib or
the product of a child's overactive imagination; hence we stop using
the ability to perceive energy. Slam bang! The third veil is firmly in
place. We cannot lift the third veil if we have become addicted to sexual
pleasure or other forms of physical sensations. Nor can this veil be
lifted if we do not use spiritual disciplines.

We create the fourth veil when we develop our emotions. An infant
is physically helpless but is totally aware of his or her feelings. You can
see the emotions that pass through a baby by watching the waves of
expressions that cross the child's face in the space of five minutes. As
we develop, we learn how to control or even deny our feelings. This
veil, created by unexpressed feelings and emotions that have not been
healed or released, masks our authentic will. Only when this veil is
lifted can we gain access to the divine will of the Creator, which exists
as a unified part of our Spiritual Essence and our personal free will.

The fifth veil is composed of our belief systems, our thoughts, mental computations, decisions, theories, assumptions, and hypotheses regarding everything we experience in life. During childhood we accept the beliefs that are taught to us by our families. We begin to alter our learned belief systems when we become teenagers, and we adopt new ideas based upon our personal experiences, not on what was true for Mom or Dad. We continue adding thoughts and beliefs that are based upon our judgments of what we think is true or false, bad or good, possible or impossible. This type of mental calculation is based upon comparison and duality. Polarized thinking and limited belief systems create a veil of mental separation. This veil begins to be lifted in stages as we remove layer after layer of dualistic beliefs. Sometimes, when we have eliminated enough of our judgments, the rest of the veil is suddenly ripped away, creating a collapse of every incorrect conclusion or false idea that remains.

We create the sixth veil of separation when we shut down our perceptions of anything that is not solid. As with the third veil, when we cannot perceive the colors, energy, or spirit connected to matter or solid forms, we perceive life solely from the five physical senses. The sixth veil differs in that it also blocks our access to other worlds, realities, time periods, and dimensions of awareness. Depending upon the individual, this veil is created at different times. For some people the veil drops in place at birth; for others the loss of extrasensory perceptions happens during childhood; and for some rare individuals the sixth veil does not exist. These gifted people who do not have the sixth veil firmly dividing the tangible and intangible parts of life are blessed with extrasensory perceptions, but they can also feel misunderstood because they can easily slip into past or future times and perceive things that others cannot. In some people these extrasensory gifts are partially shut down but can be awakened. Others do not remember using any of these abilities and must begin by developing intuition and by allowing the other veils that are being lifted to reconnect the extra senses.

The sixth veil is lifted in increments as we learn to eliminate our judgments during the first five paths of initiation. Over time, we shred and tatter the various false perceptions created by fixed ideas and limiting thoughts, woundedness and stuck or denied emotions. Every time we heal a part of our life, we experience a victory or breakthrough that frees up life force and feeds the perceptions with unleashed life force.

This newly released energy activates flashes of intuitive inner knowing and gives us the energy we need to explore the vast reaches of human and universal consciousness. New perceptions and skills begin to surface a step at a time as we reconstruct our views of reality and life on planet Earth. Our dreams may offer lucid images; we may have a vision or encounter the presence of angels. For some people, healing abilities can emerge, while others may begin to feel their energy and spirit connected to all life forms in a way never before possible.

The seventh veil of separation is created by our personal sense of individuality and the rigid concepts that delineate our human identities. We forget the truths that we understood before taking our human bodies, when we were fully aware of being connected to the Great Mystery. We are still connected, but we gain the full awareness of that state of grace in pieces as we remove the veils a thread at a time. We break the threads of separation through our personal growth and revelations, allowing us to perceive the overview of our divine connections. The human spirit finally takes its place as a limitless and eternal extension of the Creator, Great Mystery, God. Ultimately, we realize that we can walk through life and still maintain full connection to all levels of the Dream Weave.

During the seven paths of transformation, we embrace the Remembering and we destroy the threads of illusion that make up the veils of separation, keeping us from seeing the whole picture, making us believe the illusion that we are abandoned and alone. On all seven paths of transformation, every facet of truth that is reclaimed and every piece of awareness that is remembered reshapes our perceptions of our human identity and of how we interrelate with Creation. The seven sacred paths are no more than the journey home to our authentic spiritual identities and to our divine connections to the Great Mystery. When we move beyond the last illusions represented by the seventh veil of separation, we bring the authentic understanding of our spiritual natures into our human body. Some traditions call this state "heaven on Earth."

THE INITIATIONS

On the paths to remembering our oneness, we will undergo many initiations. An initiation can be anything that tests us, forcing us to look at whether or not the path we are following is appropriate or whether we want to change. Life tests us at our weak places and shows us what we need to give away and what strengths we need to keep. Depending upon our success or failure, the initiation allows us to try again or welcomes us to go beyond a former limitation. Life is the ultimate initiation in this physical world. We no longer have to look for monastic situations in which to embrace spiritual lifestyles. In many other traditions, such as the Buddhist, Catholic, Hindu, Sufi, and early Greek and Egyptian, living in mystery schools or monasteries was necessary in order to leave the outer world behind, allowing practitioners to focus totally upon their spiritual path and development. For centuries, Native Americans have found their silence and personal spirituality in the natural world while taking time apart from tribal duties or daily life. Our initiations have come through Vision Quests, Sun Dancing, Medicine teachings, and warrior training for the men and through Healing Quests, Moon Lodge teachings, Medicine or healing techniques, and Dreamer or Seer training for the women. Yet in all spiritual traditions throughout the world, humankind is now being asked to blend the world of spiritual development with daily life in order to create a new kind of initiation process that shows us how to balance both the internal process and the external experiences of daily life on planet Earth.

On each of the seven paths we encounter many hundreds of initiations. Each is a personal and individual rite of passage that allows us to change and grow. You may ask, "What does that mean?" Well, each time we go through some experience in life, we are being given a choice about how to respond to that event. If we make the choice to be dishonest with ourselves or another, we create an energy drain inside our Spiritual Essences, and we effectively limit the ability to transform our lives. Yes, we have passed through the moment where we made that decision, but not unscathed. In this instance, our initiation could be successfully passed if we were willing to be truthful and accountable for our words and actions. In Native American tradition, the ability to respond is what other cultures call responsibility.

Most spiritual paths teach us to be good people, to love others, to serve and assist where possible, not because we fear retribution, but because we want to be a part of the blessings of humankind. The internal purpose and joy sparking our desire to contribute to the well-being of our human race are fueled by the sparks of life that we carry, which are our gifts from the Creator. When we leak our spiritual energy

through being unloving or deceptive, we lose energy. The consequences are evident not only because others feel we are not trustworthy, but because we have wounded ourselves. We diffuse the life force
activating our individual spark of life, and we eventually forget how to
shine.

If we cheat or try to fool ourselves, we deprive ourselves of the energy that can propel us beyond our limited view of life. We become
lackluster and mediocre to the degree that we are unwilling to become
accountable, limiting the amount of energy or life force we can command to heal our lives.

Since each of us creates our own personal creed as we go along,
some things that seemed all right to do in younger years become un-
workable as we mature. The maturation process not only is determined
by years of wisdom and experience, but also reflects an expansion of
the human spirit. When we choose to enter the paths of human transformation, the work and the joy of learning never end; there are untold
levels of awareness in our universe.

We cannot remember why we are here, what we are to accomplish,
what place we have in life, how we can contribute, or how to find balance in our lives if we are actively being dishonest with ourselves or
others. The Remembering occurs when we are willing to create a personal creed and live by it. That personal creed can take the form of
promises we make to ourselves. For instance, an example of a personal
creed might be as follows: "I will be good to my body; I will be truthful with myself and others; I will treat all living things with respect; I
will honor the rights of all human beings to be individuals with their
own Sacred Points of View; I will embrace my faith, and I will trust the
Creator's divine guidance; I will see all experiences in my life as ways
to grow with lessons to learn; and I will strive to be my personal best
without comparing my path to others." Believe it or not, following this
simple example of a personal creed requires lots of energy, focus, and
impeccability.

When we use a personal creed, we gain a new awareness of when
and how we make a mistake and how to correct it. The process of remembering offers us solutions. When we falter or break a promise to
ourselves, it is important to forgive ourselves and acknowledge our hu-
manness. We learn everything in life by developing skills, and those
skills cannot be perfected overnight. We learn through finding what
works and what does not work. In this manner, humankind is being

given an opportunity to use the power of personal choice to learn through suffering or through joy.

As we heal ourselves, we re-member the parts of our Spiritual Essence, the fragments of our potential, that we have forgotten along the way. We do this through initiations, whether we know we are passing through them or not. Some people are not aware that they have chosen to enter these paths of growth, until the transformation experience shifts their reality, calling their attention to the NOW. The changes made in one's life can be understood vaguely by anyone who reviews his or her past and acknowledges where he or she is in the present. The more fully present and aware a person becomes, the more obvious the truth that emerges: *life is the initiation.* Every choice we make counts, every thought we have weaves the patterns of our lives, and every situation we experience influences our potential growth or stagnation.

THE GREAT MYSTERY

Remembering our oneness involves remembering how we are connected to the Great Mystery. In the tradition of the Southern Seers, we see the universe as the body of the Great Mystery, which is constantly evolving and changing. That is why we call it the Great Mystery: it cannot be limited or figured out. Everything is alive and is made of energy. Some parts also are attached to matter, having bodies or substance. Everything in our universe is a cell within the body of the Great Mystery, and all experiences of every human, plant, animal, stone, planetoid, planet, solar system, galaxy, and cosmos are recorded inside of this massive, omnipotent consciousness.

The omnipotence of God is spoken of in all major religions and is based upon the following principle: everything that exists in this universe feeds the Great Mystery through the connective tissue of consciousness, which is made of energy. Most human beings cannot see this energy and usually have to wait until they put their bodies to sleep before the interaction can occur without the mind's static interfering. But this divine connection and exchange can also occur at any time when human beings enter the silence, fully stopping the internal dialogue of the mind. The circular flow of giving and receiving divine communication can be accomplished when we choose to still the mind or when we sleep. The process of connecting to the universal consciousness occurs whether we are aware of it or not. We can choose to enter the stillness consciously, or we can slip into the silence while sleeping and dreaming.

Our life force streams from the Great Mystery, flowing to us and through us. That stream of energy can be a trickle or a mighty river, depending upon our willingness to open and receive the gift. If we deny the existence of that flow, we are denying the source of our life force and denying also that we are extensions of the beauty that the Creator placed in all of Creation. All paths of spiritual evolution begin here. My teachers taught me that there is one law that applies to all worlds, seen and unseen, all life forms, and all states of awareness. The Great Mystery spoke to all life saying, "You will evolve." How all life forms evolve is the sacred mystery that is ever unfolding. With human beings, the way we grow and evolve is determined by our choices and our willingness to become and to embody the energy and divine potential given us by the Maker of All Things, the Great Mystery, God.

There is nothing more powerful in life than experiencing the Great Mystery's universal oneness firsthand. This step on life's road cannot be fabricated, cannot be engineered, and cannot be faked. The steps that lead to that universal understanding of life's dance are earned. In that moment of wonder, separation no longer exists, and we know that we are beautiful parts of the whole, as is every living thing. The steps leading to this turning point are as unique as each individual.

No religion, culture, race, or philosophy has the only way. Believing that there is only one way and that all others are doomed is a false foundation that promotes further human separation and heartache. We often adopt our beliefs from others or from a concept we have heard all our lives but have never put to the test. The word belief contains be lie. Inner knowing relates to something that we have questioned, experienced firsthand, and found to be true or workable. If we want to corner ourselves into stagnation, we can continue walking a tightrope that stifles our ability to grow by confining our lives to a linear, unvarying sameness.

In our ancient Native American traditions, we have been taught never to question another person's connection to the Creator. That personal experience is very private, very individual, and very sacred. How every person experiences the Creator or God is no one else's business. If the individual is told through dreams or through spiritual inspiration to follow a certain path in his or her unique way, that message must be honored. If that path of experience differs from tribal tradition or the customary habits but hurts no other living thing, it is accepted. Every human being must stand on every spoke of the Medicine Wheel of Life, and each is given the opportunity to shun or to embrace the lessons being presented.

Once we have found something that helps us to grow, we might feel tempted to insist that others follow our personal path. This attitude gives no elbow room for further growth. A Cherokee Ancestor once asked, "How do you destroy a righteous person? Give that person *one follower.*" Seeking to have control over others is deadly. By insisting that others follow our lead, using "my way or the highway" thinking, we limit our own growth potential.

Seen from outer space, the Earth is a beautiful blue ball traveling around the sun of this solar system. The orbital path of our planet is different from those of the other planets that also travel around our sun. No scientist would ever think to criticize the differences among planetary orbits; those orbits are simply there. Yet many people resist the idea that our universe supports different orbits as a part of a divine plan. Just as orbits, planetary patterns, and universes evolve, so do people. Our solar system reflects a model in which all planetary paths vary, yet all revolve around the sun's light in the center. Is it so hard to imagine that all human beings also travel on different paths around the sunlight, which feeds us physically, and the Creator's light, which feeds us spiritually?

No matter how far we travel in life, one truth cannot be denied: we always come back to ourselves. We cannot change others, but we can change ourselves and how we view life. There is no limitation to the journey of the human spirit. We will find our own individual paths, and we will always return full circle to our personal truths, even if those truths have changed as our understanding grew. We come into our physical lives to experience the cycles and seasons of human experience, and we move into another circle of nonphysical experience when our bodies die. Tapping the Dream Weave allows us to understand the unseen circles of energy that influence and define our waking experiences, showing us how to come full circle and how to dance the next level of our personal growth cycles.

The unique ways that we choose to express our personal Medicines or strengths will define how we dance through our lives. One truth remains constant; we are *dancing a dream* whether we acknowledge it or not. The rhythms always change, the movement varies, and we can choose to either tiptoe or stomp through the tulips. My teacher Cisi Laughing Crow said, "Fireflies dance in the twilight like human beings dance between good and evil. People forget that balance and harmony are found when they recognize that humans are just like the fireflies; even in the darkness everyone has a light, but each person must choose to let it shine."

CHAPTER 3

The spirit intervenes, changing our dance with destiny, delicately urging the heart to open and to serve.

—Berta Broken Bow

▲▲

FIRST PATH OF INITIATION

Sacred dawning of my spirit's fire,
I open beyond self-centered desire.

I choose to serve and to be
A shining example for all to see.

I honor the spirit in all living things.
I commit to the life that honesty brings.

I seek the truth that lives in me.
I respect the truths that others see.

I give to others with a happy heart
Asking no return for gifts I impart.

I open my heart to others in need,
Walking my path as I plant love's seeds.

—Jamie Sams

The First Path of Initiation
The East Direction on the Medicine Wheel

IN OUR Native American traditions, the first path of initiation was originally introduced as a rite of passage into adulthood. Young girls and boys faced various ceremonial tests representing the end of childhood. For females this passage was usually at the time of their first menstrual flow, and for young men it came around their thirteenth year. Ceremonies varied from tribe to tribe, but most involved a test of bravery for the boys and an introduction to the mysteries of woman's Medicine for the girls. After these ceremonies, boys were admitted into the men's council and girls into the women's council in order to listen to their Elders and to learn about the adult responsibilities of being of service to the tribe.

The clarity and illumination offered by these rites of passage were found through becoming responsible for the well-being of the tribe as a whole. Young people learned how to put away negative or childish emotions and to develop the ability to respond responsibly. The death of childhood and the birth of adulthood marked a new path that began in the East Direction of the Medicine Wheel. It signaled the dawning of the process of nurturing and honing the young person's gifts into talents that would benefit that person and the whole tribe. This process allowed the individual to find his or her own path, with the best mentors the tribe had to offer providing guidance in the areas of the individual's makeup or personality showing promise. Everyone was served by teaching and through learning, without hidden agendas; the better the student became at his or her chosen role, the more everyone benefited, including the teacher, who passed hard-earned expertise on to the next generation.

Although this type of tribal harmony is rarely found today, we can use the same philosophy in our modern lives by encouraging the young to find their gifts and by becoming mentors and good role models for the next generation. By teaching how to serve and by serving others ourselves, we begin to see the global family of Earth as our tribe, the human tribe.

THE MEDICINE WHEEL GIVES US STRUCTURE

The Medicine Wheel is a Native American symbol of the life cycles that all human beings transit during the Earth Walk of physical life. Each of us will stand on every spoke of this wheel in our growth process. We all begin in the East, which is the place of sunrise, the metaphorical dawning or birth of our lives. We travel the Medicine Wheel time and again with each new cycle or phase of life. We touch the lessons of the East Direction every time we encounter a point of clarity, illumination, and new beginnings. The big AH HA that occurs when we see though some illusion or discover some new data that brings our former chaos, indecision, or confusion into clarity is the essence of the East. From that new viewpoint, we are able to begin again because we have experienced a breakthrough. New ideas are born, we embrace refreshed purpose and intent, and we awaken to the puzzle pieces falling into place. Some new part of ourselves replaces the old self, which had trudged through the quagmire of challenges existing prior to the big AH HA. These are the gifts of the East Direction, and, fittingly, the first path of initiation begins in the East. Many lessons begin in this first path and will continue with new twists, turns, and greater understanding as time goes by.

Each path of initiation may have begun at an earlier stage of growth and may continue on to other stages as well. We can embrace the lessons of a particular path time and again with deeper understanding at each new level of initiation, or we can avoid certain lessons and encounter them later on another path. We are each unique in our choices and our willingness to confront certain aspects of our behaviors and personalities. There are no rules as to how we are to experience our various stages of growth, nor must we fully understand and conquer a challenge before we are allowed to continue other lessons in progress.

One person could be blind to some very basic lessons on the first path while completing other lessons on the third path.

One basic truth about these seven paths of initiation is that we are always given the opportunities we need to grow. We can recognize the open doors or deny certain lessons and avoid challenges for a time, but those lessons eventually reappear. If we think that we have mastered one level, just because we have experienced some lesson appearing on another level, Coyote, the divine Trickster, will usually show us how wrong we are by giving us a "pop quiz" in some unexpected area of our lives.

BEING RESPECTFUL

We might discover a lifestyle that gives us a sense of well-being and purpose. We may feel quite smug about the way we have handled our life and how we are succeeding in our chosen endeavors. If our smugness makes us feel self-important, we may be asking for a rude wake-up call teaching that zealotism can border on arrogance. The pop quiz can be set in motion when we return to our family home for a holiday, finding that no one in the family is interested in why they should change their lives and adopt our new lifestyle or spiritual practices. The reactions of our family can bring us disappointment or further judgments of disdain, creating a need for some internal examination. Unfortunately, some people choose to adopt a messiah complex, insisting that others conform to their views or practices. When they refuse to look at their overzealous behavior, the trap slams shut and the pop quiz begins.

Sometimes family situations can create confusion and despair. We return home to realize that Uncle Harry still treats us like a two-year-old. Father and Mother may talk as if they believe we have nothing important to say. Another relative may openly criticize our behavior, lifestyle, appearance, or life choices and not realize how cruelly it damages our newfound sense of well-being. No one is quicker to bring up old issues or half-forgotten pain than members of one's own family. Our choices of responses to these situations may range from humility to open rebellion. The initiation in this situation lies in choosing how to respond. We can choose to be hurtful and retaliate with rage, or we can choose not to respond at all. Serving our family does not mean criticizing their lifestyle or behavior. We can serve in many ways, but

we always serve with dignity when we return love in the face of conflict, maintaining an attitude of respect.

These pop quizzes are reality checks. They can create fury or restore
the humility needed to realize the falseness of one's sense of self-
importance. As my friend Terry Allen sings in one of his songs, "My
ego is not my amigo anymore. . . ." Whether with seriousness or
humor, patterns of self-importance and arrogance will force open
some new doors of unexpected learning opportunities. If we choose to
hold on to our all-too-human need to be grandiose, the lessons behind
those doors may not be pleasant. Faulting others for being who they
are keeps us from realizing that we may have adopted their same behavior to unthinkingly belittle others. The Golden Rule of "do unto
others as you would have them do unto you" is founded in the fact
that we do reap what we sow, and if we are drawn into behavior patterns that hurt others, we will be hurt in the process. Belittling another
literally diminishes the energy in our body, leaving us with less energy
to use for creating joy in our lives.

It is important to remember that every time we think we have no
more to learn in any given area, it is our weaknesses, not our strengths,
that will be tested. What an opportunity! These are the lessons that give
us the biggest surprises. Usually, these personal lessons make me sit
and laugh at myself until I can see the unlimited value of humor along
the way. I have learned that one of the greatest gifts we have as humans
is our sense of humor. The mind's ability to thwart and the ego's ability
to confound our perceptions are conquered only by the ability to laugh
at ourselves in the face of gotta-be-right seriousness. Big belly laughs
break the stranglehold created by our false sense of self-importance. If
we take our life paths of initiation too seriously, refusing to laugh at
our human folly, we will surely succumb to learning only through tragic
or painful events, forgetting that the ultimate test of any initiation is to
also learn through joy.

Remembering that all lessons in life are about finding balance is a
tricky task. Often we are tricked into learning something new when
our own behavior creates the need. In the Native American tradition,
we call this trickery Coyote Medicine. Coyote teaches us how to blend
the sacredness with irreverence to achieve balance. By laughing at ourselves, we diffuse the seriousness and break the stranglehold that limits
our energy. Laughter reweaves our fixed thoughts or ideas in the Dream
Weave, disassembling any walls of rigidity. When we have a good belly

laugh, we succeed in freeing ourselves from stuck energy. More energy moves through us, and instead of being uptight, we are able to continue exploring life and our individual potentials. We always have a choice, and when we say yes to the opportunities being offered, we can sidestep unrealistic fears and the ego's mind traps.

WAKE-UP CALL! HOW MANY TIMES HAVE YOU HIT THE SNOOZE BUTTON?

Some events can change the course of our lives forever. These wake-up calls do not have to be huge occurrences; they can take the form of any event that shows us the need to pay attention. Whether we see these wake-ups as good or bad, easy or difficult, the experiences force us to change. A close call can do this, depending upon how soon we react or respond to its subtle warnings. When we slide past a close call without harm, we sometimes choose to hit the snooze button, ignoring the purpose of the close call until we encounter another situation that jars us into a state of awareness and forces us to give attention to some area of our lives.

We all have seen people who get into serious trouble and life-threatening situations begin to pray for the first time in many years, making all sorts of promises to God. Yet the moment they pass through the crisis, they forget or refuse to honor their promises. Completing this first path of initiation depends totally upon our recognizing and honoring our wake-up calls. The wake-up call might be a simple whisper of the heart or an overwhelming sense of joy. It might come as a burning desire to invent or discover something that will help humanity, or it could be a warm glow that envelops us when we give to others. We can also awaken when we have a spiritual experience, some mystical or unexplainable occurrence, or a miracle in our lives. In all cases, the awareness that we have begun the paths of initiation is not present unless we acknowledge the wake-up call and respond to these omens of spiritual awakening. Only later do we begin to realize that these wake-up calls are the first messages sent to us by our own Spiritual Essence. Those significant taps on our shoulders will continue throughout all paths of initiation.

More radical wake-up calls can take the form of near-death experiences, the loss of all material possessions, or the loss of people we love.

Or we might become desperately unhappy and realize that we have to change something behaviorally or spiritually. In all cases, something happens inside of us that makes us decide to look further, to follow the path of finding what works for us. Eventually, the first path will teach us that being of service to humanity gives us a newfound freedom and sense of well-being. The religions of our world ask us to be good and kind. On the first path of initiation we learn that it is just as important to be good for something. Everyone has gifts to share, talents that are needed. How we use these abilities teaches us about our personal Medicines or inner strengths. These lessons show us how to use well what we have to offer, teaching us how to develop our Medicines to heal ourselves so that we can awaken to our spiritual and human potentials.

Laughingly paraphrasing one of my teachers, I ask the question "How many times have you hit the snooze button?" We slip in and out of states of awareness that urge us to go beyond our former limitations and to quit thinking solely about ourselves, embracing the idea of "we" instead of just "me." The power of free will and personal choice determines how we respond to life's wake-up calls. Sometimes when we see or feel the red light signaling a warning, we deny its existence. We can see the changes we need to accomplish either as a terrible burden or as a wonderful opportunity. We can blame God, life, bad luck, our childhood experiences, our families, and other external elements for our unhappiness, or we can accept the challenge of evolving beyond our mind's tendency to get stuck in past regret or fear of the future.

CHOOSING TO BE OUR PERSONAL BEST

The common thread that is woven in the Dream Weave during the first path of initiation is the desire to create change in one's life. The wake-up calls that signal the need for this change can occur at any given point in time or at any age. When we hear and respond to life's wake-up calls, we begin to question, becoming aware that there is more to life than what we have been experiencing. Every human being is faced with these questions: Who am I? Why am I here? What are my gifts, talents, and abilities? How can I use those gifts? What is my role in the world around me? As we find the answers for ourselves, we can begin the process of awakening and becoming aware of the overall plan that embodies Creation and our place within it.

Some ways of thinking or learned behaviors are passed from generation to generation. These *generational patterns* or family belief systems also must be examined to see if we are demonstrating dysfunctional behaviors that limit our effectiveness. We cannot lend a helping hand and be instruments of compassion if we get angry at every small upset. We cannot be effective if we help others in order to receive recognition. We all carry patterns we learned through observing our families and hearing their opinions on life. We might have fears about money if our relatives barely survived the world wars, poverty, or the financial insecurity of the American Depression. Some families believe that women cannot succeed in business or that men should not work in child care or meal preparation. In all cases, the first path of initiation insists that we look at ourselves and rethink our value systems, discarding outdated beliefs that keep us from becoming our personal bests.

The first-path lessons begin when we have the desire to serve and we follow that desire by committing to being of service. The Southern Seers' principle of "Preservation of Oneness" is a universal truth found in nature and within our universe. Balance in all things brings oneness. The first relationship we learn to honor is the respect we give ourselves. If every life form uses 51 percent of the energy it contains for self-preservation, it will survive. When we are willing to commit to 51 percent service to self and 49 percent service to others, we have achieved a balance that allows us to be effective in life. Whether we have service-related jobs or whether we volunteer makes no difference. The commitment to making our world a better place for everyone is the key to any path of service. On one level, we agree to be role models, and because of that devotion to being our personal best, we are forced to examine our personal integrity, our willingness to change and grow, and our commitment to doing what is needed when it is needed, serving with a happy heart.

CHOOSING TO BE OF SERVICE

Every time that we choose generosity, compassion, and being of service, we set in motion a chain of events that catapults us into a series of lessons and growth spurts comprising the first path of initiation. The first step on this path is *the desire to be of service*. The second step is *the decision to be of service*. The third step is *personal devotion and commitment to making the world a better place for everyone.* When we move toward being of service, any self-obsession or feeling of being a victim will shift, and we can achieve a more balanced perspective in life. When we see how others are often in far worse situations than our own, and when we see how we can help, we view our personal problems from a totally new perspective. The world may not change, but our perception of it and how we experience it will be radically altered.

Some people follow a certain life path in order to attain money, fame, power, respect, and recognition. There is nothing wrong with these goals. In the process of life, these people will uncover many challenging and revealing discoveries: for instance, they might find that when the goals that they originally set are accomplished, they still do not feel happiness, inner peace, and serenity. A balance is needed on this path, a balance that supplies the ingredients necessary to attain the sense of well-being. How those elements are discovered is individual and unique, but eventually the path of service will become more than a photo opportunity used to influence others.

Some people may choose a life path in order to prove to their families that they are worthy or successful. Others choose to excel in order to prove someone wrong who had a bad opinion of their prospects. In the beginning, we all follow our life paths for different reasons, but somewhere in the process we weave different dreams to support our growth.

Many people feel the desire to be of service early in life; for others it comes later. Some choose to become health care professionals or researchers, teachers or public servants, fire fighters, law enforcement officials, or other service-related professionals. These career choices offer these people the opportunity to give back to the communities where they live. Just as in any life, these caring individuals will find that they too must change and grow. The tests commonly presented on these paths of service are about continually creating and recreating that original desire to serve, which might have diminished as the path became simply a career or a way to support one's family.

Many people who have chosen to be of service do not know that on this first path, they eventually will have to make another decision that alters and expands the primary decision to serve. Even though they wish to serve, they may hold an internal judgment about service. For example, they may not truly wish to serve the people in need who are of another race, sexual preference, religion, or financial status. The judgment itself produces a huge loss of personal energy that waters down their original desire to be of service. The internal split between the spirit's desire to serve and the mind's judgments can create a form of ineffective stagnation.

The judgments inhibiting service are patterns that usually were learned in childhood; people are not born with hatred or prejudice. So one of the first lessons when deciding to serve humanity is to look at the excess baggage we hold in the way of judgments, limiting ideas, and negative thoughts. We cannot be effective if we volunteer to serve only when it pleases us or only when the people in need meet our judgmental criteria. When we serve with judgments, the energy found in the circle of giving and receiving is broken.

This revelation regarding our unseen excess baggage and limiting thoughts begins a process that continues throughout all seven paths of initiation. Through a constant weeding-out process, we address all negativity, judgments, abusive thoughts, and actions, whether they are

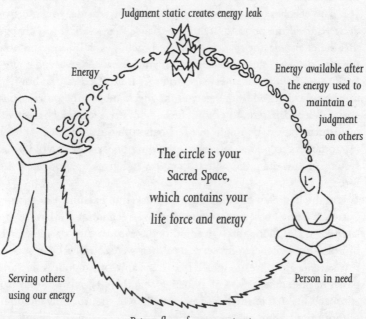

Judgment static creates energy leak

Energy

Energy available after the energy used to maintain a judgment on others

The circle is your Sacred Space, which contains your life force and energy

Serving others using our energy

Person in need

Return flow of energy sent out

Sacred Space Circle

directed toward ourselves or toward others. To begin the process, we must first be present enough to notice when we are engaging in those types of thoughts and behaviors. Everyone has a different way of handling their negative habits, and the best approach is to eliminate as many as possible through personal choice, not because someone else forced us to change.

For some people, the desire to change is enough to actually change their habits. For others, tracking down when they started thinking a certain way and letting go of the past is effective. Others make a personal creed that can be added to over time, and they stick to those promises. All of these solutions are valid. If we are determined and have the intent to change, transformation will occur. Every time we let go of some limiting behavior, we free up the life force available to us. The freed life force contains bursts of energy, the fuel that propels us into new experiences, levels of transformation, and clarity that we never believed were possible.

As these changes are made, the Dream Weave responds by opening new avenues of opportunity. For instance, if you always believed that you hate beaches because your family hated the seaside, you effectively deny yourself the opportunity to experience the ocean. If you change that belief and decide that you can like beaches even if Mom did not, the new decision shifts the patterns of your Dream Weave, and energy floods into your Spiritual Essence. You might not be aware of how things have changed or understand the mechanics of the process, but you will feel different. You might feel a new sense of vitality, creativity, or inspiration, or you might just feel better physically. The act of opening to new perceptions, rather than holding on to stubborn old belief systems, funds the mind with inspiration and gives the body new life force.

On the first path of initiation we are asked to examine our personal "ways of being" based upon what we have been taught or have assimilated from childhood through adulthood. We must then decide whether or not those belief systems serve us. When we choose to be of service, if we are to grow, we are forced to discard any limiting ideas that are based in prejudice, as well as all beliefs that there is only one way to approach life. For example, if we are willing to mentor only children without physical disabilities, we have denied the original intent to serve humanity. If we insist on using the information we learned by rote repetition in any area, we have negated any new principles or ideas that could inspire us further. If we are educated people and feel that others are stupid because they have not had the same educational opportunities, in feeling superior we have lost our purpose instead of seeing an opportunity to teach and share our knowledge.

During our lives we often lose the wonder and the excitement that gave us our original intent and purpose. Every time we can be reminded of why we want to continue to serve, we are given a rebirth of purpose that fuels our strength to carry on. We cannot control how or when we will encounter the renewal process. We can find rebirth though others acknowledging our efforts, through unexpected blessings in life, or through our own love for humanity. Any return to clarity takes that which has gone a bit stale in our lives and gives it new vigor. Many events can bring us full circle, returning us to the East Direction on the Medicine Wheel, where we get a well-deserved booster shot of inspiration.

THE FINAL BEGINNING

The turning point on the first path is when the first veil is beginning to lift and we sense that our lives have a purpose and that we are here for a reason that we may not yet fully understand. My teachers called this process "the final beginning."

This occurs when we finally turn and face the Creator, the Great Mystery, God, and acknowledge that our life cannot be lived fully without the connection to the Divine Presence that made all life. We realize that we have a soul or spirit that connects us to the Great Mystery. This moment is called "the final beginning" because from this point forward we are willing to acknowledge that we are spiritual beings who happen to have human bodies and that we are connected in some unknown way to a Higher Power that influences our lives in mysterious ways.

When we come to this realization, any concept that humans are the dominant species in the universe begins to shift. We know that we have carnal bodies like animals and that the blood that flows through all bodies in the human and animal kingdoms is the color red. We have been taught that our human brains have reasoning abilities and intelligence that make us different from any of the animal species. We know that we have emotions, tactile feelings, and physical urges because we have felt them since birth. We physically feel the human needs for air, food, water, physical touch, sexuality, and shelter from the elements. We emotionally desire companionship, nurturing, love, acceptance, and happiness. These are common traits found in the human species. However, not all human beings understand or feel the presence of the human spirit, whereas animals and plants are aware of that life force or spirit instinctually.

Many people have been taught that they have a soul, while others believe that there is no spirit or soul and deny the presence of any type of Higher Power, God, or Creator. When we acknowledge our souls or Spiritual Essences, our perceptions of ourselves begin to take on an added dimension and the first veil begins to dissolve, allowing light and definition into our consciousness.

When we come to the point of the final beginning, we acknowledge that being of service to humanity can have ties to a far greater divine or spiritual purpose than we formerly imagined. Our spiritual purpose is continually revealed as we embrace the paths of human initiation, rediscovering the parts of life and the universe that extend beyond the five basic senses.

During the first part of this path, we encounter the general lessons and initiations that shape our original decision to be of service. We commit to being of service and learn to find a balance in giving to others while maintaining our personal growth. We eliminate individual behaviors that limit us and ideas that hinder our effectiveness. We add energy through broadening our viewpoints on life. On this path we learn to hone our skills and to find our places as role models. We choose to become our personal best without having to insist that others follow our lead. We embrace the "we" rather than the "me" and desire good for all people. We look at our lives as being growth opportunities that offer challenges to increase our awareness and our inner strengths.

EXPANDING THE TUNNEL VISION

In the next stage of the first path of initiation we begin to understand more of what it means to be of service to ourselves because all that we are and all that we embrace weaves the experiences we have in life. Because we have acknowledged that every human being has a soul or spirit, we begin to see that we must honor the spiritual aspects found in every part of humanity. We strive to learn patience and to understand the cultures, ideas, and philosophies of others who think differently from us. We open ourselves to commitment by personally dedicating our lives and energy to service without the need for reward or approval. We develop self-reflective skills that teach us that all experiences in our lives are a direct result of the thoughts, feelings, and ideas that we embrace, understanding that those unseen parts of human nature contain energy. The energy of internal conflicting thoughts and feelings directly influences the harmony or discord of the experiences in our daily lives.

On the first path, we may encounter internal discord before we find our own rhythm of harmony. There are no coincidences or accidents in human experience. Everything happens for a reason and is created so that we can grow from the experience. When we are hitting every green light on our paths, we are in balance and life becomes synchronistic. When we are out of balance, the disharmony is evident and we are given a subtle wake-up call. If we correct the imbalances, we flow with life once more. If we do not pay attention, the challenges become harder and the wake-up messages become more difficult to experience.

WOW, THAT WAS WEIRD!

If we allow ourselves to experience the unusual without judging it or discounting it as being too weird or unreal, we can open ourselves to new horizons. In ancient Viking lore, "the way of the weird" referred to the manner in which their gods intervened in human lives. The Vikings accepted that the unexplainable mysteries and miracles encountered in life were due to divine intervention. But modern people often forget that the hand of the Creator passes through our lives and cannot be explained.

One turning point amid the lessons of the first path comes when we receive an acknowledgment of gratitude from someone who may or may not know us. Their words of encouragement change our perspective in an instant. Something clicks inside of us, and we realize that what we are contributing can make a difference. Suddenly we realize that our life really matters and that we have found a life path that will feed more than just the brain and the ego; it will feed our heart and our soul. An influx of energy bursts through us, and we enjoy a sense of satisfaction, spiritual accomplishment, and self-esteem. We may relate those feelings to remembered childhood joys or to the first time we felt that we had authentically succeeded in doing something that we had worked diligently to accomplish. These feelings gather enough momentum to create a kind of magical synchronicity that has not happened to us before.

Some of the uncanny situations that occur when we are in balance and experiencing the synchronicity of life may startle us. It might be something as simple as thinking of a friend and hearing from that person soon after we have the thought. Or perhaps we have an idea that we want to develop and put into action and we spontaneously encounter others with the skills or information needed to implement our innovative concepts.

Our experiences can also include unexplainable flashes of knowing that something is going to happen before it occurs. We hear someone calling our name and upon looking around find that no one is there. We feel that someone we care about is in danger or needs help and if we pay attention, going with our intuition, we may find that we were right, arriving just in time to offer our assistance.

My teachers considered these experiences to be the beginning of the stirring of spirit inside the individual. Parapsychologists have adopted many labels for the paranormal occurrences of this first path, including déjà vu, precognition, telepathic messages, psychic intuition, and paranormal phenomena. Over the past centuries, experts in metaphysics, religion, the occult, and the lore of the ancient mystery schools have called these experiences Shakti energy, the birth of intuition, taking the hand of the Holy Spirit, being baptized in the spirit, the initiation of the soul, spiritual awakening, and various other names.

In the case of déjà vu experiences, we may dream of doing or feeling something and not remember the dream, which is held in our subconscious until, at a later date, we find ourselves actually doing and feeling the same things in the location revealed in our dream. We may not remember the original dream, but we may suddenly remember that we have experienced the situation before and become very perplexed. In other instances, we may have recurring dreams that come true, frightening us and making our reality seem really spooky. Upon waking from a dream, some people have answered the phone and found that the person on the line was telling them about the exact sequence of events that they had just dreamed.

These little miracles continue to surface and can startle us into believing that something is happening that we do not understand, and in fact it is. The moment we acknowledged that we were spiritual beings, that spiritual life force energy was activated in our lives. Since spirit is the connective tissue that runs through all parts of our universe, by acknowledging the existence of our own spirits, we have allowed ourselves to enter the river of spiritual energy that connects thought, emotion, feeling, and physicality. We begin going with that flow instead of paddling upstream. We begin to flow with an unseen force that shows us our spiritual connections through synchronicity.

If we do not have a clue as to why things are changing or what understanding brought the flow of spiritual synchronicity into our life, we may accept it offhandedly until the mind tells us that what is occurring is not normal or is just too weird. Resistance and fear can surface when we feel that we are no longer in control. Our mind may shout that "the reality boat" is being rocked without our expressed consent, and it may insist that we will drown in the tide of these sudden unexplainable events. Some people feel that they must try to control the strange course of events. Others simply want to stop the synchronicity and avoid the shifts that are taking place in their reality because it terrorizes them. Some people keep themselves so busy that they can ignore the wake-up calls and maintain the status quo instead of going with the flow.

BECOMING A SPIRITUAL WARRIOR

The courageous person who is willing to accept the sudden unexplainable shifts of perspective in his or her life has to make a commitment to becoming a spiritual warrior. You may wonder what that means. In the tradition of the Southern Seers, my teachers taught me that the spiritual warrior is the brave individual who is willing to turn, no longer seeking external enemies, to face the enemies within. These internal opponents can include fear, arrogance, envy, jealousy, bad behavior, dishonesty, and a multitude of other human weaknesses. That life commitment, when we promise ourselves to go the distance and live our lives as spiritual warriors, can be one of the most profound and scary steps we ever take. Once we make that commitment, we begin to flow with the synchronicity of events that defy the regularity we have come to expect from life, and magical experiences begin to happen that change the course of our life forever.

Although most people experience this turning point much later in life, I was fourteen years old when I made this commitment. I was volunteering after school and on weekends at the local Catholic hospital. One Saturday the nuns showed all of the teenage volunteers a film on childbirth that included an actual birth and step-by-step procedures. From that moment forward, I knew that I wanted to help brings babies into the world. I began to dream about becoming a midwife/nurse. I even thought about volunteering at the Baptist hospital, where all maternity services had been moved because our small town could not support two hospitals with maternity wards. I knew in my heart of hearts that this was going to be my life's calling, because I was having dreams in which I was delivering a baby. I never thought it was strange that in my dream I was still fourteen years old or that I was delivering a baby while the mother was lying on the floor of some tiny room that barely had any light. But it was just a dream, right?

Two weeks later, on a Saturday, I was entering the elevator in the Catholic hospital, on my way to the floor where I volunteered. I looked at the pregnant woman who was next to me as the door closed. She suddenly screamed, "Stop, the baby's coming!" I hit the elevator stop button between floors and helped her lie down and remove her panties. The baby's head was crowning. I was not panicked in the least and told her not to worry, I knew how to deliver a baby. The baby came in less than two minutes. I took off my half-slip, wrapped the baby, and put him on her stomach with the cord still in place, covered her, started the elevator, and stopped it on the third floor. I got my head nurse, and the medical team took over from there.

The pregnant mother was Catholic and from out of town, and she had no idea that there was no maternity ward at the Catholic hospital. The cab driver just dropped her at the front door. This child was her seventh. I was young, naive, and very lucky. The synchronicity was astonishing since I had seen it all happen in my dreams, step by step. I was a heroine in the new mother's eyes, and all of the nuns and my head nurse were amazed, lauding me with abundant praise. I knew then that I could make a difference in the world.

BENDING WITHOUT BREAKING

The older we grow, the more we tend to become set in our habits, our outlooks on life, and our mental assessments of what is possible. Flexible attitudes show us that by allowing the pendulum of life's experiences to move, finding new points of balance that include the unexplainable, we can move beyond our former fear and rigidity. The more flexibly balanced we become, the less chaos we encounter along our paths. Harmony is not created by having only one musical tune; rather it is the blending of many tunes that creates a symphony of sound. Individual tunes work together, creating beauty rather than discord. Balance is found in living harmoniously, with flexibility, accepting the weird events that surface as a part of the mystery that is beginning to unfold in our lives. When we accept that we are experiencing divine intervention instead of feeding our fear by trying to control the outcome, the synchronicity simply follows.

The flashes of insight are no more than spiritual symbols or messages giving us encouragement, telling us that we are in sync with the path that is unfolding in front of us. The balanced spiritual warrior accepts the encouragement without hesitation and handles any fear or arrogance that may arise, humbly accepting the Creator's gift and the encouragement being offered. Taking things in stride and becoming our own counsel is another skill that begins to emerge on the first path. The more we develop this skill, the easier it becomes to maintain balance.

Instant discord is also found on the first path when we are out of balance. Serving out of a false sense of duty or with a grudge can produce experiences where anger flies in our faces because others sense our lack of harmony. We can encounter disapproval for our best efforts when we hold self-hatred or self-critical views. Our internal ideas about ourselves will always be reflected back to us in a negative way when we are doing something in order to get praise to bolster our low self-esteem rather than from the joy of being of service.

If we believe that we are victims, we hold internal images and feelings that can create our unconscious need to be victimized or emotionally beaten up by others. When we find our sense of self-worth through successful service to others, we dismantle the web of victimism. We begin the process of reclaiming our balance with the decision to honor ourselves by finding our gifts and by acknowledging those talents as being worthy, without comparing ourselves to others.

STAYING IN BALANCE

On the first path certain supporting activities allow us to proceed with grace. Listening is very important. When we listen to our words and detect anything negative or judgmental about our manner of speaking, we can discern where we are hampering our personal progress. We naturally expand by listening to our internal thoughts and by eliminating any belittling or critical thinking regarding ourselves or another. We also need to listen to the words of others and really hear what they are saying, expressing how they view life. If those ideas are negative, we must be careful not to adopt those ideas in order to be accepted; we must maintain our personal viewpoints of harmony. If we hear words that demean others, we have the power to walk away or to comment with something positive rather than supporting negativity. This also teaches us to eliminate gossip or rumormongering from our lives. There is no need to leak our life force by contributing to that type of behavior; it serves no one.

Breaking old habits is difficult, but the rewards are greater than we might suspect. On the first path we learn how certain activities drain our energy and how other positive choices give us needed life force to accomplish our dreams and goals. Imagine a river of life force that flows from your body into the world of your thoughts and feelings before it enters your life's activities and returns to your body. You might be startled at how many tributaries flow away from you due to courses set by your thoughts and feelings. Your personal river of life force may be as mighty as the Mississippi, but the energy you lose by sending your thoughts and feelings into the Dream Weave with tributaries made up of past regret, old fears, judgments, negativity, and generational belief systems will drain that river of life force until you become weak or fearful of life itself.

Every time we face the enemies within and decide to change a negative behavior to a positive one, we call our own energy back from negative thoughts or feelings, and we are given the gift of new life force. That life force has effectively been recycled, creating a circle that feeds us with energy. We become stronger because we are serving ourselves by increasing the life force we have available. The return flow of life force ensures our physical health, psychological well-being, balanced attitudes, emotional security, spiritual purpose, and overall wholeness.

This process is the first in many that teaches us the value of acknowledging the unseen energy of the Dream Weave. The threads of life force connected to the Spiritual Essence are deposited any place that we send our energy, positive or negative. All emotion is energy-in-motion. Our thoughts contain that same energy, and we have personal free will to invest that energy anywhere we see fit. Becoming aware of how we invest our life force is a task in itself. Once we recognize where we leak energy on negative thoughts, feelings, and behaviors, we can easily reclaim that part of our life force and reinvest the energy we reclaim into areas that serve ourselves as well as others.

The balance found in the circle of giving and receiving is an initiation in itself. This lesson teaches us that if we are selfish, the flow of receiving tends to dwindle. The more generous we are with others, the more we tend to receive from others as well as from life. But if we never take care of ourselves, putting the casual desires of others before our basic needs, we burn out, becoming depleted and ineffective. Balance is the key to our successful rites of passage. Every change we make in our lives is a rite of passage, a turning point where we choose to change our lives. We find new points of balance through the personal effort of testing what works and what does not work for us as individuals. In all cases, when we ignore one area of our lives and focus solely on another, we deplete our energy, hindering our forward progress.

The daily balancing acts in life are familiar to everyone, but most of us never know until much later that we are in the early stages of training, learning how to manage more than one dimension or reality at a time. This concept may sound "way out" or crazy to some people, but the seen world of what you know as physical reality also contains the unseen worlds of energy. We are constantly being touched by spiritual influences that alter our perceptions. We don't usually recognize it until we have encountered it many times. The two worlds of the tangible and the invisible come together like a busy intersection; one world contains matter and unwittingly uses the energy of the other world without understanding it or accurately perceiving the forces contained therein. As we grow, we become more aware of how those two worlds affect our lives moment by moment and decision by decision. On the later paths of initiation, the two worlds expand and begin to reveal other unexplainable and nontangible aspects of life. Our understanding expands to the degree that we are willing to look for and to find the complex weave of our universe, which is constantly evolving inside of the Great Mystery.

Somewhere along the first path, the primary lessons of the second path of initiation begin to appear in our lives. These dovetail, giving us a simultaneous transition into further growth. I'd like to remind you that we continue to develop our skills of the first path and add the lessons of the second path to the ones we are already learning. There are no full stops or graduations marking a shift from one path to another. Each path unfolds into the next and is continuous. Perfection is not a part of any of these paths, but doing our personal best is what determines our impeccability in life. To acknowledge our mistakes and to try again is all that is required. There are no failures except in our own eyes.

When nothing seems to be changing, we have merely encountered a point of temporary stagnation, or we may have come to a point in our lives where we need to retreat or regroup, collecting ourselves before we continue life's exploration process. The doldrums will always pass, and we will have some kind of breakthrough, coming to the East Direction once more, finding a big AH HA that brings further clarity, giving us a rebirth of purpose and new determination, allowing us to find the unfolding path and synchronicity once more.

CHAPTER 4

When human beings finally discover their own humanity,
they reel from the shock of finding that they must learn to
live up to it.

—Cisi Laughing Crow

▲▲▲

THE AWAKENING

Sacred Mystery,
Open my eyes so that I can see,
The part my judgments play in me.

Accept my grateful words of praise
For the love of life that's set ablaze.

I recall my spirit to the sacred fire
Where burns my heart's purest desire.

I banish all jealousy so I may replace
Envy's burden with the state of grace.

I will offer kindness in the face of pain,
Leaving revenge in the shadow's domain.

I embrace forgiveness so I will know
The grace of blessing every friend and foe.

—Jamie Sams

The Second Path of Initiation
The South Direction on the Medicine Wheel

THE South Direction on the Medicine Wheel is the place of the return of trust and innocence, the place where our faith is tested or proven, and the place where we have the opportunity to recapture the wonder of being alive that we once held as children.

For centuries, my people have taught those willing to hear that human beings, the two-leggeds, are a part of the Earth. We belong to the Earth Mother whether we think we do or not. On the second path, it becomes evident that we are a part of the Earth when we learn to feel the heartbeat of the Earth align with our own. For many people, this is a life-changing event. Some feel the heartbeat; others sense it in other ways, such as a sparkling synchronicity when everything they do begins to flow magically in a natural rhythm. When the rhythm of the human heart begins to vibrate at the same resonance as the Earth's energy field, synchronicity happens. As indigenous people, we have held this sacred truth for centuries, and we did not need to have scientific data to support our inner knowing or ancestral wisdom. Now, this simple truth is supported by scientific data gathered from many different facets of research.

Gregg Braden, a geologist and the author of *Awakening to Point Zero*, recently released data that scientifically explains the phenomenon that human beings experience on the second path of initiation. The Earth Mother's energy resounds and is measured as electrical units per second, which are called hertz. These pulses are the heartbeat of the Earth Mother. In 1995, the Earth's resonant energy field vibrated at 7.4 to 8.6

hertz. By 1997 the hertz level increased to 9 hertz and then jumped to 9.9 for three weeks in March, raising human consciousness.

When human beings begin to make changes in their lives that eliminate negative behavioral patterns, their hearts begin to put out a higher rate of hertz. Synchronicity with the Earth's energy begins to change their personal experiences of life in general. We call this synchronicity Grouse Medicine because of the spiraling flight of the grouse. We continue circling the Medicine Wheel of life, level by level, as we learn life's lessons, creating a synchronistic process that continues if we do not allow fear to alter the flow.

On the second path, our heart continues to open to new possibilities through the phenomenon of synchronicity. When life becomes hope filled or seemingly magical, we tend to look at what we are doing right that has allowed change to occur. From these observations, we are urged to continue the beneficial changes, improving our behaviors in order to remain in the joy-filled state we are experiencing. We often begin to perceive life from a different vantage point, and we become more sensitive to the mannerisms we use when we interact with others.

Some people begin self-help or self-improvement regimes that assist them in maintaining the positive changes they are embracing. Others may find new levels of awareness in the form of heightened sensations or acute astuteness emerging at the oddest moments. In the face of this synchronicity, some people find themselves surrounded with new friends who are experiencing the same magical feelings, and by sharing their experiences they are urged to explore the journey together.

When we are finding balance on the second path and are actively working toward becoming our personal best, we go through many rites of passage. Every time we move forward, counting a personal victory over some former challenge or limitation, we find that our efforts have produced a harvest of personal miracles. Things that we once believed we could never accomplish are suddenly within reach as we jump one hurdle after another. This is not to imply that no concerted effort is necessary; on the contrary, we become able to gain momentum only to the degree that we are willing to face our fears, taking on greater challenges by employing the deep reservoirs of untapped personal courage.

AWAKENING THE PERCEPTIONS

Every human being has many sensory perceptions, which are developed in different fashions. For this reason it is important that no one accept these examples as the *only* ways in which the synchronistic aspects of the second path can be experienced. There is no singular way to view, feel, hear, or perceive the unseen energy that begins to appear when we embark on the lessons of the second path. In fact, some people sense this newfound harmony with life without seeing anything at all. Other people may begin to feel energy shifts in a more intense way; when they are around negative situations they may feel the fight-or-flight syndrome in their bodies and become confused by the array of emotional and psychological waves accompanying the emotions emitted by others. This hypersensitivity is the beginning skill of an empath, a person who clearly feels the emotions belonging to others. Some people with extra-sensitive hearing or feeling are able to tap the unspoken languages of the natural world, communicating with animals on a conceptual, feeling level. On the second path, many people find that the senses are heightened from time to time and they gain a new respect for every living thing. These occurrences are not stable at this stage, and many people become frightened out of their wits and try to stop it from happening again, or they believe something is desperately wrong with them.

When this synchronicity with life begins to occur, it is evident that a new two-way communication has begun. At first this communication can be a form of intuition. The small, still voice within our being, which has always been there, is synchronistically communicating with the Earth Mother and our body, allowing us an opportunity to relate to that inner voice with a newfound trust. If we have ignored the gut feeling or sense of knowing that we have encountered earlier in life, we have created a pattern in the Dream Weave that will take time to fully overcome, but that victory is a second-path lesson that opens new worlds of wonder to everyone who puts forth the effort. We are being asked to trust our senses as we did when we were children, before life presented experiences and reasons for us to shut off those heightened perceptions.

When we are in sync with life, the wonder continues to flow unless we ignore the fine-tuning of intuition. Discounting the gentle messages we receive through our body's perceptions creates a kind of static that keeps us at odds with life and ourselves. All intuition is a developed skill that comes through the trial and error of honoring or ignoring our perceptions. The key is respect. When we respect ourselves, we own and honor our intuition and senses. When we have low self-esteem or are fearful, we often discount the perceptions that can naturally guide us. By learning to respect ourselves and our perceptions, we begin to respect the life forms around us. We learn to honor every living thing and each life form's right to be. We sense our own Sacred Space, the space around us that includes our body, our spirit, and all our thoughts, emotions, and possessions, and we honor the boundaries of the Sacred Spaces surrounding all life.

In order to tap into this magical state of being, we must face one of the most profound challenges on the second path: embodying the form of spiritual warriors and having the courage to face our internal weaknesses and free ourselves from habits, ideas, and emotions that belong to the past. Every time we go beyond a former limitation we free some energy, which heightens our perception and shows us that the magic of life is still there, even though we had become blind to it. The rewards that seem like acts of divine intervention urge us to continue moving forward. Yes, some people get frightened along the way, but the South Direction requires us to have faith in the process and in the divinely orchestrated instances of magical or unexplainable moments.

OH, THE TANGLED WEB WE WEAVE!

If we want to commit to the paths of initiation and to gather the harvest of magical experiences that occur when we have freed our life force, we must clear ourselves of unhealthy emotions and behaviors, which cloud our clarity. If we feel that we cannot trust another person, we might be seeing ourselves reflected in their behavior. If we are actively using mind games, manipulation, control, or intimidation to bend the will of others to our own purposes, we will not be able to tap into the authentically clear intuition of childlike wonder and trust. We will continue to receive mixed messages within our gut feelings and invalid or inaccurate flashes of intuition. Confronting and correcting these behaviors is one of the required lessons of the second path. If we avoid this process, we will remain clueless when others are perceiving a situation accurately.

Deceit and hidden agendas are the precursors of stagnation. When we communicate with one another in this manner, the results are disastrous. Disentangling our energy from these behaviors can take a lot of effort, but the benefits are many. When we refuse to use manipulation, hidden agendas, controlling behaviors, or deceit in communicating with others, we begin to clear our own observations, and we accurately feel or intuit truth. We also begin to reclaim the energy we have leaked on mind games or intimidation. As that energy is freed up in the Dream Weave, we feel spurts of effortless ease, which allow us to accomplish goals quickly. As we eliminate the behaviors that muck up our emotions and thoughts, we may find ourselves making unexpected quantum leaps in our growth processes. Sudden bursts of accurate sensory perceptions can accompany the release of these types of behaviors, giving us new ways to communicate with other life forms in our world.

This process of developing new kinds of communication skills is an intuitive form of self-discovery that unlocks a multitude of hidden human potentials and allows us to interact with the natural world. Being guardians of nature and communicating with all life on our planet is our precious birthright as Children of Earth. The desire to stay in synchronicity with the Earth and to grow allows us to communicate with ourselves and our feelings. The realization that all matter is made from unseen atoms and that all atoms contain energy is a scientific way of arriving at the same understanding: all things contain life force, so everything is alive. We have been taught to believe that inanimate objects such as rocks and mountains are not living things. On the second path, when we begin to perceive or to feel energy, we know how wrong that lifeless concept is.

There is nothing in our universe that does not contain energy. Emotion, thought, intent, and consciousness are some of the forms of energy present in human beings. These flows of energy are one way that we communicate with one another, and they also are the means by which we relate to all other life forms. It becomes impossible to send or to receive any form of truthful communication if we have not cleared the lines of energy within ourselves that direct our thoughts, feelings, and intentions into the universe.

My teachers taught me that there are 357 sensory perceptions or antennae of awareness within the human being. Our conventional educational systems teach that we have only five senses and that 90 percent of the human brain is unused. My teachers insisted that once we begin these paths of initiation, new sensory perceptions are woven into the Dream Weave and that from that point, new antennae of awareness are activated. The rate of activation depends totally upon the individual. As we develop the abilities we need, we learn how to communicate with and to integrate the energetic messages sent to us from all of Creation. We are never given excessive access to the worlds of unseen energy until we are physically, intuitively, emotionally, psychologically, and spiritually ready to handle it.

CLEARING THE WILL

What does that mean, "until we are ready to handle it?" My teachers were very specific on this point. It takes a lot of energy to tap into the intangible worlds of the Dream Weave. Some people leak energy through constant sexual activity, compulsive behaviors, and addictions. Others leak energy through victim thinking or gossip. Still others leak energy on planning revenge or through using intimidation to make others cower in submission. We leak our life force every time we act on thoughts of greed or feelings of envy or jealousy. If we entertain ourselves by playing with the feelings or minds of others, we not only have misdirected our creativity or flow of life force, we have ensured that our own Dream Weave patterns will become tangled into an intricate mess that will keep us stuck in the same illusions we believed we were using only to control others.

If we actively use our personal will to manipulate or to control others, any gift of intuition that we possess will be severely limited because of our self-centered viewpoint. When people employ hidden agendas or lack integrity, they find a scarcity of available energy. There is not enough life-force present to touch the next set of lessons that will bring illumination. Some people were born with gifts of intuition, but they cannot use these abilities as they could when they were children, because they have adopted attitudes and behaviors that misdirect the energy or life force needed to accurately master the former talent or skill. Until the life force is freed, through eliminating the behaviors that misdirect its use, we cannot authentically and accurately gain access to the unseen worlds of energy existing within the Dream Weave.

How do we open ourselves to further growth? Every person may have a different method, but all the diverse processes of discovery and growth yield certain results that are common to everyone. Take the example of a drain pipe that has gotten rusted and partially clogged over the years: this is a metaphor for our human condition. Not much water can flow through that pipe until the layers of accumulated sediment are stripped away layer by layer. On the second path, we are asked to begin eliminating the accumulated patterns that have numbed our human perceptions. How we accomplish that task is uniquely individual.

On the second path we learn to understand energy. Feeling and emotions are a form of energy-in-motion that effectively flows into all parts of Creation and interacts with all other energy and eventually returns to the point of origin. That point of origin is the person who sent the positive or negative feelings, thoughts, or actions into the world through the use of personal will.

One part of the second path's work consists of continually clearing the will by eliminating the need to see ourselves as victims or by making victims of others. Hatred, revenge-based emotions, and mistrust are felt by all human beings. If we deny or mistrust our feelings, fearing that we might act on them, we will accumulate stuck energy that should be kept in motion by feeling it and releasing it without judgment. If we act on base emotions and rage against others, we are abusive, making victims of those around us. If we deny our feelings, we become victims to our guilt and shame. *Guilt is not an emotion* and cannot be moved nor easily released. Guilt is created when we adopt what we think others expect of us as our guideline, denying our own integrity and self-directed will. If guilt is present, we can examine when we adopted the idea and from which person it originated. When we honor our inner knowing and breathe deeply, we release the energy that was stuck. Healthy shame is beneficial and very different from guilt. When we know that we have done something that is inappropriate or hurtful, healthy shame reminds us that our integrity is at risk and that we need to be accountable for our misdeeds.

Any time that we refuse to feel what we are feeling, we use vast amounts of life force. All mental assessments or inaccurate assumptions stop the effortless flow of emotion that belongs to us as human beings. Allowing ourselves to feel the full range of emotions, without necessarily acting on them, is healthy. As we clear ourselves by releasing our wounds and the reactive emotions that come up when we feel hurt again, the energy-in-motion is recycled. We don't get stuck in denying our will or in refusing to feel. When we hold on to feelings stuck in

past wounds, they sour our attitudes and inhibit any kind of healing
flow or emotional growth.

There is nothing outside of us that does not exist inside of us. That
statement may be confusing to some people, but the fact is that the external picture of what we experience in physical life always reflects our
internal decisions, feelings, thoughts, and attitudes. Those unseen emotions, ideas, attitudes, and decisions determine the ways in which we
weave our individual parts of the Dream Weave. Each personal thought
or attitude is a thread of energy, which intertwines with other personal
feelings. Together, all of our attitudes, feelings, opinions, thoughts, and
ideas make up an unseen framework or skeleton for our life experiences. What we can experience in life is determined by our concepts of
what is possible and our willingness to feel. We cannot encounter the
magic in life if we do not feel and acknowledge our emotions. If we
are allowing our emotions to flow, we will feel wonder when it happens and we will know that miracles are possible. We blind ourselves to
possibilities every time we make a firm decision that life on planet
Earth cannot offer certain experiences.

YOU HAVE AN INVISIBLE
SAVINGS ACCOUNT

Where have we invested our life force or energy? We invest that energy
in our family life, children, jobs, places of worship, homes, recreation,
and health. These places of investment take up our waking hours. As
with bank accounts, we make deposits of time and energy that we trust
will bring us a dividend of happiness. We invest our thoughts also in
something like a bank account, which determines whether we will
have enough "cash flow" of creative energy and life force to maintain
all of the physical parts of our lives that we think will make us happy.
Our energy accounts go into the red when we waste energy on destructive thoughts and feelings. Synchronicity reappears the moment
we make a spiritual withdrawal, refusing to invest our life force in any
activity that energetically feeds envy, jealousy, anger, resentment, bitterness, judgment, blame, unhealthy shame, or self-importance.

How we invest the energy contained in our decisions affects our account balance. If we wake in the morning feeling blue and decide we
will have a rotten day, we have set up the energetic skeleton made of

our feelings, attitudes, and beliefs. The day will usually flesh out in the manner in which we believed it would. If we hold a belief that we can share the joy we have inside of us with others, during that day we may find total strangers smiling at us for no apparent reason. If we assume that we have kindness to offer and we follow that attitude with action, we simply feel better. We receive our own sense of well-being as a reward, even if others do not respond to us in kind.

Every time we make a decision to vent anger on another without cause, we disturb the force of energy that may be rhythmically flowing through our life. Every time we decide to act on feelings of vengeance or to return retribution, instead of feeling and releasing those emotions, we limit the amount of energy that can flow through the vessels of our bodies. The metaphorical pipes get clogged every time we insist upon revenge instead of letting go of our need to be right or to get back at another who has wronged us. Our choices regarding how to use our energy always determine our surplus of usable energy even when we are exhausted because we have chosen to operate in the red.

THE SPLASH YOU MAKE CAN TOUCH THE WORLD

My Cherokee grandpa taught me this lesson when I was seven. He took me to a fishing hole and asked me to throw a rock into the pond. He asked me what I saw, and I replied that I saw a splash. He asked me what else I saw, and I said a circle of water and another circle and another circle. He then told me that every person was responsible for the kind of splash they made in the world and that the splash would touch many other circles, creating a ripple effect. I sat and watched the water until he asked me to notice the muddy bank where we were sitting. He pointed out that one of the circular waves made by my rock was lapping at my feet, having found its way back to me. Then he told me that we all need to be careful of the kinds of splashes we make in the world, because the waves we create will always come back to us. If those splashes were hurtful, we will not welcome them back, but if the splash and the waves were made from goodness, we will be happy to see them come home.

The teachings of all major religions on our planet show us these same truths. They ask us to be loving, to respect one another, and to become influences for good. We can see the truth of these teachings when we see that energy abundantly flows through a person who has not tied up her or his life force with feelings of jealousy, envy, and the need for revenge. By contrast, people pursuing a lawsuit, for example, feel like they cannot get on with their lives while so much of their emotions, time, and energy are tied up in a court battle. The same limiting ineffectiveness occurs when we waste our energy on regretting the past, fearing the future, or battling with negative thoughts or feelings. These activities create a dam of stagnant energy inside of us that keeps us from living life in a synchronistic and abundant manner.

From the moment that we experience synchronistic joy in our lives, we are put on notice that we must become aware of every thought, feeling, and action that we put into the world, owning them all as our creations. Accountability for all aspects of our lives is a tall order. The levels of what we are willing to be accountable for continue to increase as we grow, allowing us to become more aware. Forgiveness toward ourselves and toward others is of paramount importance. If we cannot forgive others and ourselves, letting go of the wounds encountered in the situations that we have experienced, we get stuck. When we refuse to forgive, we are asking for a pop quiz. These pop quizzes can come in the form of life situations that force us to look at our personal behaviors.

Imagine a sponge that is set in a dish of water until all the water is absorbed into the sponge. The sponge cannot soak up any more moisture because it is holding on to every drop it has absorbed. When we hold on to our resentments and fears, our anger and bitterness, there is no room in our life for other thoughts, experiences, or feelings. To the degree that we do not release our negative feelings and hidden resentments, we are effectively soaked in them. The creative force of life cannot flow through us when we have dammed any part of it. This lessens our ability to embrace new experiences. When we clutch our wounds, using them as justifiable reasons for not moving forward, our life force is used to fuel our avoidance mechanisms.

Forgiveness and the release of the past open the creative flow of life, supporting all levels of mind, heart, body, emotion, and spirit. This energy flow determines the state of our health, our desire to create and procreate, our willingness to develop our gifts, and how we use or deny the life force that we are given as human beings. Prior to embracing the second path, we may be stuck in victimizing others and in feeling victimized. As soon as the big AH HA of the second path occurs, we realize that by choosing to let go of the past, our fears, and our negative patterns or reactions to life, we are suddenly funded with a resurgence of life force, which propels us into a newfound way of being and a very different way of understanding the world.

HONORING EACH STEP IN OUR PROCESS

There is no law that insists that we become perfect or that we handle every negative pattern instantly or in a specific amount of time. *Life is the initiation, and healing is a process, not an event.* The challenges we choose to embrace may take a while as we unravel the threads of old habits. As we call for withdrawals of energy that we have invested in places that stopped us from living up to our potential, we learn the step-by-step skills that unlock our abilities, and we soon have enough of ourselves present to see why we are here, what we can contribute, who we are, and how we can grow. The path that belongs to us individually will open when we adopt the idea that every challenge, no matter how difficult, is a blessing and an opportunity that allows us to reinvest our energy in learning more about ourselves and our places within Creation.

My teachers taught me that the Great Mystery cannot be solved. We cannot figure out everything in the universe or second-guess the Creator. Chaos always precedes order, and the impeccability of divine order allows our dreams to be nurtured and to be born, manifesting in our physical lives. Since we are not being asked to figure everything out, what are we being asked to do? We are being asked to adopt the faith and inner knowing that our lives are a part of an intricate weave of Creation, reflecting our personal attitudes and our willingness to express love. Every human being is a vessel of love, whether we are willing to see it or not. We have a shadow nature that can keep us from seeing that we are extensions of the principle of love. Our fears can limit us. If we invest our energy in fear-related ideas or act out brutal emotions that damage us or others, we have forgotten our proper places in Creation. The second path begins the re-membering of the parts of ourselves that we have invested in the negative bank accounts belonging to the shadow side of our natures.

Impeccability emerges as our personal integrity is reinstated, bringing a balance within the self. When in balance, we notice when we negatively invest our thoughts and feelings, and we are willing to correct our mistakes by withdrawing our life force from those thoughts, actions, or feelings. We become accountable for the development of our personal Medicines or inner strengths. Impeccability is not about striving to become perfect. If we set ourselves up for perfection, we destroy the human ability to learn from our mistakes. We can also be seduced into believing that we are never good enough, that our valiant efforts to change will never meet an impossible standard that is nebulous at best. After all, who determines what is perfect and what is not? Impeccability, on the other hand, means that we are reflecting our personal best efforts and are developing a personal creed that we can live by, changing that creed to include new revelations as we grow.

Impeccability also includes no judgments. What is right for one person may be dead wrong for another. Limiting human beings to one course of action, one path of worship, or one cultural concept is equivalent to limiting Creation. By setting up rules that lump all human beings into a set appearance or way of being, we can slap the Creator in the face and deny the varied expressions that were created in every part of the natural world, including humankind. The Great Mystery did not make any mistakes when creating our universe. Trusting that truth is our human task.

The word *universe* expresses our beautiful and diverse ways of being, uni meaning one or oneness and *verse* meaning difference or opposites. We could see a slightly different meaning in this word if we consider our human purpose to be learning oneness through duality or opposites. Could this have been the original intention of the Great Mystery when creating our universe? Are we here to learn from one another, to explore our differences, and to find oneness in embracing all of Creation without judgment? The lessons of the second path seem to support this idea by showing us how our emotions give us opportunities to use our free will. We can choose whether we are going to deny our feelings, react to everything we feel, or act only on the feelings that support our intent to heal and to evolve spiritually.

WHEN THE MIND HAS A MIND OF ITS OWN

On the second path we begin to develop the ability to see how our belief systems contain consequences. For example, if we hold a rigid idea that we will not enjoy a certain experience, we have woven that probability into the Dream Weave long before we experience it in our lives. By deciding that we will have a horrible time at any function that we attend, we set the stage for that personal opinion to become the reality. In the Dream Weave, the patterns of our likes and dislikes, as well as the mental conclusions containing no authentic experience to back them, will form a design that paints us into the corner. The lack of flexibility that we have adopted through the decisions we have made and the opinions we have held will support tunnel vision and stagnation. The consequences of the belief systems we hold will manifest in the form of a pop quiz that teaches us we have personal authority over our viewpoint.

If we decide we do not like a certain person because he or she is loud or has blond hair or comes from a certain culture that is different from ours, we have denied ourselves the experience of observation and interaction with someone who could give us a learning experience. The consequences that we create through our beliefs are not often apparent at the time. We can stop the synchronicity of our life's experiences by refusing to take a chance. If we decide we do not like a certain person before we have even met that person, we may have negated any further experiences that could come through encountering others that we would meet through that person. Our judgments would stop any interaction before we gave life a chance to offer us the blessings of synchronistic breakthrough experiences.

We effectively limit our life experiences when we refuse to see how our belief systems have created a tunnel vision. The expansion of the human spirit comes from willingness to become an explorer of life. We all have observed people who died shortly after retirement. This usually happens to people who have no plans for the future or have lived only for their job; when the job is over, they are left without a sense of being needed. Believing we are needed only because we hold a certain career position is as defeating a viewpoint as believing that our lives must follow a rigid plan that disallows any joy or continued learning experiences past the age of sixty. These beliefs and many others like them are present in millions of individuals who were taught them by their parents' belief systems. Fears of growing older, fears of being forgotten, fears of disease and death are created by beliefs such as these.

The truths of one generation may not apply to the next generation. Yet we tend to remember certain catch phrases or snips of supposed wisdom, and we adopt those without questioning their truth. Never questioning whether we are carrying untruths that belong to generational patterns of beliefs can limit our ability to expand beyond the earlier generation's burdens of ignorance.

Perhaps you heard your parents or grandparents say, "If God meant men to fly, he would have given them wings," or "I wonder who she had to go to bed with to get where she is today?" We often fear progress, new technology, new ways of relating to one another, new approaches to life. We are often trapped in our adopted belief systems. On the second path we begin to eliminate the places within ourselves where we are refusing to say yes to life because of fears or lack of experience created by the beliefs that no longer apply to our present-day situations. False beliefs can also create fearful emotions that do not allow us to find our personal will.

As the river of life moves on, we are asked to be flexible enough to use our discernment, integrity, and willingness to try new things in order to grow beyond our former limitations. The places where we hesitate show our lack of confidence in ourselves or our decision-making abilities. It comes as a great shock to most people on the second path to learn that we cannot make any wrong choices. Every choice we make in life will afford us opportunities to see exactly how we have chosen to grow. Realizing that we must live up to our humanity and the choices we have made can be a major wake-up call.

MIRROR, MIRROR ON THE WALL

In the Mayan tradition, the Great Smoking Mirror is a symbol of how life reflects our belief systems and all that we hold internally as being truth. The smoke that wafts in front of the mirror is made up of the illusions we have created through ideas of separation contained in our beliefs. The list of illusions that we have bought into through media ad campaigns, group beliefs, rumors and gossip, the judgments of others toward us, and our own need to be liked or admired is staggering. On the second path, we are asked to begin to see these illusions and to call our energy back from being invested in those illusions in order to free our spirits from the burden of carrying such limiting beliefs.

The Great Smoking Mirror is like a magician performing a sleight-of-hand trick to wake us up to our own restrictive behaviors that come from holding illusions as truth. For instance, if we believe that we are superior to others, we might be faced with a situation that forces us to observe another egotistical human being treating others with condescension and disdain. Or we might be ill used in this way ourselves, which will show us how that attitude feels when it is turned on us. After the experience we may see the truth of how our personal behavior is offensive and decide to change our manner of relating to others.

Every event in life offers reflections that can teach us about ourselves. We discover reflections in how we react in certain situations, how we feel or think, and what we are being shown through personal observation or participation. The more we free ourselves of unwanted reflections through emptying the burden basket of our belief systems, the more energy we are funded with to create new experiences that support our growth. In truth, the process is one of transforming energy. The same energy used to create something of beauty is used to create further painful lessons. No one is standing guard to enforce the manner in which we creatively or destructively use the gift of life force. We are the ones who choose how to use the energy we embody, and those decisions require that we take authority over our lives and become impeccably accountable.

Many people have told me that they did not realize that working on these issues would be so hard. I have responded by reminding them that it is no harder to let go of limiting habits than it is to endure another experience in which they feel betrayed or victimized. We betray ourselves and our integrity when we participate in situations that demean others, yet we are often horrified when the same group of people decides to target us. This boomerang effect is a part of the reflective teaching of the Great Smoking Mirror.

If we choose to enter an arena of experience that destroys rather than supports harmony, we have asked for life lessons that give us the opportunity to relate intimately to discord. If we look deeply, noticing everything that happened just prior to experiencing a form of betrayal, we discover moments where we have betrayed ourselves or our integrity or abandoned our authentic feelings. If we continually dishonor ourselves and our personal integrity, we are unconsciously asking for life to mirror back to us our lack of impeccability. These reflections can take the form of others being abusive toward us or betraying our trusts. We can place blame outside of ourselves, or we can forgive ourselves for setting the lesson in motion, forgive others for their actions, and move beyond the need for such painful situations by working on the internal places where we hold self-hatred or self-revilement. These internal betrayals are just as potent as having someone else humiliate you in public.

The idea that life is happening to us without our consent or participation is an illusion. We have woven our internal belief systems about ourselves just as surely as we have woven our judgments of others. When we are in pain, it is often hard to discern our part in a given situation, but it is always there. What we do to ourselves internally, the Great Smoking Mirror reflects in the external world. On the second path of initiation, the reflections are different from the ones that follow: in those we correct certain behaviors and look at new reflections from the viewpoints of the successive paths. On the second path we learn to trust ourselves and our experiences as being part of our growth. Ultimately, we acknowledge that good and bad luck are illusions. We learn to embrace our personal process as events that trigger our ability to heal the will, emotions, thoughts, and attitudes that have formerly hindered our growth.

DROP-KICK THAT BLAME THROUGH THE GOALPOSTS OF LIFE!

Laying blame by pointing fingers at others is the behavior that begins to be corrected on the second path. My grandmother, Twylah, taught me that every time we point a finger at someone else, three fingers are pointing back at us. On the second path, when we begin to see how we must first turn and face the enemy within, we begin to heal our lives. Without this self-reflective skill, we are not able to become accountable for our lives, and to that degree we have not freed up the energy that we have formerly used to blame others. Through blaming others or believing in bad luck, we create an illusion that dams up the flow of life force that we could use to catapult us beyond victim consciousness and into creative endeavors. Without accountability—that is, the skill of turning within instead of pointing fingers—our integrity is skating on very thin ice, and we become victims of patterns formed by blame, shame, regret, and guilt. The will suffers, and finally we shut down to the opportunities that life offers.

With this one self-reflective skill of personal accountability, it is possible to change our life forever. When we grow beyond being victims, we are no longer giving ourselves away by dishonoring the Medicine we carry, the inner strengths that were given to us at the time our spirits were exhaled into the universe by the Great Mystery.

DABBLERS AND DILETTANTES FORGET HOW TO KEEP SCORE

As we think or believe, so shall we experience life. Physicists have always said that thought precedes form. We cannot stand on the sidelines of our personal experiences and refuse to believe that our thoughts and feelings do not play a role in the game of life. When we dabble in life instead of embracing it with authentic commitment, we become dilettantes. When we wake up, we may be stunned to realize that the rules governing our experience were made simply by the unseen forces of our personal opinions, judgments, feelings, ideas, and beliefs about life.

Once we count the fouls and errors created by victim consciousness and refuse to play dirty with ourselves and others, we will begin to experience the magic of the second path. Our lives begin to heal in dramatic and unexpected ways, adding a new dimension to our outlook. It takes courage to leave the spectator vantage point and become an active participant in life's adventure. When we choose to activate the Dream Weave patterns supporting the exploration of interrelatedness and oneness, we have emptied the burden basket of aloneness and despair. To forgive and let go of the past, in order to move beyond the idea that we are casualties of life, is a sacred victory given only to those with the courage to make the leap of faith. This act of trust is the beginning of authentic power within the self. We have become willing players who know that we are responsible for our individual roles and experiences within Creation.

As we develop the impeccable behaviors that are required of us, we may falter from time to time, but each level of understanding brings skills and strengths that we can add to our personal Medicines. When we become inattentive or slip into an occasional negative pattern, we are also provided with a new wake-up call or pop quiz, which will persist until we pay attention and regain our balance once more.

When we adopt the disciplines of spiritual warriors, we must also include ways to nurture the faith and trust that we rediscover. Some of these ways include prayer, meditation, worship, and ceremony. As second-path warriors, we find support and solace through sharing our thoughts, feelings, and experiences with others who follow the same or similar paths. It does not matter which religion or spiritual practice we follow as long as communion with the Great Mystery or God is a part of our path. The spiritual challenges that are encountered along the way can include trusting that we are never alone. When life seems to be too difficult, it is necessary to gain strength and nurturance from a one-on-one connection with the Creator, the Earth Mother, and spirit. We also develop human connections and adopt an extended spiritual family comprised of other compassionate human beings who understand the spiritual path and who are committed to their own growth.

On the second path we may need to say good-bye to relationships that have become abusive or jobs that bring no joy. We may find that others do not understand our feelings or new sense of spiritual commitment and that they cannot support us in letting go of habits that are limiting or ways of being that they themselves still rely on in their lives. It can be painful to let go of our past when in letting go we are also required to let go of former friends. Being a disciple to our path can seem a lonely road, but in choosing integrity and the desire to heal our life, we must be impeccably honest, realizing that communicating with others who are also working toward spiritual growth is of ultimate importance.

When our goals change and our viewpoints change, many things fall away. In these moments we come to our personal crossroads and are asked to make decisions, reclaiming our faith. Our inner knowing tells us that there is a divine plan, that all is in order, and that the Creator is holding us in the pregnant chaos of that which we are giving birth to through our personal choices. When we release our fear of change, the magic of life returns and we transform, finding a new level of understanding at hand. Our heart and mind are strengthened and clear. Our body feels vital and more alive than ever, and we feel spiritually attuned to the oneness of life in a new and different way.

DO I REALLY NEED THIS LESSON?

As we embrace our lessons, there are times when we must use discernment to see clearly where other people fit or do not fit in our lives. We ask ourselves the following four questions: (1) How do I feel when I am with this person? (2) How do I feel just after he or she has gone? (3) Do we have similar goals, purposes, and levels of integrity? (4) Am I taking this person on as a project, trying to change his or her life instead of focusing on my own issues? The answers to these questions allow us to discern whether we are moving in the right direction or whether we should change course. When we find those answers, we should be ultimately grateful for the insights.

There are many ways to walk the second path, and all are equal. However, a few things are encountered by every traveler no matter what their tradition, religion, race, or creed. Our heart aligns with the Earth Mother's rhythm, and transformation begins. A sense of synchronicity blends with life events, creating a new feeling of wonder and aliveness. We gain a newfound respect for ourselves, others, and all living things as life experiences teach us more about what respect means. From learning the value of respect comes the desire to live life with integrity and honesty toward ourselves and others.

These lessons presented on the second path of initiation are the foundations of every path that follows. We are not asked to master every lesson at once but to remain vigilant as we walk through our lives, ever mindful of the fact that we are being initiated by every thought, word, deed, and feeling, as well as by how we relate to those human experiences. My people call this way of being "walking your talk." Talk is cheap. Anyone can talk a good talk, but it is ultimately our actions and behavior that determine our level of integrity.

BREAKTHROUGHS AND REWARDS

In many cases, the warrior candidate nearing the completion of the second path begins to experience energy in a visual way, gaining access to the unseen worlds of the Dream Weave. This paranormal activity may occur in waking or sleeping states. Often a person's physiological vision can also improve if the veils of former clouded perceptions are eliminated. This happens because the manner in which the individual perceives reality has radically shifted. Some people may also begin to see light or perceive energy around objects, mountains, animals, trees, or people, thinking that the lighter halo around an object is a trick of the optic nerve or retina. A few people with whom I have worked were so frightened by the miracle of perceiving energy that they actually believed they had a detached retina and had their eyes checked, only to find out nothing was wrong with them.

One woman saw a large swirling blue light outside of the sliding glass door of her bedroom, night after night. The presence of what she thought was a spiritual being, standing in her garden for hours, shocked her at first. She went through many fearful emotions until she decided that the presence of the blue light was a good sign. Then she began to see the outline of the luminous body, which gently showed that it was trying to communicate with hand movements. She was fascinated, but she did not understand what was being expressed. She did not hear any words, nor did she feel anything that might have given her a clue as to what was being communicated.

After many months of clearing some of her issues, she finally heard the voice of this angelic presence. She was told to pick up a pen and to write the words so that she could fully understand the messages and review them when she needed to. She admitted to me that prior to this experience, she had been deeply entrenched in the social scene in her community and had passed on lies and betrayed people's confidences to her. She believed that by discrediting others she would gain stature on the social ladder. She saw many other unbecoming behaviors in herself and began to eliminate them. The more she worked on herself, the more connected she became to her spiritual warrior nature and to the angelic presence that blessed her with encouragement.

In another instance, a young man I knew, who was reared as a Baptist in a tiny country town in the Bible belt of the southern United States, had all of his church beliefs about hell and damnation stripped from him in one event. He had been taught that anyone who had not accepted Jesus as personal Lord and Savior and had not experienced baptism through being held completely below the water as sin was washed away was doomed to eternal damnation and hellfire. He had many friends who were not Baptists, and he was unsure about the rigid judgments held by his religion. He knew many people of other faiths who were kind and good, and he could not believe that those people were going to burn eternally in hell. His heart was troubled, and he did not know where to turn to find inner peace.

One day he was walking through the woods, and a blue jay flew down in front of his feet. He stopped and watched, and the bird hopped a few feet away. As he followed, bit by bit, he was led to an area that was once an ancient Indian burial ground. He saw a cave in the bluff, and there stood an ancient Indian fanning a twig fire. The young man stood still and watched, afraid to exhale. The old Indian motioned for him to come sit by the fire. He was too frightened to comply, so the old man began praying in English. Those words of that prayer changed the young man's life forever. He listened to this Ancestor spirit talk to the Creator about private aspects of the young man's life, his inner turmoil, and how his life was to be used to help all people on the planet without judgment or insisting that they follow one particular religion. The young man was so moved that tears ran down his face, and his body began to shake. When he stopped to wipe away his tears and looked up again, the cave was empty and the old Indian had vanished, but he knew that his inner turmoil had come to an end and that he had experienced divine intervention.

OOPS! TIME FOR A REALITY ADJUSTMENT

Every time we have a breakthrough, we reassemble the way we perceive life and reality on the seen and unseen levels. When this reassembling occurs, we experience dramatic changes in our bodies, in our behaviors, and in our abilities to know things consciously without going through normal thought processes. These shifts in perception occur on every path of initiation and create a type of rewiring within us that changes how we respond to life. On the first through fourth paths, the rewiring process occurs when we change our limiting behaviors and heal our past wounds. On these paths, we are actively working toward processing and clearing our issues. When we succeed in dropping old habit patterns, or when we conquer some preexisting challenge, we feel the shift and will never be the same again. We let go of the former computations, false ideas, and unstable rationalizations, which allows us to rewire our thinking and feeling processes.

Some people who have experienced the unexplainable can fall into a trap orchestrated by the ego's sense of self-importance. As these people begin to have flashes of intuition, they may suddenly believe that the insights are signals that they are destined for spiritual stardom, psychic fame, or becoming the world's greatest shaman or oracle. But everyone on the first through fourth paths encounters flashes of clear intuition or lucid dreams; this is nothing unusual. These occurrences may be infrequent, but they are always brought about when we have freed enough life force to break through some illusory deadlock in our way of thinking, feeling, or being.

Continued intuitive accuracy depends totally on skillfully developing those extrasensory gifts. The newcomer who has experienced those gifts of insight for the first time and adopts an attitude of arrogance not only offends others but also tends to appear foolish. People who erroneously believe that because they have had these brief insightful experiences, everything that they psychically sense is going to be accurate or all-knowing are cruising for a bruising. Life always seem to find a way to humble us when our egos decide to write checks that our fledgling abilities can't cash. After the ego leaks that amount of energy on self-importance and arrogance, Coyote can find ways to show us that our life force accounts definitely are showing a howling overdraft!

There are a multitude of ways in which our lives and perceptions change when we meet the challenges presented on the second path. When we heal the limiting or destructive behaviors that cloud our perceptions of life, freeing ourselves of the behaviors that tie our energy into webs of deceit or stagnation, we are given an authentic cornucopia of new abilities and skills. We are funded with the energy needed to use those gifts as long as we maintain the integrity of our focus and handle our personal issues. Personal impeccability is a skill that is honed with time, through living our personal creeds with integrity to the best of our individual abilities. We embrace these lessons by living them, adding authentic skill and inner strength to our understandings of the second path's lessons as we interweave with them the lessons of the third path of initiation.

CHAPTER 5

*Authentic treachery is found when we abandon ourselves,
becoming deaf to the whispers of our spirits and blind to the
powerful potential therein.*

—Joaquin Muriel Espinosa

▲▲▲▲▲▲▲▲▲▲▲▲▲▲▲▲▲▲▲▲▲▲▲▲▲▲▲▲▲▲▲▲▲▲▲

HEALING PATH

Teach me how to gather
The fragments of my soul,
Reclaiming lost potential,
I seek to become whole.

Let me find forgiveness,
Embracing a new way to *be*,
Releasing the hurt and anger
Toward all who wounded me.

Let me heal my human body,
The sacred vessel of my soul,
Mending all the unhealed aspects,
I find within my Medicine Bowl.

Let me find the courage
To face the enemies within,
Healing all my weaknesses,
Honoring the warrior therein.

Let me honor my sacred promise,
To be loyal to my healing quest,
Never deserting my Medicine,
Nor the heart within my breast.

—Jamie Sams

The Third Path of Initiation
The West Direction on the Medicine Wheel

THE West Direction on the Medicine Wheel is the place of introspection and listening. The third path of initiation teaches us about healing and contains many lessons that help us reclaim the fragments of ourselves that may have been wounded or denied at various times throughout our lives. In the West we find ourselves looking at the duality of life: our fears and our loves, our strengths and our weaknesses, our joys and our sorrows. We learn how to respond to our *healthy* shame when we know we have done something that needs to be corrected, becoming accountable for our actions. We acknowledge our ability to heal when we become willing to correct our behaviors and to make amends if necessary. We learn how to release unhealthy guilt, which comes from accepting the unreasonable expectations of others. We become aware of when we are adopting self-sabotage and shadowlike behaviors, and we correct our old ways of being in order to move forward into healing potential.

The earlier lessons of learning how to observe the obvious, which began on the second path, are now approached in earnest. We begin going within the self for answers instead of seeking those bits of wisdom and truth from outside sources. On the third path of initiation we again will be required to face our fears and to look at all of our behaviors that may be coming from our ego's sense of self-importance or the shadow side's need to negate our sense of well-being. We hone our skills of discernment, and we make choices about how we want to view the behaviors of others in relation to our own behaviors past and present, determining what we are willing to experience in our individual frames of reference. This act of observation followed by decisive action is how we create healthy boundaries, which instill a sense of well-being.

As human beings, we have Sacred Space, which encompasses our bodies, our thoughts, our feelings, our possessions, and our creative energy. As we learn the next level of how to respect the Sacred Space belonging to us, we are required to look at what we allow inside that Sacred Space. The boundaries of our Sacred Space are determined by healthy or unhealthy attitudes. If we have enough self-esteem to refuse to allow abusive behaviors in our Sacred Space, we have conquered one major challenge of the third path. We learn to release the need to defeat the self with our own thoughts, we let go of the need to be critical of others, and we detach from others who insensitively direct physical, emotional, or verbal abuse toward us.

Depending on the individual, the third path can contain more lessons and the longest set of initiations. We are asked to begin the process of healing addictions, old pain or trauma, physical illness, emotional instability, unhealthy psychological patterns, childhood issues, manipulation or control behaviors, dysfunctional relationships, and any other forms of imbalance. I do not intend to downplay the number of issues that are presented to those of us who embrace the third path, yet we all must discern individually what we need to heal.

Like all the paths, this one is longer for some people than for others simply because of the differences in human experiences. We experience trauma and pain in our own unique ways. Some people heal their wounds as they occur and move on, while others carry the pain with them for years. When we heal the imbalances created from our past wounds and embrace life from our present viewpoint, we see our experiences from a new perspective. Eventually, if we can let go of the past, we are able to be authentically grateful for our wounds, our harrowing experiences, and the brutality that we may have endured. Through healing those wounds, we become *healed healers* who have embraced our own suffering and transformed our lives. Healed human beings stand tall as examples for others. Nobody can belittle the life of a healed healer. The human being who has authentically healed his or her past has an unshakable, intimate knowing of the value contained in the journey of healing the self and in the bravery required of all spiritual warriors.

I will say once again that each of the seven paths of initiation dovetails into others. It is possible to be completing lessons on the third path and the second path at the same time that we are beginning some fourth-path lessons. How each person experiences these initiations is as individual as the human being. Remember that these paths are not linear. We seem to want to view life like a ladder, but the idea of linear growth disallows the multitude of possibilities that humans are given to grow in different areas simultaneously. To judgmentally label a person as being on a particular path that we view as less enlightened that our own is an erroneous folly created by the shadow side of human nature. Some people learn the lessons of physicality through athletically developing the body; others evolve and heal through expressing their emotions; others explore human potential through developing the gifts of the intellect; and others seek the meaning of life through mysticism, prayer, and spirituality. All forms of growth are valid, and how we piece these elements together in our lives is an expression of our uniqueness as human beings.

On the third path we embrace what we call Frog Medicine in our Native American traditions. Frog teaches us to cleanse the old through clearing our thoughts, behaviors, and feelings. Frog teaches us that shedding tears can be the first step of this cleansing transformation. The purification process represented by Frog Medicine is the ability to cleanse all that keeps us from healing and to refill ourselves with new energy, renewed purpose, and feelings and thoughts that support our intent to change. This two-step process of cleansing the old and refilling with the new will be present in every step that we take toward healing our lives on the third path.

Bat, the Mayan symbol of rebirth, is another Medicine that we are asked to embrace on the third path. After we have purified the aspects of our lives that no longer serve us, we are reborn, leaving the past behind. Bat teaches us to respect the rebirth process as we learn how to operate from our new Sacred Point of View. We have earned the new beginnings in our lives, and we are required to shelter the seeds of our personal potential that we have planted through our own efforts. Bat hangs upside down in the cave, like human babies do as they await birth in the womb. This upside-down position is also a metaphor for how we must sometimes change everything in our lives, turning it all topsy-turvy, before we can be reborn into our new states of being. During the rebirth process, as in our mother's wombs, we hear the echoes of every thought as well as the double heartbeat. The double heartbeat signals the harmony of our heartbeat as it melds with the heartbeat of the Earth Mother, who encourages us to continue healing our lives.

TRANSFORMATION AND THE NUMBER THIRTEEN

In many spiritual traditions the number thirteen represents transformation and healing. The Jewish and Muslim calendars follow the thirteen moons of the year. The Native American tradition honors the thirteen moon times or annual menstrual cycles of women, the Thirteen Original Clan Mothers, and the thirteen crystal skulls, which represent the human cycles of discovering our personal Medicine and being transformed into our potential by becoming our visions. In the Christian tradition the number thirteen is represented by Jesus and his twelve disciples, Jesus being the shining example of actualizing the transformative power of divine love on the physical plane. The Mayans also honor the number thirteen and are guided by their calendar, which shows the transformation of human consciousness. Ancient pagan religions and newer spiritual traditions that have begun throughout the world in the past three thousand years have all acknowledged the tipping of the scale that transforms the mundane into the magical events of healing.

Several years ago I was back on Cattaraugas Reservation in upstate New York visiting Grandma Twylah, and I went to a remote area surrounded by bluffs that overlooked Cattaraugas Creek. I desperately needed to be still and to allow the water to cleanse my weariness. Too many people in need of healings and not enough energy to fulfill the needs of others had taken a toll. I sat on the stone shore of the creek and thanked the Great Mystery for all the blessings of my life and for allowing me to feel the beautiful changes that occurred in the lives of others when they began to heal. I felt that I had fulfilled the part of my path and my spiritual obligations that involved actively being on the road, but I wanted to make sure that the traveling part of my path was complete. I asked the Creator to let me know when that time arrived so I could make the changes that were required of me. Then I closed my eyes and rested for a few minutes.

I felt a shadow cross over my body, and I opened my eyes, looking up. I was shocked to find not one, but five eagles in the sky above. I sat bolt upright and watched as another eight eagles joined the first five in the next few minutes. Thirteen eagles were circling me, and I cried tears of joy. I knew that the eagle had been hunted to near extinction in the East, and this was an event that marked not only my rite of passage and change, but also the spirit energy of the eagle returning to the

Seneca people, the Iroquois Keepers of the Western Door. When my friend Wata, Evening Star, came to collect me fifteen minutes later and saw seven or eight of the thirteen eagles that remained above the bluffs, we hugged each other and marveled at the gifts of spirit we had both been given that day. That was the day that my path changed and a new kind of service began in my life, allowing me to turn over my former duties to others who were ready to come forward and assist in humanity's healing process. I knew that I had come full circle and no longer needed to be on the road.

BE AWARE OR BEWARE!

As we learn to listen to our thoughts and observe the many types of internal voices that are projecting those thoughts within our minds, we may encounter some unpleasant realizations about how our behaviors are controlled by the thoughts we entertain. We learn to identify the voices within our minds that come from pain or woundedness, pride, or shame. We may find situations where we give our authority to others who are seemingly more enlightened about life, or we may think that we know it all and become stubborn, arrogant, or boastful. We may discover that we have invested our self-importance in areas that allow us to use our career or social positions to open doors, and yet we are not happy. We can also discover that in our own woundedness, we have no sense of self at all and that the enemy is the self-defeating attitudes we hold or the internal voices of self-hatred that we adopted while growing up. We can also discover that we have picked role models or teachers that are wrong for us. We can suddenly realize that the groups we are associated with have become rigid, self-serving, or controlling. All of these resulting points of clarity are the products of introspection, and if we are willing to change, they can radically alter the way we live our lives.

WHAT DO YOU MEAN, ENLIGHTENMENT HAS TRAPS?

At the midpoint of the third path we often discover that we have all of the answers about what is right for our personal growth process within us. This realization may make some people feel totally insecure or un-sure of themselves, while others can begin to feel superior or omnipo-tent. Both of these feelings are the forerunners of *enlightenment traps*. Enlightenment traps appear on our paths when we have disallowed al-ternatives and options that could release us from the prisons that we have created for ourselves through fixed ideas and by giving our au-thority to the shadow sides of our natures. For example, when a person believes that anyone who eats meat will never become spiritual or reach enlightenment, this idea creates an enlightenment trap that dis-allows others the use of free will or an alternate way of experiencing life's initiations. If that person later comes to the realization that food does not control the spirit and that all human beings have the right to decide for themselves how they want to evolve, the enlightenment trap is broken. That person may still feel that vegetarianism is right for him or her personally but will no longer insist that meat eaters are inferior or are committing crimes against nature.

Enlightenment traps appear much more frequently on the third and following paths than on the first two paths of initiation. Life seems to test us to make sure we will use properly the energy we reclaim with-out being seduced into abusing our personal authority. On the third path we are beginning to reclaim the fragments of ourselves that were shattered through traumas, shocks, abuse, addictions, physical illness, and emotional pain. The reclaimed parts of ourselves, which previously had gone into numbness, denial, shock, or some other form of uncon-sciousness, carry with them many threads of unused energy, and this energy can be reactivated to give us new life force when we heal those parts of our past.

For example, if we have been worn down in any kind of abusive re-lationship and believe that we are unworthy of love, that judgmental idea is carried in the part of the self that was wounded. When that frag-ment of self is healed or reclaimed, the idea of unworthiness may re-appear at a later date, frightening us into believing that the results we have worked so hard to gain do not last. This belief is an enlightenment trap at work and could signal one of life's many pop quizzes. If the fear of being unworthy reappears in a situation that resembles a past event, it may be testing us on whether we are going to buy into old fear pat-terns. All that is truly occurring is that we are being given an opportu-nity, in the present, to review the old shadow beliefs that were created due to past hurts so that we can release those untruths that no longer apply to our present state of health. If the fear is released rather than embraced, the pop quiz is passed with flying colors.

The third path of initiation can get tricky, because in order to begin this path we may have had to agree to embrace all parts of ourselves, examining the attitudes, life situations, and fragments of ourselves that keep us from healing in a conscious manner. My teachers used to joke about this path by saying, "Dive deeply, but don't hold your breath!"— and then they would roar with laughter as I looked seriously confused. They were referring to another enlightenment trap on this path. As we learn how to process our denied feelings or past pain, it is easy to forget to breathe, meaning we can become obsessed with finding reasons for the least little thing that occurs in our lives, trying to label every daily occurrence so that all of the pieces are tidy in our minds. This activity will create BLACKOUT. Nothing is clear when we lose consciousness, and we do lose consciousness when we don't allow ourselves any breathing room. By obsessively needing to figure out why things occur in our lives, we can effectively cut off our spiritual circulation.

One person I knew was constantly explaining why other people had to go through their life experiences. He would say, "Oh, that happened to them because they didn't . . ." and then he would fill in the blank. He would actually get angry when people who came to him for healings did not get past the issues they were trying to handle as quickly as he expected them to. His self-importance was an astonishing example of an enlightenment trap at work. He was so sure he could see what each of his clients needed to handle, having labeled every client's issues with cementlike judgments, that he allowed no elbow room for divine intervention and healing to occur authentically.

Any person who has chosen the path of being of service has also committed to facilitating change by allowing the Creator to work through him or her. We cannot control how the Great Mystery chooses to work through us. Our egos would love for us to believe that we are personally and wholly responsible for another person's healing or change, but nothing could be further from the truth. In any given situation, all people and all elements present work together within the context of a combined intent to actualize healing at its own time and in its own manner. We are effective only if we humbly allow ourselves to be used as instruments of healing. We cannot predict how the healing will occur, but we can add to the equation our life force and our intention to be of service, gratefully acknowledging all the people and spiritual forces present.

That brings us full circle to the Native American saying, "The Great Mystery cannot be solved!" If we knew the reason for everything that happened to us, life would be boring. Not only that, but such knowledge would eliminate the free will that allows us to change our attitudes and minds and to reweave the patterns of energy that have formed our individual parts of the Dream Weave. Through the simple act of allowing God, the Creator, the Great Mystery, to be the Higher Power, limitless possibilities and miracles become available to us. Why would we ever choose to control the way the mystery unfolds in our lives? The shadow side of human nature thrives when we limit our trust or when we need to control the way things should happen. To do so is to negate the power of the Great Mystery in our lives. Control of that sort is like playing God and is another enlightenment trap. It creates attitudes, thoughts, and feelings that do not serve further growth but allow the shadow side of our natures to control our perceptions and our experiences.

ALLOWING THE GREAT MYSTERY TO TOUCH OUR LIVES

The appearance of miracles or divine intervention are startling at first, since they are usually unexplainable instances of sparkling synchronicity. Grandmother Twylah told me a story about her life that showed how the divine intervention of the Great Mystery affected her decision to share her wisdom with the people world over. She had come to a time in her life that was particularly difficult, was working hard to make ends meet, and had four children to keep her busy. One day a man called and asked for her by her maiden name. He told her that when she had been taken from her family at the age of six and sent to a foster home, he had met her grandfather, Moses Shongo. They had walked along a creek, and Grandpa Shongo had come across a stone. He had picked it up, held it to the sky, and asked the man if he would to give it to Twylah at some point in the future. Grandpa Shongo said he would have crossed over when the man remembered to give Twylah the stone, but she would need it when the time came.

Twylah had already healed of having been blinded during high school and crippled by the anesthetic given to her while she birthed her fourth child. At the time the stranger called her, the burdens she was carrying were overwhelming, making her feel confused and worn out. She had no energy left to help others. Her greatest heartache in life was that her grandfather, who had passed her his Medicine, had died while she was in a foster home and that she had never been able to say good-bye. When the man gave the stone to Twylah, she saw that it was perfectly round and black with a broad white line forming the center. Any stone with a different-colored line running all the way through it is called a Sacred Path Stone. In that moment, Grandpa Shongo's spirit was reaching out to tell his granddaughter to stay on the path, lending her his strength from the spirit world.

In facing those shadowy passages that could lead us into despair, we must acknowledge that if we do not allow the mystery of life to flourish, we will not be able to see the little miracles of support offered to us by the spirits of nature. We must also observe how disdain and condescension toward others is created by the ego and the intellect. When we assume that we know more, have experienced more, are better off, or have a view of life that is superior to that of others, we have forgotten that every traveler on life's road is a messenger. To regain balance in these situations, we are required to pass through a few life experiences that may reveal how we have created our own enlightenment traps.

If we do not acknowledge how our attitudes have created a chaos of imbalance within the Dream Weave, and if we do not understand how those internally held viewpoints and feelings are affecting our lives, we will create difficult challenges to overcome in our life experiences. One example is the loss of the material things that make some people feel superior. The symbols of wealth, power, influence, and position are slowly eroded from the life of any person who has gotten to a place where he or she has begun the initiation process and has erroneously invested his or her energy into false images of power or success.

This lesson applies to all people in all walks of life. Any of us who relate our worth to what we do for a living can lose that false sense of self when the wake-up calls ensue. We possess dignity and honor if we take pride in all that we do, no matter how humble our roles. If we use our roles in life to make us seem important in our own eyes or in the eyes of others, we lose our authentic identities. The spiritual warrior fully understands that every human being is a perfect creation reflecting the limitless aspects of the Great Mystery, and that he or she is required to relate to all human beings from that perspective of dignity.

Anyone on the third path who has invested his or her identity with a false sense of self is sure to create a way for the chains of illusion or delusion to be broken. I have seen people on this path demonstrate various ways of letting go of old identities. They can flow into healing, or they can go kicking and screaming, blaming the Creator for their bad luck. Whichever route they choose, those false illusions of unaccountability will shatter eventually.

When I committed myself to this healing path, the man I was in love with left my life, I lost his child, which I was pregnant with, I lost my job because my employer went bankrupt, and my monthly paycheck bounced. I sold all of my furniture and anything else that would give me the money to travel to Mexico to study with my spiritual teachers. I had to let go of my dreams of being a wife and a mother and heal the heartache in my life, but I still had my connections to the Creator, the Earth Mother, and to the Ancestor spirits. It took a while to heal the wounds of my broken heart, but I found joy in the face of my pain because I had discovered that I was rich beyond belief when life reawakened my sense of what really mattered. As I healed, I was blessed daily with dreams and visions of why my path had changed, returning me to what the Great Mystery had intended for me to do with my life.

I knew that I had to heal myself and that I was to endure many trials by fire in order to fulfill my promise to serve. I had already experienced some of these. At nineteen, I contracted mononucleosis, and for years I suffered from chronic fatigue and a high blood level of Epstein-Barr virus, which the medical profession did not acknowledge as a disease until fifteen years later. This condition was complicated by getting undulant fever in Mexico when I ate unpasteurized dairy products. For the next nineteen years I lived with a daily temperature of 101 to 103 degrees. At the end of three and a half years in Mexico, I fell through an adobe roof and was paralyzed for three weeks, and I had to wear a steel back brace for the next six months.

I was being asked to endure the emotional, physical, and spiritual burdens placed on my shoulders. There were many times I believed I would not make it through these Dark Nights of the Soul. It was during this time that I learned the value of letting go and walking away from anything or anyone that kept me from healing. I developed an endurance and a faith that carried me through sixteen years of fevers in a healing process that still funds my life with strength today.

I am not saying that this devastating form of letting go is necessary for every person on the third path, but I have seen various forms of this lesson occur in people's lives. Clearing a way for healing to occur happens eventually in each person's life, but how each individual's story unfolds cannot be second-guessed. Every human story includes letting go of the past in one way or another. This death of the past can be a pleasant experience as well, particularly if we flow with the changes in our life in a gradual manner. Some of us, however, learn through the University of Hard Knocks, and I happen to be one of those students.

DID LIFE HAVE TO HIT ME WITH A TIDAL WAVE BECAUSE THE DRIPPING FAUCET DIDN'T GET MY ATTENTION?

Hard knocks come to many people in order to allow them to change their life paths dramatically and quickly. I have observed many people in positions of fame or wealth, who could have used their positions for the benefit of others, become so self-absorbed that they did not know how to share or give back. I have seen others who genuinely offered help and then did not follow through, breaking promises to people who trusted the offered assistance. Some of these people had reached the third path of initiation, yet they ended up in dire straits when they could not become introspective and accountable for their behaviors.

One publicly recognized person had a habit of going to meet many spiritual leaders of all different faiths, thinly veiling his insecure need to be acknowledged as an evolved soul. This man did good works from time to time and helped various organizations and individuals. On the third path when the authentic hard work of introspection was required, he adopted another behavior, avoidance. This confused man felt spiritually superior to others and sized up every person of goodwill who came into his life, mentally assessing whether or not the person was his spiritual equal. He used people to his advantage and then discarded them, never seeing how his abuse of authority was creating huge tangles in the Dream Weave. I was deeply saddened because I knew that the tangled web he unwittingly had woven in his arrogance would one day appear on his doorstep.

No matter how important or successful a person becomes, no one can control the unseen worlds of spirit in the same way that they control employees, spouses, or children. We cannot manipulate the Dream Weave. The web of life that we experience is precisely woven by our internal attitudes, thoughts, feelings, and judgments. Trying to buy our way into a state of enlightenment is ludicrous and impossible. Good works will not change the web of life if we are behaving like tyrants when dealing with other human beings. If we hold secret judgments, the net of our entangled energy will reflect the internal wars raging between our shadow and our light, effectively strangling the best-laid plans for success. We need abundant courage to see exactly what we are creating with every thought, attitude, or action. Any effort to cheat or slide by unnoticed has to die before authentic healing can occur.

On the opposite side of self-importance, we encounter people who have suffered greatly in life and have no sense of self-esteem at all. They may be so deeply wounded that the third path continues the second-path opportunity to find the courage necessary to reassemble their sense of well-being. Some, in the face of incessant human tragedy, choose to revile the sacredness of life and do not care if they destroy themselves or others. For these people, the first and second paths have involved learning to see hope for the future for the first time in their lives. By the time they reach the third path, their task is to reinforce the self through treating themselves and others with profound respect. These people usually appreciate what others take for granted, since the smallest of blessings was once denied them. Prior to the original wake-up call that brought them into the paths of initiation, their lives might have been what most people would consider living nightmares.

If all that we have experienced in life is suffering, poverty, humiliation, and pain, we often continue the abuse by adopting it as our personal behavior. In such instances, seriously wounded human beings find that by reaching out to others from similar backgrounds who have changed themselves, they are given a new foundation on which to rebuild their lives. This sense of extended family gives people a form of support and can change them forever by showing them that they are valuable and worth loving. The path of reclaiming self-worth is a hard one and requires perseverance, but the person who finds the courage to walk this path is powerful indeed. Healing from the depths of despair, including memories of violence and abuse, can infuse a calm strength in those who have walked through that storm. When others would panic in the face of danger or disaster, a person who has already experienced far worse can garner the strength necessary to rise to any occasion.

Often it is painful to watch people go through their growth processes. When someone we love is learning through hard knocks or heartache, we may hurt too. If she or he is racing at speeds up to mach 10 with his or her hair on fire, heading for a brick wall, how are we supposed to respond? We can issue a warning, speaking up as long as we are prepared for the possibility that our message may fall on deaf ears. We can remain silent and observe. We can retreat, allowing that person to learn in his or her own way, choosing to observe from afar. If we do not approve of the person's behavior and we feel it is destructive, we can step out of his or her arena of influence. If the person is an addict, we can intercede with other family members in order to get him or her into recovery. All decisions about how to respond are individual, but in all cases we are asked to hold no judgments, praying for this person's highest good, turning the situation over to the Great Mystery. Letting go of how others *should* heal is a third-path lesson.

In the tradition of the Southern Seers, this transformational process of healing our internally held imbalances is called Shaman's Death and Rebirth. The death of false ideas, the end of destructive illusions, and the termination of relationships with people who support inappropriate or unhealthy behaviors will all appear in this cycle of initiation. The death cycle can also include Dark Nights of the Soul, which force us eventually to look at the growth opportunities we are being given by undergoing the death-and-rebirth cycle. If we deny this third-path transformational process, refusing to see it as a way to develop endurance, or Elk Medicine, events in life will continue to challenge us until we become willing to pick up the gauntlet and surrender to the healing process with grace. The ensuing Dark Nights of the Soul become more intense if we continue to deny the warning signals that life presents to us. Health can suffer; at this stage of initiation the stomach, liver, spleen, and intestines are the weakest because they reside in the same area as the Dreaming Body, which contains our life force and the connections we have to the unseen worlds of thought and feeling.

WE SENSE OUR WORLD THROUGH THE DREAMING BODY

The Dreaming Body is shaped like a luminous egg residing within the torso of the human form. The bottom of this egg rests on the pubis, and the top is just below the heart. From the center of the egg, approximately three inches above the navel, hundreds of tiny golden threads of energy, which are our human sensory antennae, spread into the universe in every direction. These are the energetic threads connecting us to our intuition and allowing us to understand and feel the world around us. These same threads extend into other unseen worlds; through them a person who has healed enough of his or her life can perceive reality beyond the usual frames of reference.

The Dreaming Body is our connection to the Dream Weave's world of feelings, intuition, inspiration, and ideas. All perceptions of the seen and unseen worlds begin with the golden threads of the Dreaming Body and end up as sensations or impressions. Whether we are sleeping or awake, this luminous egg of the Dreaming Body collects life force and feeds us the energy needed to fund our creativity. We can enjoy full use of the Dreaming Body only if we have freed ourselves from old patterns of limitation. When we allow those limiting habits, ideas, or attitudes to die, we are reborn into new levels of understanding and clarity. We then are able to use the universal energy coming from the Great Mystery to feed our physical bodies and our growing range of perceptions. As we heal, the tiny golden threads unfurl into larger and larger areas of experience, allowing us to continue to free ourselves from the tangled threads created by hurt, trauma, or abuse. By becoming introspective and embracing the death-and-rebirth process, we become more able to operate effectively in life and to use correctly the energy being given to us. As we reclaim and heal the wounded fragments of ourselves, we rediscover self-esteem. Then our personal authority and effectiveness in life expand dramatically.

How many threads of perception are activated in new states of awareness varies from person to person based upon how much that person has healed. When a person has been traumatized or wounded, the threads that reached out to others recoil into the luminous egg of the Dreaming Body. Whether they remain tangled and knotted or open again to awareness depends on whether the person has healed wounded feelings, embraced forgiveness, brought the wounding situation to closure, and become willing to open again to his or her sensitivity. If the person remains shut down and does not allow healing and forgiveness to release the areas of blockage within the Dreaming Body, the old unhealed wounds can be seen as gaping holes by those who perceive energy.

I had the first experience of reopening the perceptions of my Dreaming Body when I came to an authentic place of forgiveness about having been violently raped when I was nine years old. As I healed, the golden threads of my Dreaming Body began to unfurl. I began to see tiny cometlike or sperm-shaped lights in the open air every time I was in bright daylight. I had seen colors around people all my life, but this visual phenomenon altered as my awareness changed. I also began to see lines of energy, which I perceived as red and magenta, appearing between my body and the object I was viewing. The grid looked like a schematic of the inside of a radio or television, with bright lines of energy delineating the mazelike overlay like a color transparency between me and the world. This was a signal to me that past wounds were healed and that I could reclaim the magic of life.

EXPANSION VERSUS ABANDONMENT

When we fear experiences foreign to our upbringing or avoid situations that our peers consider unacceptable, we are actually afraid of being alienated. When we see only one tiny aspect of life as acceptable, that limited avenue of experience becomes the only safe path we can endure comfortably. We can expand that comfort zone if we are willing to adventure beyond the limited perceptions of needing to fit in or to be accepted. If the only validation we have received in life has come through being one of the crowd, it will be hard to leave this comfort zone. Some of us base our behavior on a fear of punishment, others on the need for love or approval. If we have suffered heartache, we might resist change because we fear being alienated or criticized, abandoned or ignored.

Confronting our fear of abandonment is one of the most difficult challenges on the third path of initiation. On this healing path, we may need to let go of the places we have lived if we are to find a new identity. It is difficult to move beyond a certain lifestyle if everyone we have known all our lives has fixed ideas about how we are supposed to act, how we are supposed to look or feel, and how we are supposed to live. If we begin to change and we notice the people in our lives are becoming distant, we are being given an opportunity to make choices. We can choose not to abandon our healing process and our growth potential, or we can succumb to peer pressure and deny our need for change by stuffing our feelings. If we do not feel strong enough to leave and to implicitly trust ourselves, we can continue working on getting stronger, or we can stay in denial and numb our senses through refusing to feel the internal discomfort and self-blame.

If we choose not to abandon the self, we have effectively woven new patterns into our life experiences that will support us in forward movement and healing. But the moment we abandon our inner knowing that we need to change, we have woven threads into the Dream Weave that will present us with the lessons we need to learn about abandonment issues. These lessons may take many forms: our lover might have an affair, our spouse might ask for a divorce, a group might distance itself from us, a friend might stop calling.

Those abandonment scenarios are wake-up calls. We may be asked to look at ourselves, discovering the event or the thought where we have abandoned our personal integrity, our feelings, our sense of self-esteem, or our personal creeds. By abandoning ourselves, we have woven threads into the Dream Weave that have put us out of balance with our intuition, our sense of well-being, and our inner knowing. If we ignore the small, still voice within us whispering that something is amiss, it becomes easier to slip into illusions or denial, blaming others for our pain or loneliness. If, however, we acknowledge where and when we abandoned ourselves, we may agree that we no longer choose the company of people who are leaving our lives. "Sometimes life just happens when we are making other plans," giving us an option we may not have seen. The alternate path that appears unexpectedly can urge us to grow beyond our former lifestyles and identities, aligning with new people who allow us to be ourselves.

Every time we suddenly find new options or alternatives when our path had seemed impassable, we have broken through some former illusion. Sometimes the illusion is lifted by divine intervention, while at other times we actively let go, or something that was a blurry mess comes into focus. Those times can be marked by the unusual appearance of some animal in nature, visions that result from a ceremony, spirit signals found in the natural world, dream encounters, visitations from spirit guides or angels, or a sudden feeling of the burden being lifted for no apparent reason. Sometimes reading or seeing something turns on the light in our heads and brings us the big AH HA as the puzzle pieces fall into place.

HOME IS WHERE YOUR HEART LIVES WITHOUT FEAR

A few years ago I endured several confrontational pop quizzes where wounded people, riddled with human hatred and ignorance, attacked me. I was publicly rebuked by strangers, who happened to be Native American, for being a mixed breed, and I was attacked by bigoted white people when I wore my Indian regalia for ceremonies in public places. I emotionally collapsed after one book signing where a born-again Christian, who believed that Native American teachings were of the devil, tried to stab me in the back with a hunting knife. I felt unprotected, and the wounds of dealing with ignorance and prejudice brought up the feelings that I did not belong anywhere and that it was not safe to be a loving individual who honored every spiritual tradition. I was reminded of similar incidents that had happened to me seven years before and the dream that had helped me heal at that time.

In the dream, Grandpa Shongo told me to come to the reservation and go to Cattaraugas Creek and he would help me find my protection stone. Finding the protection stone is very sacred in our tradition. Once in a lifetime will people find the stone showing how to heal their lives, keeping them safely connected to the Earth Mother until they cross over to the other side. I went back to "the rez" and found the part of the creek I'd seen in my dream. I searched the sandbar for forty-five minutes and then sat down and tried to communicate with Grandpa's spirit. I told him I was sorry that I could not find the stone. I felt his presence and a hearty chuckle. Then a tiny voice came from the sandbar, saying, "Here I am, here I am!" I started digging in the spot I heard the sound coming from, and I saw the tip end of the stone sticking up from the sand. When I uncovered the whole rock and washed it off, I was amazed.

My personal protection stone had once been mud, and hundreds of thousands of years ago sea shells, twigs, crustaceans, and other impressions had been etched deeply into it before some ice age or volcanic activity had turned it to stone. As I examined it over the next few hours, I discovered more and more within the markings. Three of my totems were etched in that stone and represented the Medicine that I walk with in my life. Other symbols reflected aspects of my gifts of the spirit and personality traits. I was startled as Grandpa Shongo's voice boomed in my head, and I jumped like someone had goosed me. He said, "This is who you are. You belong to the Earth like this stone. Your blood is a mixture of different parts of humanity because your life is to be used as a bridge between people that will show unity between races. You never need to be ashamed of not belonging, because you belong to the Earth." In that moment a healing began, and it continued to reveal itself a bit at a time for many years.

The Mayans used the onion to represent the layers upon layers that are peeled away to reveal the spiritual essence of the healed human being. It is natural for humans to grow and change, to move in different directions from the patterns developed in childhood, but it is the courageous human who is willing to embrace the work required to strip away the layers of the onion needed to reach authentic freedom. We reach this kind of freedom when we see every adversity or challenge in life as a way of tempering the warrior nature into bright, strong courage, inner knowing, and truth. We learn that the layers of the onion are peeled away when we embrace life with all its many joys and sorrows, understanding that all experiences are valid initiations that give us the power of choice. That ability to discern allows us to choose how to relate to the events in our lives and to move through the doors that those experiences have opened for us.

Our shadow natures would like to portray doom and gloom in every instance of suffering or in all painful encounters, telling us that we are not strong enough to survive or to continue. This internal shadow talk is the mind's ability to thwart our forward movement. Every fleeting thought that is self-defeating or contains self-hatred dampens the human spirit's ability to overcome the barriers at hand. Succumbing to the influences of the shadow can infuse us with hopelessness, helplessness, and despair. By noticing the shadow thoughts when they occur and by consciously changing them, we alter their content and effectively eliminate the shadow's control.

Eventually on this path, we let go of our fear of dark forces or evil and come to a place of understanding where the dark and the light are seen not as separate forces but as part of the same universe. This perception offers us ways to learn through observing and experiencing opposites. Just as we would never know what heat was unless we experienced the cold, so also dark or evil motivates our search for light, wholeness, and inner peace. The shadow side of human nature gives us an alternative. Grandmother Twylah said, "There have always been 'the people' and 'those people.' We should be grateful for 'those people,' because without them, 'the people' would have become lazy and never stayed on the path." Spiritual warriors acknowledge inappropriate negativity as a challenge. We can see what we do not want to emulate, and we choose the path that is more beneficial and aligned with our goals.

For instance, on a day when we are feeling vulnerable, we might think, "I cannot achieve, I am not worthy of succeeding in this area of my life." We are given the choice of believing that negative idea presented by the shadow or reweaving that idea's thread in the Dream Weave by disagreeing. If we choose to believe the negative, we have given our authority away and shunned our free will. If we choose to disagree, we can replace the thought with a more positive one, and we can call our energy back from investment in self-negation. One way to reclaim our energy and our authority is through making this simple statement: "All parts of the Great Mystery's creation are made in wholeness. I honor the wholeness in me as I revere the perfection placed in all living things."

What we resist will persist. One big enlightenment trap on the third path is denying any inappropriate behaviors we may be demonstrating. Every human being has a shadow side that must be acknowledged. If we insist that we have no shadow behaviors, we are denying that we are ever impatient, jealous, angry, fearful, envious, dishonest, bossy, judgmental, controlling, manipulative, or critical. All human beings are responsible for their light as well as their shadow, and without recognizing both parts of ourselves we cannot heal. When we can authentically see where we use our shadow to define our light, we can embrace the shadow to achieve wholeness. We then can purify our behavioral imbalances and attain new levels of understanding and longer periods of balanced harmony.

The goal of life's initiations is not to master rigid rules of perfection. The goal is to become impeccably aware of all our thoughts, feelings, and actions so that we can achieve harmony and oneness with everything we experience in life. Embracing all the feelings and thoughts means embracing the good and the bad, the light as well as

the shadow. In this integration process, we discover the value of our
free will and the power of personal choice. We can choose to give our
authority to the negative or to the positive. Every time we choose to
change our Sacred Point of View, adopting the role of the unbiased observer, we release judgments that could hinder our ability to heal.

SPEAK NO EVIL

Indigenous tribal cultures worldwide practice forms of etiquette that
are as individual and diverse as the tribes themselves. One thread running through many tribes is the practice of speaking no harm. The
habits of working in silence or singing while at work and using story-
telling to fill the community's need to come together in groups and
communicate leave no room for careless, hurtful words or gossip. The
understanding that all words reflect and create positive or negative energy in the unseen worlds keeps negative chatter from bringing discord into daily life. By using silence as a way of being, tribal people are
given access to clear minds, which allow energy to be seen. Other
worlds existing within nature are open to them through this silence,
and consequently there is more harmony within the tribe. When energy is not leaked through negativity, boundless inspiration is available
for creating dance, stories, and ceremonies that celebrate every individual's role as a cherished member of the tribe.

When he was on the third path of initiation, the modern-day mystic
and inventor Buckminster Fuller came across the realization that negative feelings, critical thoughts, and abusive behavior drain life force.
Near the end of his military career, he became acutely aware that his
personal addiction to alcohol and the ensuing rage-filled behavior were
destroying his marriage and his family. Seeing the abuse his shadow
side was dishing upon his family, he tried many ways to change and
failed. Refusing to be victimized by his shadow side, he finally resorted
to using himself as a guinea pig. With his wife's agreement, he had a
doctor wire his jaws shut so that he could not verbally abuse anyone.
His diet was monitored, and his wife fed him all his food in liquid
form through a straw. During this voluntary period of silence, he discovered that he was forced to acknowledge his addictions, his destructive feelings, and his negative thoughts without being able to escape
through his former denials or by projecting abuse onto others. Mr.
Fuller healed his shadow, and in return he was funded with boundless

ideas and inspiration. Many of the inventions we credit him with, such as the geodesic dome, came to him during this time of silence.

On the third path of initiation, we begin to realize that everything we think, feel, dream, and do contains our life force. That life force energy is propelled by our intent and motivated by our personal will. We cannot operate successfully in life if we do not have enough energy available to us. If we have invested our energy in criticizing ourselves or others, we have drained the bank account of life force that could be used for inspiration, physical vitality, or creativity. The more aware we become of how we are investing our energy, the easier it becomes to reclaim that life force and to funnel it into areas that allow us to manifest the dreams we hold in our hearts. Patterns of behavior that have leaked energy through negative ideas or critical feelings are the property and realm of the shadow.

We encounter human shadow behavior in a multitude of places. We can observe it on the television news, which reports the crimes occurring this week; we can see it in common greed; we can watch it in movies where the bad guys play out horrifying violent events; and we can notice it in the hypocrisy or back stabbing found in the workplace. If we allow these behaviors to control our view of life, our observations will depress us, make us fearful or angry, give us nightmares, or create a lack of hope. We can view life as black and white, but if we do so, we invite an enlightenment trap to appear. The radical judgments required to see all of life as cut-and-dried segments of "us and them" will create entire webs of dead-end thought processes and lead to stagnation. This is not to say that we are asked to encourage criminal behavior or to become used to violence, but rather we are asked to observe the places within ourselves that still hold shadowlike behaviors. If we acknowledge that all human beings have light and dark sides, we have taken a step in the proper direction. If we choose to work on the places within ourselves that need change rather than pointing a finger at others, we will not change society, but we can change ourselves.

As we move through the process of confronting our own shadowlike behaviors, we evolve in our understanding of the wholeness within human consciousness. My teachers showed me how humans can slip into fear and how fear allows the shadow to gain authority over our thoughts, feelings, and viewpoints.

The infinity symbol in this figure is also called a Möbius strip, after the German mathematician who discovered its unique geometrical

NOW

PAST
Lived

FUTURE
Will live

Add regret and lived
becomes devil

Add fear of the future
and you are willing evil

THE GIFT
The Present Moment

Infinity Symbol

properties. This symbol, however, is ancient in origin and has been used by indigenous people for centuries to show how the two worlds of seen and unseen, matter and energy, are linked as two circles that have no beginning and no end.

FEAR IS THE ENEMY OF BEING PRESENT

My teacher Joaquin Muriel Espinosa drew this symbol in the earth with a stick and made the line at the nexus. Above the line he wrote NOW. That state of being fully present occurs when we are in balance with ourselves and with life, serene and at peace. He designated the left loop as the past and the right loop as the future. He showed me that if our thoughts and feelings from the past are haunting us, we cannot be fully present. He then pointed to the future and told me that if we fear the unknown of the future we are also out of balance because we have invested our energy in what could happen rather than what we are experiencing at present. In both cases we have negated the value of the moment and cannot derive the pleasure that the Creator offers us in the NOW. We cannot receive the immediate blessings of happiness and contentment when we invest our energy in regret, fear, or expectation of doom.

For years I worked with those images and made some other discoveries of my own. Since "the present" is the gift that humans are given by the Great Mystery, I began to see that in the English language there were also some anagrams that further explained the phenomenon of slipping into shadow thinking or negative feelings.

If we regret things we have done in the past or how we have lived, we invest our energy in going backward in time. The word lived spelled backward is devil. We create our own internal devils and the demons of regret or self-blame when we get stuck in past events that haunt us with thoughts of how we could have done it differently. The letters from lived and live also make up two more applicable words, veiled and veil. These anagrams show us that the past is veiled when we get stuck in regret, and we veil the future when we allow our fears to alter the present.

If we do not catch fearful thoughts when they appear, they collect and we can slip into fearing the future or the unknown. By investing our energy into the fear of how we will live in the future, we often procrastinate and leak creative energy that we could have used to accomplish what we need for today. By falling into this shadow trap, we create our own evil or gloomy outlooks of what the future will hold, because we have worried about a future that is not yet formed, influencing what will come through our negativity and fear in the present moment. In so doing, we put the future before the NOW and go backward again. The word live spelled backward is evil. Every time we fear the future, we are giving our authority, our will, and our life force to the shadow, allowing that energy to be used in a backward manner, creating our own fears by giving them the use of our life force. The spark of life that shines inside of us is diminished because we are leaking life force into the past or into the future.

COYOTE TRICKS US INTO HEALING

In the tradition of the Southern Seers, any act of personal sabotage is directed by the shadow and is Coyote Trickster Medicine of the highest order. Most of us are not aware that we are engaging in this form of conflict because we believe we are intending one thing, but in actuality we are investing life force in opposing ideas and feelings simultaneously. Nightmares usually appear when uncertainty, created by self-sabotage, mirrors the duality we have consciously or unwittingly embraced. Polar opposites in talk and action also mirror our acts of self-sabotage. When we are saying one thing, thinking and feeling another, and acting in a totally different manner, the art of self-sabotage can give an internal voice to every fearful or wounded fragment of our personality. The task of mending these opposing pieces of self begins on the third path.

Coyote is the totem that can present us with back-door lessons we do not expect in order to make us realize exactly how we are thwarting ourselves. Doubt and indecision hound every person who is actively hoping for positive results and secretly fearing failure, making mental lists of how and why something is too much to hope for. Deadly seriousness can overcome any person who is desperately focused on a desired outcome or has been trapped in the high drama of his or her personal life. Coyote Medicine will appear in some form in order to break the seriousness, reflecting the ridiculous nature of our human folly. Coyote laughs when we become as serious as a heart attack, reminding us that seriousness is twice as deadly as any heart attack because we lose heart all together. Having heart and using heart energy makes belly laughter possible and that lightness of being that supports all types of healing. If we remain stuck in our seriousness, we will develop diseases that will kill the body in order to release the spirit from the prison created by our own refusal to embrace joy.

On the third path is it paramount to learn to laugh at ourselves and our self-importance, arrogance, high drama, or false sense of indispensability. Those who are learning the lessons of personal authority or spiritual purpose on this path often stray into the false impression that they are the only chosen ones or that they have been designated to change the world because of their special abilities. The lessons connected with this phase of development show whether our humility is in place and whether we can wear our power lightly. All too often the know-it-all syndrome comes into play, and the pseudointellectual talks from a position of authority but cannot live the philosophy he or she expounds upon. Coyote is the great equalizer, tripping us up in many different ways in order to reveal exactly where we are sabotaging ourselves.

THE CEMETERIES ARE FULL OF PEOPLE WHO BELIEVED THEY WERE INDISPENSABLE

Some people on the third path get stuck in giving to others until no life force is left to maintain their own health. This is another enlightenment trap. A friend once told me that the cemeteries were full of people who believed they were indispensable. On the third path we are shown exactly how we overextend ourselves, and we are asked to make healthy boundaries so that we attain balance in giving and receiving, rest and activity. This gift of balance is found in the archetypal lessons of Otter Medicine balancing work and play and is also provided by the trees, the Standing People, in lessons of giving and receiving.

Learning how to say no is difficult for those who have tied their personal sense of worth to the role they hold in their chosen careers. We can see this pattern in all arenas of life, whether in parenting, in climbing the corporate ladder, in service-oriented jobs, or in the healing arts. The idea that we are indispensable can lead to denying that we are human and that our bodies need attention. The Superman or Superwoman identity can hinder us by producing illnesses that force us to slow down and pay attention. When we start to pay attention, we may notice that our behavior was motivated by wrong goals, such as money, acclaim, the need to be needed, and fear of failure.

During the second through fourth paths, some people who are healing their lives choose occupations that support other people in their healings processes. They might become massage therapists, family counselors, psychotherapists, hands-on healers, or psychic or spiritual counselors. If they are not careful, these people can be faced with a particular type of enlightenment trap. Having an occupation that offers income based on the neediness of others can lead to fears of losing income if a client heals and no longer needs the service provided. Also, the energy required to do enough sessions to pay the bills can be staggering and can leave these healers too drained to maintain their own health. Having more than one source of income allows any person in these fields to keep from falling into the traps of fear about money issues.

LOSE THE EAR WAX AND THE INTERNAL CHATTER

Listening is a mainstay lesson of the third path. Authentic hearing comes when we can use every part of our bodies as ears. To digest the essential points of any situation, we are asked to listen with more than our ears, using all our perceptions and being fully attentive. Observing the obvious is a part of listening, as is absorbing and understanding another person's words and intent. If we are thinking of what we will say next or how to reply, we are in the future and are not present enough to understand, digest, or integrate what the other person is trying to convey to us. We effectively destroy the circle of communication the moment we are not attentive, lessening our potential to learn and to grow through sharing feelings and information.

Listening to our own words and counting them as sacred is another lesson on the third path. Our own spirits hold us accountable for the manner in which we make promises or commitments and for how we use our words to influence, manipulate, control, or encourage others. Speaking words that we think others want to hear or playing mind games is deadly at this stage of development. The third-path consequences of this behavior will boomerang, causing the resulting initiations to become more radically chaotic and to erode any honor that we hoped to embrace through our lessons. The pop quizzes and enlightenment traps devised by the shadow will contain stronger implications if we cannot hone our integrity, striving for further impeccability in our lives by refusing to feed shadow behaviors in ourselves or another.

When vows, promises, or commitments are not honored, others can withdraw their goodwill and supportive energy, with a sudden accompanying loss of synchronicity. I observed the downward spiral of energy create a multitude of hardships in one man's life. He kept breaking his promises and being arrogant until others simply withdrew their life force from him, with no harmful intent toward him, and chose to reinvest it in other areas. The withdrawal of goodwill was so substantial that his former synchronicity vanished and his life hit the skids. Even then, he did not realize that his own behavior was creating the problems that he blamed upon fantasy opponents.

WHY DO I FEEL LIKE A RAW NERVE ENDING?

At certain times on all these paths of initiation, acute sensitivity to noise, violence, smells, electronic devices, light, and other elements in our personal environments can make us feel sick or like we are going crazy. This ultrasensitivity usually begins on the third path as we are reclaiming parts of ourselves that had to shut down if we were to survive. When those fragments are reclaimed, we may find that our sensitivity and our sensory perceptions are so acute as to become physically painful. This is normal. The restructuring of our perceptions of life is a part of the healing process. If we fear the changes occurring in our sensitivity levels, we might develop environmental illnesses at this stage of development. The sensitivities will balance out if we do not label them or feed them with our fear that something is wrong with us. The more we hold on to rigid judgments regarding physical symptoms we experience, the harder it becomes for those conditions to balance out in a natural way.

Judging others also sets us up for one enlightenment trap after another. Some people use their sensitivities like a merit badge to show how spiritually developed they have become. Others judge those who eat certain foods, drink liquor, or smoke tobacco, proud of how pure they have made their lives by conquering their own addictions. We can develop an entire system of mental judgment by projecting onto another what we believe is right for us. These thoughts affect our own immune systems as surely as physically abusing our bodies can impair our health. In some cases we might develop allergies because of our judgments.

If we look at cultures outside America, we find that they are not disgusted with the natural smells of the human body. We have been programmed by our soap, perfume, and deodorant commercials to judge the human body's smells as undesirable. On the third path we are asked to review any sensitivities stemming from judgments we may have adopted from group thinking, the media, or advertising campaigns, such as which body types are desirable and undesirable, which cars and clothing "spell success," and who is to be coddled and courted because he or she is important or famous. These sources of input can control our inner knowing through powerful visual images, subliminal messages, and the conscious or unconscious consumption of the illusion-filled belief systems being presented to the public.

The third path teaches us how to maintain our individuality and our personal integrity in the face of modern technology and the world's seductions. The challenge is to respect who we are and what we feel is authentic personal truth and to maintain our Sacred Points of View. The balancing act between what we are asked to accept from the stimulus we receive and what we derive from our inner knowing can present many challenges to our sense of integrity. We dive deeper into the introspection process and observe how certain beliefs within mass consciousness can be controlling our free will or can be altering our

Sacred Point of View. We are given the opportunity to see what we want to keep and what we choose to give away.

HONORING OUR PERSONAL TRUTHS AND INTUITION

The third path yields a harvest of blessings that allow every person to use inner knowing and personal power. How we use authentic self-esteem and our personal authority in life constitutes another layer of lessons that can test us on everything we have learned. As we weed out the various catch phrases and group beliefs found on our paths, we find our own truths and we begin to experience heightened senses of intuition, which allow us to trust ourselves and to respect our individual sense of what is right for us personally. We do not accept blanket truths without exploring personally whether those statements have validity.

These skills of observation, feeling, hearing, and sensing things from the viewpoint of personal authority open new doors of awareness. These intuitive skills can be used in the healing arts, in business, in counseling, in the arts, in parenting, or in any other field of endeavor. To strictly appoint the development of intuition to solely one area would be foolish. How a person uses his or her increased capacity to understand life and self is a matter of personal choice. But I would like to share some examples of various ways that the healing process can assist us in all areas of our lives.

When we learn to trust the intuitive part of our nature, we become more able to understand that we are constantly inspired to take certain paths in our lives. Inspiration is a form of taking spirit into the self. You may ask what spirit is. In our Native American traditions we see spirit as the life force energy that is the connective tissue between any living thing and the Great Mystery, the Creator, God. Every time we breathe, we re-spirit the body through respiration. Every time we clear the mind and allow ourselves to be still, we can become inspired because we allow spirit or universal life force into our Sacred Spaces. As we continue to heal our lives, we become more aware of the occurrence of intuitive flashes urging us to explore all aspects of human potential.

Honoring our intuition is the key to living in synchronicity with all life and the Great Mystery. How much attention we give to intuition, seeing it as a creative force, determines the ease with which we find the universal flow of life. When we allow that flow to become a harmonious part of our personal rhythm, we instinctually know things. We all have heard stories of people who were warned intuitively against boarding an airplane that later crashed. There have been countless stories about how paying attention to intuition changed the course of someone's life forever. Without being too dramatic about the importance of intuition, I will simply say that those messages are available to anyone who has cleared the chaotic chatter from the mind. Intuition is divine guidance that comes into play when we listen or feel. That guidance becomes a natural part of our lives as we continue to develop the skills connected to the intuitive part of human nature. Our certainty and self-trust flourish, and our view of life dramatically changes as we allow our senses to be honed to new levels.

The blessings gained through intuition allow us to grow by leaps and bounds. We learn how archetypes within our world can assist us in sorting out who we are, where we belong, and how we can use our gifts, talents, and abilities. I developed three divination systems to teach people on the healing path how to use their gifts of intuition. *Medicine Cards*™, written with David Carson, use the archetypes of the totems or power animals to reflect to the reader how he or she can learn about the personal Medicine or inner strength available to him or her and how to use those gifts in a balanced way. The *Medicine Cards*™ *Just For Today* is a minideck of the animals, giving short daily reminders of ways to focus our intention and use our intuition. The *Sacred Path Cards*™ uses Native American symbols as the archetypes that represent the life lessons and challenges that we all encounter on the seven paths of initiation. These tools allow people to explore their personal gifts of intuition, giving a blueprint of how to learn to trust the human transformation process a step at a time.

Needing to compete with another who has similar knowledge is one of the seductive enlightenment traps that can appear on the third path. Far too often we are drawn into the arena of competition because we want to prove to ourselves that what we have learned is superior to what someone else knows. This form of competition occurs when we feel threatened, and it can bring old patterns of jealousy into play. When we feel that we have accomplished a lot and are beginning to use our newfound gifts of authority, we may fall prey to the shadow's need to be acknowledged. If we criticize others for the manner in which they present their knowledge, we have succumbed to our own lack of certainty. In this instance, we may not approve of another person's behavior, but it is not our place to demean anyone else. If we have truly healed, we can remain respectful of that person's Sacred Point of View even if it rankles or counters what we believe is appropriate.

THE ARMOR USED BY THE SPIRITUAL WARRIOR

The third path also offers lessons in Armadillo Medicine, or boundaries, which shows us how we feel when our own boundaries are not honored as well as why we should honor the boundaries of others. If a person does not feel comfortable being asked to discuss personal information, that boundary should be honored without any comment that could make the person feel ill at ease. If we are actively embracing our own healing process, there are times when we may feel vulnerable or ultrasensitive. It is totally inappropriate to force anyone who is feeling that raw to interact with others in loud or boisterous activities. On the third path we are asked to develop our intuitiveness and sensitivity to the degree that we can respectfully observe the boundaries of others in this manner. These boundary lessons are a part of honoring the Sacred Spaces of others and respecting our own physical and emotional boundaries as well.

As we learn more about what is appropriate for us individually, we gain more of ourselves through the healing process. We are then asked to extend the same compassion and understanding toward others. I observed one woman years ago who was very sensitive when she was experiencing personal trauma or hurt, but who acted loud, rude, and inappropriate when someone else in her circle of friends was vulnerable or hurting. She was swept away with the high drama of a situation and gossiped about the person, who was already traumatized. She never realized how hurtful her lack of boundaries was to those of her friends who eventually heard the intimate details that she had dished out without thinking.

When she was confronted with being the source of these hurtful rumors, she would say only that she heard it from others, and she refused to be accountable for having passed the information on. This woman would scream and yell and slam the phone down when confronted with her behavior, laying blame outside herself. This behavior pattern is far more common than we would like to think and is an example of another way we are held accountable for our thoughts, words, and use of authority. If we gossip, we are misusing our authority and we are raping another person's boundaries. When the tables are turned and we are the recipients, we receive the full impact of how that behavior feels.

From time to time, all of us are drawn into commenting on something that may not be any of our business. The lessons can be very painful if something we said is twisted by another or is repeated in a rumor that hurts other people. Learning who to trust with confidences can take time and some hard knocks. Learning how to be careful with statements of our personal opinions requires that we be fully present when we are speaking to anyone. The fact that today's media will misrepresent facts and misquote people's statements in order to get a sensational story is a sad situation and shows that integrity is at risk in all segments of humanity. We are not asked to point fingers but rather to look at our own behaviors and to correct the patterns that we do not like.

During the third path we often meet up with other lessons regarding boundaries. Crow Medicine is a Native American concept that teaches us about Divine Law. Crow shows us that if we focus on the positive, we are given more positive experiences. If we focus on the negative, the shadow side of human nature will be fed by our negativity and will come alive, feeding our experiences with further negativity. These lessons can apply to internal mental criticism or to external verbal rebukes that demean ourselves or others. There is a big difference between acknowledging what is imbalanced or inappropriate and then working to change that behavior, and beating ourselves up with self-revilement or self-hatred. It is just as inappropriate to allow our shadow nature to strip us of our dignity or shame us into hopelessness as to allow it to convince us we are superior. In all situations, we feed our life force to the positive or to the shadow and give our authority to one or the other, harvesting exactly what we have fertilized with our life force.

The set of lessons that Crow brings into our lives may ask us to find positive things to think or feel about all people and all situations. We do not have to judge any person's shortcomings, but instead we can learn to see any situation or person as a magnificent teacher. Any person who is misbehaving can be showing us what we do not wish to become or how not to do something. Through thanking the person for the lesson, we can learn to honor the fact that every human being is a messenger or teacher for us. We are also asked to use discernment, or Owl Medicine, and we are given the choice to forgive and to let go of past pain. It is our choice whether or not to allow the offenders, who have been forgiven, access to our Sacred Spaces at any time in the future. I would like to say, however, that it is not necessary to let a coyote back into your hen house to attain spiritual enlightenment!

THE VALUE OF OBSERVING THE OBVIOUS

On the third path we learned that the value of looking for something to admire in ourselves or in another person, strengthens our boundaries in the Dream Weave and deters negativity from entering our thoughts or feelings. This prevents those negative threads from entering our physical lives by being spoken as words. My teachers called these kinds of boundaries spiritual or Dream Weave boundaries. By protecting the parts of our Sacred Spaces that are seemingly unseen but that contain thought, feeling, energy, and dreams, we are using a spiritual form of preventative Medicine. We are required to use vigilance in monitoring all that we allow inside our Sacred Spaces. We are asked to feel every emotion that influences our human experience and to move those feelings through us and release them as neutral energy. In this manner we are beginning a fourth-path lesson, which allows us to experience all of life with ease.

Gratitude and communion with the Creator continue to be integral parts of the third path as we allow spirit to assist us in purifying our thoughts, emotions, behaviors, and attitudes. We are asked to return thanks for every blessing in life and to honor the steps of our personal healing and the healing taking place in the lives of others. We learn to pray for the well-being of all human beings no matter how they are living their lives. We send love to those who have hurt us, and we draw our strength from that same love. We gather together with others who will pray with us, and we share our healing experiences. We ask for guidance and the strength necessary to stand tall in a loving manner, even in the face of our greatest fears. We learn to become the one who watches, observing all that comes into our experiences from the view-point of an unbiased witness.

By observing inappropriate behavior without entering an arena of conflict, we are able to sidestep negative encounters. When we look at any situation and are grateful for the teaching being presented, we have prevented ourselves from being labeled or targeted as the enemy. If we engage in conflict by pointing out the bad behavior of another person, we have chosen to enter a metaphorical boxing arena, which can set us up for attacks of all kinds. On the other hand, we can do what a friend of mine once suggested: she told me that she simply and silently thanks the person by saying, "Thank you for letting me know you better."

LAUGHTER SHIELDS US AGAINST HARMFUL INTENT

In today's world, the most powerful form of spiritual attack is envy and jealousy. Some people believe that black magic, bad spells, curses, sorcery, and witching are the most harmful spiritual attacks on others, but all those rituals are propelled by jealousy or envy, the need for revenge or retaliation. I have felt and seen how ugly, unstaunched, hate-filled emotions can harm the energy fields of others. This battering in the unseen worlds of the Dream Weave can weaken a person's spiritual boundaries and eventually make that person ill or accident prone, particularly if the person targeted is also leaking his or her energy on fear, hate, bitterness, or envy. The revenge-oriented rituals that the inept dabbler practices are a misuse of Raven's Medicine of magic. Dabblers who use spells and curses, directing harm toward other human beings, will have their bad intentions boomerang, creating more harm in their lives.

No harmful intent can flourish in the face of laughter. Laughter is the lubricant that keeps negativity from sticking. We break the stranglehold of any malicious intent when we do not fear it but rather engage in laughter, joy, and love. The more skillful we become, disengaging from negativity, the stronger we become spiritually, emotionally, mentally, and physically. Fear of the shadow will allow negative energy to gain the upper hand in our daily life as well as in the energetic realms, where our nightmares reflect our subconscious fears or the negative

feelings we are entertaining. If we can embrace the fact that all life contains shadow and light, the fear of what we think evil can do to us
dwindles until it no longer affects us through our own judgments.

At various points on the third path we are given opportunities to
see how far we have come in developing a personal sense of well-being
and in using our personal authority effectively in the world. This discovery occurs each time we are tested on how we will use the authority we have gained, the expertise we employ, and the influence we have
available. We get a real close-up look at our weaknesses in the process,
as if Coyote placed all of our personal garbage and ragtag issues under
an electron microscope!

I know firsthand what a humbling experience that can be. Looking
at our own shit magnified at close range changes our mind's perspective of self-importance forever! Coyote laughingly told me that this
equalizing event was the first psychedelic experience every person's
ego went through during the initiations of the ancient mystery schools.
If we make choices that include lording our skills over others or trying
to exercise control over situations and people, we will immediately encounter this type of pop quiz.

If we feel that we are strong in one area and we misuse those abilities, the results can affect other areas of our lives where we are not so
strong. For example, if we finally have been promoted into a manage-
ment position but have not matured emotionally, we may make unreasonable demands on others to test out our power. This unfortunate
choice of action can start a chain of events that becomes more than
humbling when we are called on the carpet by the boss. Or we may
not know how to drop that same petty tyrant behavior when we leave
work, alienating family members or friends. The pop quiz can occur
when no one wants to share our company any longer.

Learning how to handle the authority we have earned or the success
we have attained is a third-path lesson. Handling fame or acclaim of
some sort includes learning how we can be seduced into becoming a
petty tyrant, an arrogant snob, or a know-it-all. All of these ego-oriented
behaviors are third-path enlightenment traps. They seduce us into believing that we must adopt behaviors that we assume to be those of a person
in a position of authority, public acclaim, or wealth. Nothing could be
further from the truth. The authentic, healed human being, who has embraced his or her personal authority and wears his or her power lightly,

demonstrates humility and compassion in a respectful manner. When we release our need to be recognized, the gears of our belief systems are stripped and authentic being replaces mental attitudes.

THE DOMINO EFFECT: THE BARRIERS COME TUMBLING DOWN!

Active processing of personal issues that results in victories over our former limitations can be viewed as a domino effect. Imagine a line of dominoes standing on end, creating a path across a table with lots of curves and twists. When you take your finger and tip the first domino over, the entire line crashes down, one after another, until the entire bunch has fallen. The results of clearing one of our personal issues can be seen in the same way. When we remove one false idea or behavior pattern from our lives, the first domino gets knocked over, and all of the intricately connected habits, issues, or false ideas connected to the first one come tumbling down.

Our hearts open time and again as we let go of the patterns that keep us in fear or pain. We learn how to keep our hearts open for longer periods of time as we grow and experience new wonders at every point of personal transformation. Sometimes we have to be totally exhausted and at our wits' end before we can authentically receive the blessings being offered. The following story is an example of how I found one of those heart-opening events in my life.

I had been traveling for months, and I was depleted from the constant giving that accompanies teaching and facilitating healings. I was in Washington, D.C., and was so tired and emotionally exhausted that I went to the back of the Unity Church parking lot and cried before my lecture. I thought if one more person asked me for *anything*, I was going to break in two. I looked down at a pile of gravel being used to fill in potholes and saw a stone that called to me. I picked it up and saw that it was in the shape of a heart. On the face of this heart-stone was a deeply etched symbol commonly found in ancient mythology, the double-sided ax of the clan of warrior women. Just as I was realizing that this was the symbol for the heart of the warrior, I heard the Earth Mother's voice saying, "The heart of any spiritual warrior knows how to be strong and how to help others, but it is the wise woman who takes rest and nurturance before her heart becomes hardened to others or to her own human needs." I will always carry that stone with me as a reminder to be as openhearted with myself as I am with others.

On the third path our personal views of reality are restructured, and we experience dramatic changes in how we respond to difficult situations. The situations that could have brought us to our knees in the past, we now tend to handle with ease. We are fully responsible for these changes and for giving ourselves permission to experience life in a different way. When we remove the massive amount of connected responses that we mentally and emotionally adhered to during our lives, we create lots of space for changes to occur in our thought processes and emotional responses. We claim our personal authority over knee-jerk reactive behaviors when we choose to respond rather than simply react. As we free ourselves from the programmed reactions that came from our woundedness or from dysfunctional patterns exhibited by our families, we gain more personal authority. Our former perceptions and emotional responses are literally rewired time and again as we eliminate the old mechanisms that reinforced the brain circuits of our learned behaviors.

Our personal breakthroughs teach us how to see present challenges or difficulties in a new light as we learn to acknowledge the opportunities we are given to stretch beyond our former limitations. Our understanding of how we operate in the world is increased as we gather more of our awareness and balanced self-esteem into present time, using those gifts to discover harmony and wholeness. New points of balance are achieved as we heal and refine our lives. We continue to redefine who we are and how we choose to live, changing directions when life urges us forward. The Shaman's Death and Rebirth becomes a matter of shifting gears as we become more flexible in our thoughts, actions, feelings, and modes of operation. Genuine compassion and authentic humility can bolster our progress throughout the remaining paths.

CHAPTER 6

Human beings have five elements that stifle the spirit's ability to soar; unwavering seriousness, self-importance, lack of imagination, the mind's negative chatter, and fear.

—Berta Broken Bow

▲▲▲▲▲▲▲▲▲▲▲▲▲▲▲▲▲▲▲▲▲▲▲▲▲▲▲▲▲▲▲▲
WISDOM PATH

Wisdom's fire flashes,
With scorching flames,
As the trials by fire
Test all that I claim.

Coyote comes calling
To see what I've learned.
Can I play with wildfire?
Or will I get burned?

Will I be threatened?
Will I need to compete,
Allowing self-importance
To cause wisdom's defeat?

Can I share all my wisdom
With the intent to inspire,
Allowing others the right
To claim their spirit's fire?

When Coyote comes calling,
I'll be prepared as he arrives,
Finding balance through laughter,
Amidst the snares that he contrives.

—Jamie Sams

The Fourth Path of Initiation
The North Direction on the Medicine Wheel

THE North Direction on the Medicine Wheel is the place of wisdom. The experiences we have gathered in life and how we have learned from those events form the essence of wisdom. We learn to incorporate the intellectual knowledge we have by walking it in our lives with impeccability. The North Direction offers us an opportunity to review all that we have learned and to learn how and when to share that wisdom with others. The fourth path has been walked by many travelers who have offered new wisdom to humanity as a gift of insight. The vast worlds of consciousness, energy, and spirit in our universe are accessible because some human being had the courage to enter the unknown and to become the adventurous spirit who was willing to find out what uncharted potentials were available to humankind.

The unspoken languages of the animals, plants, stones, and elemental spirits in nature bring us further wisdom about our human roles in the natural world. We discover how to detect the beautiful gifts being offered to us by the life forms on the Earth Mother and how we can apply their lessons to our lives. The realms of angels, spiritual guides, and unseen forces of consciousness offer divine inspiration. In the North Direction of the fourth path we incorporate all the messages we receive from the spiritual consciousness of other life forms into our personal understanding of life on planet Earth. These lessons of wisdom allow us to perceive that all life forms in our universe are more than biological or geological forms; they all contain consciousness or spirit.

For centuries, humanity barely touched the beginning lessons of the third path of initiation, and a rare few completed those lessons. The fourth path was followed by fewer still, and on the subsequent paths, the fifth through seventh, many initiates lost their lives in the effort. Today, the picture is totally different. The territory has been charted by countless individuals who have opened the Dream Weave for all of humanity to safely enter the realms of consciousness formerly unknown to the masses.

Every life-form in our universe has a Sacred Space, which includes the physical matter of its make-up, the spirit or consciousness connected to it, and the viewpoint it represents. Human beings have a Sacred Space that also includes personal thoughts, emotions, possessions, and an experiential viewpoint on life. The Sacred Point of View is where we assemble our perception of personal reality. Our Sacred Point of View shifts every time we alter our viewpoints of *what is possible* and *what can be experienced*. We continually expand our perceptions of accepted reality when we undergo experiences in our lives that cannot be explained through the sets of rules and regulations dictated by science or the accepted reality of the masses.

On the fourth path we are asked to integrate experiences of things, such as consciousness or spirit, that cannot be physically proved by measuring their weight, texture, or content. This path includes realms of undefinable situations that must be understood through the heart because the intellect cannot embrace that which is not tangible except through feeling and personal inner knowing. On the fourth path, individual experiences take us beyond conventional education or intellectual expertise.

Every time we rediscover the wisdom contained in the unseen forces in nature or the divine hand of the Creator blessing our lives, our Sacred Points of View are radically altered. Every time we have encounters with spirit in dreams or through meditation or visions, we feel a presence that can neither be denied nor explained to others who have not tapped into those levels of awareness. Every time we go beyond our former limitations behaviorally, mentally, spiritually, or physically, those successes offer us abundant new life force.

This next figure is a visual image of how we use the energy we have gathered to access more than one lesson and path of initiation at a time. Each of the paths of initiation is symbolized by a finely tuned gold watch, containing many separate wheels. Each of the tiny inner wheels represents the issues we are working on personally. Each watch contains all of the wheels, or issues, that we must face in order to complete our growth on that path. We learn to see those issues from every direction as the wheels turn. All of the lessons or personal issues on a path of initiation have a separate wheel that interacts with the other wheels and the skills that we embrace.

The watch may appear to be running slow or fast, depending upon the individual's process, but the timing is always correct and perfect according to the Great Mystery's sense of divine order. The level of difficulty, rhythm, and mastery that operates in each of the wheels is determined by our willingness to embrace our life lessons.

We have access to all seven watches, or paths, when we have collected the skills needed to move to the next path while maintaining the

Paths of Initiation

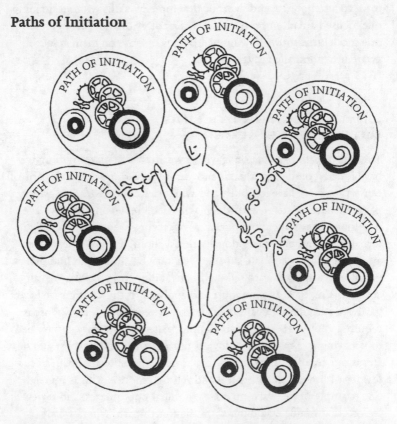

We are learning lessons from different paths at the same time. All lessons that we encounter require the use of energy and give energy back to us.

turning of the former wheels. Those skills, and the life force energy that accompanies them, come from the Dream Weave and are available to us as we free ourselves from our limitations, having mastered the lessons of a particular path. We are required to explore all the cogs of every wheel of experience that we choose to embrace. The cogs represent all the skills that we learn step by step until we master them. We are allowed to move forward into a new area of consciousness when we develop the skills needed to encounter that level of awareness. We also must have the courage and willingness to explore those new areas.

By being mindful of the skills and the wisdom that we have attained, we can usually keep the former wheels of personal mastery impeccably moving in rhythm. We then have enough energy or extra life force to attempt new endeavors or develop new skills without draining our focused attention from the tasks currently at hand. This figure is one model that shows how human beings operate on many levels of awareness simultaneously.

COYOTE COMES CALLING WITH A SLY SNICKER

The fourth path of initiation is where we are tested on everything we have learned on the prior paths and we are forced to see which parts of our wisdom we have forgotten and which we continue to use, which parts we have mastered and which skills need reviewing. At this stage of development we often find ourselves observing events that rekindle internal reactions, either emotionally or psychologically. When we view an unjust or inappropriate situation, we may be stunned to find our emotions swaying toward self-righteous indignation or fury. We can count this reaction as a pop quiz and apply all of the wisdom we have garnered in order to regain balance *before* we respond. If a response is required and we lash out in an inappropriate way, we have succumbed to behaving in a manner that lowers our personal effectiveness and destroys our balance, throwing us into reviewing the second path's lessons of how to creatively feel and release emotion. This is merely one example of the wake-up calls, continual pop quizzes, and review lessons that can be encountered on the fourth path, where we are tested on our use of wisdom.

On this path we are asked to discern *when* we should share what we have learned and *how* to impart that information to people without being too complex or giving them too much information for their level of understanding. It is an invasion of the Sacred Spaces of others to blurt out information or advice that was not solicited. This unbecoming behavior can come from overenthusiasm or spiritual arrogance or lack of sensitivity, but in all cases it is a signal that the person giving the information has not learned this fourth-path lesson. We are asked to learn the value of respecting the boundaries of others and not having to be the supreme authority. If we are in a position where others look to us for advice, resisting the urge to add input or sage wisdom when it is not asked for can be a paramount lesson. I have personally stuck both feet in my mouth when nobody had asked me for my opinion or spiritual advice. People who were smug about what they thought they knew resented the input. Others, who held hard to their limiting judgments, verbally attacked me. The beginners, who were asking some simple question and received an explanation on every aspect of how things fit together, were overwhelmed and confused. Oops! Zipping the lips can be a hard-earned virtue.

Because we have found a certain astute level of healing and balance in our lives during the prior paths, the divine Trickster is now going to test us on our wisdom to the fullest extent of our capacity. If you can imagine a circus person spinning several plates on the end of sticks, balancing all of them simultaneously, you have the picture of a person who is actively walking the fourth path. Each spinning plate represents a set of skills earned through successfully mastering life's lessons. Those skills are spinning in motion as the initiate adds new wisdom and abilities to his or her experience, while also adding unexpected elements to test the degree of expertise that he or she has attained.

On the fourth path, Coyote watches us spinning the plates and comes over to pee on our leg. Do the plates all fall to the ground and shatter? That depends upon the level of focus, concentration, and certainty we can count as our own. Some people who are beginning the fourth path become flustered or disgusted at the metaphorical urine splashing on their leg; they might have to go back and review some earlier lessons. Other people have seen Coyote from the corner of their eyes and are prepared. Others might let one auspicious plate slip, crashing on Coyote's head just before the Trickster lifts his leg. How we

respond depends totally on our sense of humor as well as on the level
of wisdom we have gained.

Joaquin Muriel Espinosa, my teacher in Mexico, was an authentic
adept. I saw this man change his body's appearance in front of my eyes
so that he would not be recognized by his students when he wanted to
observe them unnoticed. He came from the Toltec and Yaqui Dreamer
lineage and was of Mayan, Aztec, and Yaqui blood. Joaquin was an
amazing trickster. One of the lessons of the fourth path that he taught
me will forever be branded in my memory as the biggest lesson I have
ever encountered in the value of humor. Before this lesson, I believed
that integrity, expertise, authentic skill, and credible information were
the only tools needed on the fourth path. Dang, was I surprised!

It was a warm day outside of San Luis Potósi in the high desert of
Mexico when I went with Joaquin to an area near a deserted mine
shaft. He asked me to sit silently and to focus on a question I had been
repeatedly asking him for days, which he had avoided by not giving
me a straight answer. I thought he was sitting nearby, in silence. After a
while I heard whispering sounds, and my attention was drawn to the
mine shaft, where it seemed the sounds were coming from. I became
curious, and then my emotions dropped into fear as the unearthly
sounds continued. The opening was about twenty feet in front of me,
and as I looked, I saw my own face seemingly floating in the darkness,
whispering something that I couldn't hear properly. Fear mounted as I
felt a rush of bile shoot up into my throat and a knot form in the pit of
my stomach. I nearly heaved when I saw the ghostly apparition of my
own death mask floating, without a body, in the pitch darkness of the
shaft opening. I was feeling waves of panic, unable to take my eyes off
what appeared to be my own face, which looked withered and blue. I
was shocked beyond my own panic as the whispers suddenly changed
to a resounding yell. The face changed and laughingly yelled at me,
"The answer ain't out there, Jamie! It's in here, but you're too afraid
to look!"

The death mask vanished, and Joaquin jumped from the darkness
and roared with laughter. The look on my face must have been hilarious to him. After realizing what had happened, I was caught up in the
laughter, finally getting the message I was apparently sending myself
through a Trickster lesson. We must face the death of *who we think we are*
before we can go within and know that nothing is really outside of us.
The answers to the heart's questions have to be experienced internally.

When our hearts move beyond the fear of not being able to trust our perceptions to be accurate, we begin to honor our own inner knowing and to claim the wisdom we have rightfully earned.

HEY, COYOTE, LIGHTEN UP! I'M DANCING AS FAST AS I CAN

Some people might think it unfortunate that the further we go in our human growth processes, the more is required of us. They fear the level of mastery that is required at various stages of initiation because they get overwhelmed when life seems to batter them beyond their toler-ance. Those who have made it to the fourth path have gained wisdom from having lived through those Dark Nights of the Soul and chaotic times when everything takes unbelievable effort. We often acquire the gifts of strength required on the paths by successfully passing through harrowing experiences or personal pain. Endurance, authentic spiritual humility, and unswerving dedication are prerequisite skills for fourth-path lessons. Human beings find the road more than a bit rocky if they are not actively using the basic skills and spiritual disciplines that give a firm foundation of faith to every path.

The four basic skills that form spiritual foundations are: (1) focus-ing on positive thoughts without judgment; (2) taking a time of si-lence or prayer; (3) having an attitude of gratitude and counting our blessings; (4) recalling our energy from any activity, thought, or feel-ing that feeds shadow behaviors and reinvesting our life force in posi-tive viewpoints.

When we are on the fourth path we may find ourselves in the com-pany of people who behave like dogma-filled pains in the ass. These folks can be worthy opponents or petty tyrants, or they may be totally unconscious of the roles they are embracing. These situations mirror to us the Coyote backdoor teachings, showing us that people can assume the roles of teachers without knowing that the lessons they present through their behaviors are not in harmony with their words of sup-posed wisdom. These people can be magnificent teachers because they demonstrate the improper way to behave and a rare quality of tunnel vision that is astonishing. The student who is an astute observer can learn untold lessons, allowing him or her access to wisdom unwit-tingly presented through a teacher's backdoor behavior.

At this point on the fourth path we are tested on whether we have gained a sense of humor through our lessons with Coyote or whether we must develop beyond the seriousness of taking everything personally. The ability to be grateful for the hilarious examples that life is presenting to us takes some effort, particularly if we are required to laugh at ourselves as well. The fourth path is about sharing what we have learned, but many people begin teaching workshops or seminars in various fields when they are just approaching the lessons of the second or third paths. They may be looking for a form of affirmation or seeking followers. Some people are teaching so that they can learn the life lessons that are not included in the subjects they are teaching. Some people teach in order to share what has worked for them in their development process. Others are cutting-edge inventors or specialists in their areas of expertise. In all levels of teaching Coyote presents seductions that will hound the path of anyone who becomes an opinion leader or teacher in any field of endeavor.

When I was a student, I experienced a Coyote lesson that came full circle in later years. When I was twenty-four, Cisi and Berta taught me the patterns of sound heard in the walks of certain animals. They used the drum and beat out these rhythms so I could understand the part sound plays in the energy of an animal's spirit messages. After many weeks, they put me in a room in total darkness and sat in another room beating out the rhythms in fainter and fainter patterns, allowing me to discern the subtle differences and to perceive spiritually which animals came to me. I saw many amazing animals walk into my perceptions, and some gave me gifts of wisdom that I took to heart.

I was deep into the visions and did not notice that the drumbeat had stopped. I finally realized that I had drifted far from my body, and I felt the gentle hands of the grandmothers massaging my limbs. Trying as hard as I could, I forced myself to return to my body, and just as I felt like I was coming out of the trancelike state, taking a big breath, the light was switched on. There in front of me was a sight that made me laugh so hard I was flooded with life force: Cisi's hundred-and-nine-year-old backside was exposed three feet in front my face! Cisi was four-foot-three, seventy-five pounds, toothless, and had the tiniest wrinkled butt you can possibly imagine. The technique was certainly effective, and it did get me back into present time. Berta was laughing so hard I was sure that she would succumb and cross over to the other side on the spot. She was nearly twenty years older than Cisi, as far as they could reckon.

Nearly twenty years later, when I was teaching a workshop in San Diego, I had led the participants on a journey of guided meditation. The workshop would be ending when we finished the journey. I looked around and was horrified to see most of the people were sleepy eyed and totally ungrounded. I realized they were about to leave and confront driving on the California freeways. I had to take responsibility for getting them grounded quickly. I used a very gentle tone of voice to get their attention and told them that I was going to reveal a very sacred form of Native wisdom found in Moon Medicine. Suddenly every person's attention was on me, and I could feel the expectation rise as I briefly paused in silence. The Coyote in me whipped around and dropped her drawers, and I mooned everyone. The hilarious scene that followed will remain in my mind forever.

I got to see all sorts of judgments and expectations come falling down like a house of cards when some people rolled on the floor screeching with laughter. Others who had certain expectations of what a spiritual teacher should or should not do simply stared aghast for a moment until they saw everyone else's reactions, which made it okay for them to laugh. The value of shocking someone into being present through laughter is the gift of the naughty child within us, who gets to really play!

The ability to go beyond taking ourselves seriously or insisting that everyone else be bound by the same seriousness is an unbelievable gift of the spirit. Outrageous behavior has a proper use that is just as sacred as the inner stillness and communication with spirit. Wisdom comes from knowing *how* and *when* it is appropriate. In that brief instant, I knew it was my best shot at getting those folks centered. I also knew that I had no attachment to what others thought of me personally, that the wisdom of the Medicine stands on its own. I also was able to avoid being trapped on a pedestal of expectations on which some people like to put spiritual teachers.

We are all teachers, and we are all students. As we spiritually expand with everything that we experience, we learn to count every human being on life's road as a messenger, and we begin to hone the skills of acute observation to razor sharpness. Through these gifts of being fully present and observing the obvious, we are able to apply our accurate perceptions to our lives and to the further development of discernment skills. As we continue to hone these observation skills, we learn to continually remove any personal expectation, judgment, preconception, or bias from our Sacred Points of View.

DANG IT ALL! I DON'T WANT TO FLUNK THAT POP QUIZ!

Many pop quizzes and enlightenment traps related to teaching will appear whether you are a teacher or not. These lessons appear on the fourth path because wisdom is a sought-after commodity in today's world. Even if you are not publicly teaching, if you have reached the fourth path, you have developed successful skills that others admire and wish to learn. At some point, there will be a pop quiz on these issues from the viewpoint of being a student or a teacher.

Pop quiz number one happens when a teacher is put on a pedestal by one or more students. When the teacher demonstrates any normal human behavior that shatters the student's image of perfection, the teacher can become the target for anger, hatred, covert gossip, and blatant antagonism. This happens fairly often in teaching situations in general, but I feel that it occurs with more regularity in any area that concerns spiritual growth. It is amazing how human beings tend to project their own moralistic ideas of perfectionism on to any person who is willing to teach anything pertaining to spiritual growth.

How a teacher responds to the resulting lessons is up to the individual. When I was teaching many years ago, I saw the overview of this pop quiz only after I had been battered by the unhealed projections of students and the neediness of people who could never get enough attention. I had already changed the focus of my personal path and was taking time for myself and my family. I had stopped traveling to teach groups, except on reservations, when I was asked to speak or teach by the Tribal Elders or Human Resource directors. I changed my focus so that I could write and clone myself through my books without having to be on the road all the time.

Coyote gave me a rare opportunity see something I had not noticed before. I was approached by three women who asked if I would share some teachings with them. I had declined originally because I do not take personal students. After three weeks of their pleading and phone calls, I dishonored my own boundary and personal path by agreeing.

I shared over four hundred hours of quality time, and in return, I was given three $1.59 bags of Bull Durham tobacco and a hidden gift that did not surface until later. I was teaching these women to become self-empowered, and they did not tell me that they were also following the teachings of a Native American man from a reservation, who had taught them a rigid set of rules to keep them submissive and helpless. Unknowingly, I contradicted his viewpoint, and the women decided that since he was born on a reservation and I was not, his knowledge was the only true and authentic wisdom. The basket full of jealousy-directed criticism and judgments filtered back to me when others repeated what had been said by the three students. Coyote was showing me that if you dishonor yourself and your boundaries, what you are sharing will also be dishonored or belittled. I was stunned at my own acts of self-sabotage, having set myself up for the Coyote lesson, but I learned how to respect my Sacred Space, and I was given a gift of seeing one of my personal blind spots.

One of the women came to me a couple of years later and wanted to unburden herself and apologize. She told me things that all three of the women had said about me behind my back. She asked me to forgive her jealousy and envy, which had fueled her actions. She admitted that all three of them wanted a man to tell them what to do. I forgave her, and we are friends to this day. I had been blind to the jealousy and envy of others, and I did not recognize these women's resentment when it was staring me in the face. This lesson was a big wake-up call for me.

All teachers are confronted with students who want to show how much they supposedly know, comparing what they have learned from others to what the teacher is presenting. If the teacher tries to defend any portion of what she or he is sharing, Coyote will come to call. One of the easiest ways to handle this situation is to ask these students if they are willing to listen to another point of view. If they are not, tell them that they are free to leave and return to the teacher they are touting as being superior.

The proper use of wisdom is a tricky thing. We need to know when to let people make jackasses of themselves and when to stop them from disrupting a learning situation. Every teacher encounters high-maintenance students who need lots of attention because of their basic insecurities and need for approval. If you give too much, they can suck

you dry and drain the energy of the entire group with their constant
rambling questions, which may or may not apply to the subject at
hand. Every teacher must learn how to handle a variety of situations
that boil down, essentially, to boundary issues. The teacher is the person in charge of setting proper boundaries, which will allow learning
to occur. Guidelines for what is and is not appropriate are maintained
for the benefit of the entire group, not only for the teacher. If these
boundaries are dishonored, chaos can ensue, destroying the focus and
intent of the learning experience or severely restricting the amount of
informative data that could have been shared.

Any person who is an instructor, teacher, team leader, facilitator, expert in a field, or lecturer has to face some or all of these lessons. Certain teachers seem to be bull's-eye targets for Coyote adventures, while
others seem to avoid any major conflicts. That is not to say that the
minor conflicts do not knock even the most congenial teachers off balance from time to time. The personality of the teacher has a lot to do
with whether she or he encounters Coyote's lessons or gains experience in milder, more gentle ways.

If a teacher is even-tempered and serene, never confronting or challenging the student, nobody's buttons get pushed and the student has
absolutely no idea what the teacher is really thinking or feeling. If a
teacher is boisterous or passionate, earthy and a bit irreverent, the
stereotypical ideas of what an enlightened teacher should be can shatter, and some student's buttons invariably get pushed. If the teacher is
too formal and inflexible in his or her viewpoint, the students that return to learn from that person are usually heavily invested in the need
for decorum, dogma, discipline, and precise rules that encourage rote
learning and disallow individuality. We can learn from every kind of
teacher and every kind of student. How much we learn is derived from
how we view or feel what we are experiencing at any given moment.

WHEN THE MIND HAS AN EGO
OF ITS OWN

Another fourth-path enlightenment trap preventing authentic wisdom
from being attained by teachers is the trap of consciously withholding
needed information. My Medicine teachers in Mexico taught me that
we are only as skillful and impeccable as the teachers who taught us. In

order to maintain their position of being the enlightened one or king of the mountain, many teachers feel that they must delete or edit the content of what they know and what they are willing to share with their students. This perpetuates the teacher's false sense of self-importance and creates new generations of inept students, who usually adopt the arrogance or weaknesses of those who taught them. My teachers taught me that the authentic adept, healed healer, or wise teacher will always work to ensure that his or her students are equally or more skilled.

When I was in college I observed professors who demonstrated jealousy when they encountered a student who was exceptionally bright. These students often outwitted the professor by posing questions that were valid and thought provoking but threatened the professor, who had never ventured beyond his or her own belief system. Any teacher who is unwilling to say "Gee, I don't know" has not completed the wisdom path. Having to be the sole authority who has an answer for every question under the sun is an enlightenment trap. Know-it-alls and pseudointellectuals who use complex terminology and ambiguous concepts to confound others are not the keepers of authentic wisdom.

The fourth path is where what we have learned must be integrated and used with heart. Knowing something intellectually does not make it wisdom. Integrating thoughts into concepts that are lived daily is the path of wisdom. The gifts of authentic wisdom require a marriage to occur within each individual. The head and the heart have to be used in equal measure if we are to attain wisdom. In many people, the body/mind/heart split is a mechanism that creates denial. *Thimking* is a coined, humorous term that addresses the machinations of the mind that keep us from understanding and incorporating thought into wisdom. When the mind thinks it knows something but the heart is uninvolved, we do not feel how the information or experience impinges on our lives. If we think and feel, we find balance instead of inappropriate thinking or *thimking*.

I have seen countless people who could espouse the most profound and wise concepts yet who, when confronted with a situation that could have been easily solved by applying the exact principles they preached, were lost and clueless. This example of *thimking* occurs frequently on the earlier paths of initiation. If it is not handled by the fourth path, Coyote can wallop us with a dilly of a pop quiz, life lesson, or Dark Night of the Soul. The message is "get out of your head."

If we do not blend the heart's messages with the intellect, we may be forced to open our hearts through pain, sorrow, or grieving.

I saw one person, who refused to come from his heart and used his intellect as his defense mechanism, denying and enduring one wake-up call after another. Longtime friends drifted away. His marriage was constantly on the rocks. After seven years of near breakups, a tragedy forced him to acknowledge what was really important. When his teenage daughter, who was Daddy's little girl, was killed in a boating accident while he was driving the boat, he finally got the message to get out of his head. With a heavy but open heart, he authentically began the lessons of the second and third paths.

This man had served his community, had helped others with psychological counseling and healing, was well versed in a multitude of subjects, had developed many of his artistic talents, was a good provider for his family, and had healed certain aspects of his own life. But his intellect had overridden his heart to the point that he used professional boundaries with loved ones, never allowing himself to be vulnerable or human. He had pigeonholed every possible solution and response to life inside the academic concepts of psychology. When he became a university department head, this man believed that he could not appear to learn from others or embrace alternate views while maintaining his intellectually superior status in the eyes of others. He was tied to the false idea that if he did not appear to be precise, proper, and professional at all times, his reputation would be permanently damaged or destroyed. This instance is a perfect example of how some people can complete a few fourth-path lessons and still have the majority of second-and third-path lessons to learn.

WAS 1 BLINDED BY BEING BLISSED OUT?

As we embrace the lessons of the fourth path, we are required to see exactly where we have sabotaged ourselves. We can become so caught up in our own growth processes that we forget that others may not be coming from the same level of integrity. We can experience many disappointments when we project our level of understanding and healing onto others who may not be healed at all. When we are in states of joy, we often see others' potential rather than where they truly are in their present stage of development. This lack of discernment occurs when we are not paying attention, and it can bring some interesting and some-times painful lessons.

Many years ago I hosted a spiritual gathering at my home, and near the end of the evening I went into my bedroom, only to find a woman who was the owner and editor of a spiritual magazine going through my chest of drawers like a spy or thief. I was so stunned I just watched her until she looked up, embarrassed at being caught. I asked her what she thought she was doing, and she tried to bluster through the direct question without answering, then hurriedly told me she had to go. This type of abusive invasion of the Sacred Space of others happens more often than we would like to acknowledge and reflects a host of discernment issues we may not have addressed. Being blissed out or too openhearted without the use of proper discernment can be emotionally lethal. As we heal our lives, the pendulum of emotions can swing from unhealed mistrust into being far too trusting. The Dream Weave provides us with boundless energy and true joy when we have let go of our pasts. Our task is to use the energy appropriately and to balance it with large quantities of discernment and acute awareness of the obvious.

I used to joke about "bliss bunnies" who had found a spiritual path and had become blinded by the light, seeing nothing around them until it fell on their heads like a ton of bricks. I resembled that description myself from time to time because I was blind to others' hidden agendas or covert intentions until I was deeply and profoundly hurt by people I had trusted. The balancing act of respecting your own boundaries and recognizing where people are in their development is a supreme Coyote lesson. I always see the potential in people rather than what they are being in the moment, so this is my personal lesson. On the other side of those lessons, I continue to trust people until they prove otherwise, expecting nothing from them so I will not be disappointed if they demonstrate a lack of integrity.

As we hone these abilities of discernment and learn where we have self-created blind spots, we are often shocked into realizations that alter our perceptions of reality. In the face of heartache, it is far too easy to discard the former breakthroughs where forgiveness allowed us to regain our balance. Coyote tests us time and again on our willingness to reenter the flow of life, wiser and still coming from our hearts. Patient observation of the authentic behavior of others, before we rush into situations that we do not fully see, is a precise skill. We are asked to respect our Sacred Spaces, to have appropriate boundaries, and to be willing to let others be who and what they are at any given time, observing and responding appropriately. This skill requires that we be fully present in all situations at all times, unless we want to blunder into a Coyote lesson, which can appear as a painful reminder of our lack of balance and personal impeccability.

I have seen many openhearted spiritual people fall prey to get-rich-quick schemes, con artists, controlling teachers, and cults. Whether they were convinced to follow those paths out of greed, fear of scarcity, loneliness, or lack of discernment makes no difference. The power of personal choice allows us to choose *where* and *how* we want to invest our energy. Coyote gives us the pop quizzes that define our levels of discernment regarding the personal choices we have made. Snares of these kinds teach us how to use the power of personal choice, and they give us the lessons we need to discover our own internal rhythms and the connections to our own wisdom. They teach us how to trust our intuitions implicitly. Every time we dishonor ourselves, we set in motion a pattern of energy that allows us to see exactly how we either wove a web of tangled events or breezed through a situation by trusting the inner knowing we earned through experience.

Often we blame others for our bad luck without acknowledging our part in refusing to honor the warning signals we received along the way. Not being fully present and ignoring our inner knowing are usually the first missteps in creating patterns of self-sabotage. One student of mine lost everything her parents had worked for all of their lives by investing it in supposed rare coins that turned out to be nearly worthless junk silver. The person who talked her into cashing in all the municipal and government bonds that her parents owned was someone she knew and trusted from her church. The man disappeared after she had cashed in the last bond, leaving her and her widowed, elderly mother penniless. During the process of selling her parents' bonds, many friends had tried to show her that she was being duped. She angrily asked them to leave her house and never return. The result of refusing the advice of longtime friends and ignoring the warning signals was devastating.

Denial can appear at every stage of initiation. We are constantly tested by life, and we can be snared if we are not paying attention. It becomes easier to spot our patterns of self-sabotage and lack of discernment as we undergo the lessons along the way. How we handle our tests depends upon our ability to recognize the potential scenarios and to apply the discernment and wisdom that we have gained through experience. It is quite a task to hone perceptions to the degree needed to become skilled at staying out of the way of sabotage and others' hidden agendas. Once we have achieved this task, there still is no guarantee that we will not be tested on our discernment from time to time, but we will have garnered a level of expertise that can keep us out of Coyote's line of fire.

OOPS! WHERE DID 1 DISAPPEAR TO NOW?

The fourth path also presents us with the lessons that teach us not to give away our sense of well-being or healthy self-esteem. We are required at all times to honor ourselves and the healing we have accomplished. It is very easy to lose ourselves in a relationship, whether it is an intimate relationship, a friendship, or a teacher-student relationship. Some people give all that they have and are to their families, spouses, partners, lovers, or humanity in general. There must be a balance, and Coyote comes calling when we have dishonored ourselves.

In a relationship where we are losing ourselves through constantly acquiescing to the needs of the other and denying our own needs, our self-worth and self-esteem are at risk. The sense of self that instills a healthy respect for both partners is often tested by Coyote when one or the other seemingly loses interest in the relationship. This lack of interest can occur when one partner has lost his or her self-esteem, becoming a "yes" person, or has lost interest in having a Sacred Point of View of his or her own. In any relationship without two viewpoints, there is no room for learning. Two separate tunes are required for harmony to exist. This melding of musical notes allows the tunes to interact; the two Sacred Points of View fully represented create a balanced third viewpoint. When one viewpoint is lost, the chemistry between two people begins to diminish and the relationship can die. Those who bring no new interests or views to a relationship often fail to see that by dishonoring what they have to offer, they have killed the parts of the self that gave needed life force or spark to the relationship.

All relationships require that we be in alignment with ourselves. If we have diminished our dedication to our personal growth or have dishonored our basic needs or personal worth in order to serve a mate, we have adopted a misguided behavior that will eventually erode the foundations of our relationship.

The Southern Seers tradition names many kinds of relationships with life forms both seen and unseen and views them as circles within circles. One's primary relationship is that of the self to the Creator. The next circle is self to self: the body, mind, spirit, thoughts and feelings, intuition and dreams. The third circle is the relationship of the self to other humans. Many circles exist within this one, starting with one's mate, then the circle of family, then a circle of friends, then one of acquaintances. More circles include our co-workers, our community, our country, and all people who are the Children of Earth. The fourth set of circles contain the self's relationship to nature: the plants, animals, stones, waters, mountains, valleys, deserts, jungles, forests, and plains of the Earth Mother. This fourth band of circles includes our connection to the sparks of life or spirit contained in all of these forms, as well as to the preservation of the Earth's resources. The fifth set of circles contains our relationships to other planets and stars, which embody spirit and life within our universe. The sixth set of circles is our relationship to the unseen worlds of awareness that are contained within us and exist within universal consciousness. The seventh circle reflects our relationship to the unborn worlds of consciousness, which are given birth though our willingness to become aware of their existence and our ability to relate to them, exploring the constantly evolving consciousness within the Great Mystery.

If we are to master the art of expanding our relationships to all parts of Creation, the first three circles of relationship must be sound. Our relationship to the Great Mystery, God, the Creator, is primary. To maintain this circle we must honor our connection through returning thanks and through communicating with the source of all life. The second circle of self to self is maintained by honoring the needs and health of the body and seeing to the needs of the spirit, by feeling all emotions and releasing or detaching from anything that limits our growth. We are also asked to monitor any negative mind chatter and to transform our self-destructive thoughts into positive inspiration. By calling our energy back from negativity that we may have placed in the Dream Weave, we recycle the same life force into productive or creative activity. The third circle of self to others is made strong through personal integrity and being lovingly respectful toward others while maintaining our personal Sacred Point of View.

OPEN YOUR HEART AND KEEP
THE RHYTHM GOING

The Golden Rule of most major religions is the yardstick used by the third circle of relating to others. In Native American traditions, we refer to this same principle as "walking a mile in another's moccasins." On the fourth path, we not only are asked to relate to others as we would be related to, we also are given the opportunity to stand in another's shoes and to feel all that that person feels, to carry that person's burdens, and to see life from that human being's Sacred Point of View. By so doing, we become the instruments of compassion that the Creator intended self-realized human beings to become. We do not give ourselves away when we are compassionate. We actually extend our consciousness and caring into other Sacred Points of View while maintaining the integrity of our first circle of self to the Creator and our second circle of self to self.

The image of the person spinning several plates at the same time on the ends of sticks gives us a clue as to how we can do it. The stick on which the plate is spinning is the key to grounding our wheels of experience. If we understand the principles intellectually but we are not walking those principles in life, plates will fall all around us. But if we connect those principles to our daily life, we can use the wisdom as a way of being or living life. Through the integrity of our thoughts, feelings, and actions, we are afforded more energy or life force, which is the fuel that keeps many plates or levels of knowing effortlessly spinning in unity.

OUR DREAMS HOLD KEYS
TO FOLLOWING THE PATH

One fourth-path technique to keeping all the plates spinning in unison lies through our dreams. The Dreamer in indigenous societies is a holy person who serves the tribe through his or her ability to tap into the unseen worlds of consciousness or spirit while sleeping. The skill required by the Dreamer is the ability to interpret the dreams and to understand fully the message or wisdom offered. Then the Dreamer is required to deliver the pertinent information to the tribe without altering or editing the content. The Dreamer is like an antenna for communication with spirit, having no personal agenda but instead allowing correct and valid information to flow through him or her from the Great Mystery.

Dreams are used in many spiritual traditions as a guideline for self-improvement and growth. Dream Circles are groups of people who come together and share what they have dreamed, seeing the similarities of their metaphors dovetail into universal wisdom, as well as sharing the individual messages so that all can come to a further understanding of spiritual growth. People in these circles will encounter many similar dreams and symbols, tapping into a level of awareness that applies to humanity as a whole. These signals portend a shift in the planetary consciousness and benefit everyone.

Both of the women to whom I dedicated this book have been a part of Dream Circles for years. Connie Kaplan and Neela Ford are experienced Dreamers whose different systems for understanding the Dream Weave were shown to them personally through the wisdom of their dreams. Although their methods differ from each other's and from the training I received, the impeccability of their information stems from universal truth. I highly respect both women, and I deeply honor their contributions to humanity's search for the energetic maps or blueprints that allow us to go beyond the known borders of our physicality and into the invisible worlds of expanded consciousness. I want to include some of the viewpoints of these two dear friends, viewpoints that are found on the wisdom path.

Connie Kaplan is a counselor who has brought forth information from the Dream Weave that assists people in understanding the spiritual levels they are transiting in the Dream Weave and how those lessons apply to the soul's commitment and to what the person has agreed to do while in human form. Connie has directed Dream Circles for years, and I would like to share a common fourth-path lesson that she has relayed.

Many times on the fourth path people will dream that a teacher they revere comes to them to impart information necessary for them to move forward at that moment. Connie has taught her students that they are not really seeing her appear to present a teaching; they are projecting the wisdom that they themselves have encountered as coming from an outside source. We both believe that on the fourth path, this projection of one's unacknowledged inner knowing occurs when the person dreaming is not owning that the wisdom is coming from her or his own inner place of wisdom, tapped into through dreaming. The dreaming student needs to acknowledge that the teacher in the dream represents a part of himself or herself that owns the wisdom presented. This wisdom is coming from his or her own consciousness, which becomes available through the Dream Weave.

This is one of the full-circle lessons that we are given on the fourth path: owning the authentic wisdom that is available to us when the first three circles of relationship are sound. The healthy relationship circles of self to Creator, self to self, and self to other human beings open the fourth circle, which allows us to connect to the spirit in all life forms. We therefore can be open to the messages of wisdom that come to our spiritual awareness through those open doors. Once again we are reminded by Coyote, "It ain't out there, buddy! It's in here!" As we open ourselves to the vast worlds of consciousness that are available, we gain access to the inner knowing and wisdom that we have always carried as eternal spirits who exist within the Great Mystery.

Neela Ford is a healer who uses aromatherapy to clear the pathways of consciousness, stuck emotion, and limiting thoughts that can impair a person's ability to tap into the Dream Weave and the Remembering. Neela reminded me that one fourth-path lesson occurs when people have a dream in which they are trying to escape an animal. The Totem they are running from in the dream usually represents the inner strength, or personal Medicine, that they need to own in order to move beyond some challenging situation at hand that terrifies them. In this instance, the power animal is using a metaphorical chase to show us that we are running from ourselves and from the talents that we can embody if we learn to see those qualities within ourselves. The task is for the dreamer to turn and face the inner strength that he or she has denied and to use those talents or gifts in the current situation. We can face the animal in our dream, or we can see the message and follow the wisdom by consciously using the Medicine of the animal that is trying to get our attention.

People who are not normally connected to the messages sent through their dreams will find that on rare occasions on the fourth path of initiation, certain gifts of wisdom will appear as vivid or lucid dreams. These dreams are usually wake-up calls sent to us when we have ignored the need to enter the silence or when we have caught the "busy disease." The hustle and bustle of daily activity may have robbed us of the ability to clearly receive life's messages or warning signals. If we are not familiar with the principles of dreaming and interpreting the metaphors or messages presented, we need to write these dreams down and meditate on them. If we ignore the gifts of wisdom that we are being offered, Coyote is sure to come calling.

On the fourth path we are constantly tested. We are given lessons that can shake the foundations of all that we have held to be true. Old belief systems are radically changed as doubt or overconfidence rattles our unstable beliefs. Our Sacred Points of View will continue to change until firsthand experience hones those shaky thoughts into inner knowing that is rooted. Based upon our experiences, we decide whether to open our hearts or to close them, whether to give away our authority or go through the experiences that give us the authentic wisdom that makes us strong. If we decide to embrace the challenges we are presented with and to develop our inner knowing to a new level of understanding, no matter how hard it may become to endure the accompanying lessons, profound dreams will follow.

These dreams are lighthouses that can guide our way beyond all that we have known or held to be true. The fact of this kind of support being sent from all other levels of consciousness within the Dream Weave is an initiation in and of itself. The unseen assistance, which urges us to become more than we think we are, is one form of divine intervention. At the most critical points in our spiritual development, we are often given dreams that make us curious enough to venture further into areas we want to understand. Coyote, the divine Trickster, relents by offering needed assistance just when we are about to give up or quit trying. The shaky, infirm ground will support us, and the path will rise to meet us when a dream appears giving us symbols or messages that contain the next clue to a mystery or the support we need to continue awhile longer.

GOING BEYOND THE EXPLAINABLE AND REMEMBERING

This turning point on the fourth path is an alignment with the brave heart of the warrior inside of us that urges us to continue the process of discovery. We make a conscious or unconscious decision at this point in our development that determines whether or not we will be able to tap into the life force required to experience the fifth through seventh paths. Fear can stop us from saying yes, as can any denial we use to handle our personal issues in the moment they arise. The make-or-break point in the path is not always clearly defined. We can use the same avoidance mechanisms we used on earlier paths, when we got frightened by the unexplainable feelings and experiences that were too unreal to be fully embraced. Or we can align ourselves with loving intent and adopt an attitude of acceptance, trusting the presence of the Divine Mystery, whose wisdom is far greater than our own.

When I was embracing fourth-path lessons, I was practicing holding the stillness and silencing all my thoughts one evening when my perceptions changed. I saw myself walking through the snow in a long white buckskin dress. I could hear my moccasins crunching in the snow, and in the distance I saw a buffalo standing at the edge of the meadow. I walked over and sat at the buffalo's feet and looked into its deep brown eyes. Its steamy breath covered my face with a gentle vapor of moisture that formed tiny crystalline ice flakes on my face but kept my body warm. I returned thanks for being blessed by this creature, who was my personal Totem, and suddenly I felt our minds join. I looked up to see that the buffalo's eyes had turned sky blue and its brown fur was radiant white.

The scene changed: I was sitting in the South Direction of a council fire circle of Native American Elders. I was taught many things by these wise people, and then I was instructed to stand in the fire at the center of the circle. When I stood in the fire I was spun by the blue-orange flames into another council, and again I sat in the South, the place of learning. I looked around the table of pewter-colored stone and saw that it was surrounded by Sky People, extraterrestrials. It took me quite a while to calm myself as I looked around the circle and viewed seventy-five different species of beings. A few human beings were there as well, and I recognized Buddha, Jesus, Kwan Yin, and various other females who I thought only appeared in mythology as archetypes. I was reminded of the spiritual commitments I had made before I took my physical body, and I was given loving encouragement to continue. As the scene began to evaporate I felt that I had been deeply honored and profoundly humbled. The veils of separation were dissolving, and I was becoming spiritually whole again. This vision was a turning point for me on the wisdom path.

On the fourth path we also find new ways to release the "forgetter mechanisms" or veils of separation that cloud our inner knowing, and we discover alternate ways to tap into the Remembering. Forgetter mechanisms are common in the form of abandoned personal dreams. For example, if you were humiliated by an elementary teacher who said, "You will never learn to play an instrument; music just isn't your thing," you might have adopted that lie. The lost potential creates a forgetter mechanism that keeps you from learning music because you believed the lie presented by an adult authority figure. The forgetter mechanism may bleed into other ideas regarding music in general, and you might even find music oppressive later in life.

In the traditions of my teachers, the re-membering occurs when we begin to reassemble the parts of our inner knowing that we lost by taking the risks involved in being human. Birth into a human body is similar to taking an entire universe of information and consciousness, shoving it onto a microchip, and placing the particle containing all that wisdom inside a tiny human body that has no control over its own movements for quite a while. (See chapter 2 for detailed discussion on the veils of separation.)

That birth experience alone is enough to create forgetting. From that point on, our daily human experiences present enough shocks that we become aware of less and less of our inherent potential. How's that for a Coyote trick? You have to learn to gain control over your growing baby body, then learn to deal with all the emotions of growing up and all the judgments of others who tell you something is right or wrong, no matter how you see it with your child's eyes of wonder. We learn and adopt habits based upon the families we have and the cultures we grow up in. No wonder we forget! Then, later, we learn to drop everything we picked up that does not support us and reassemble all the beliefs that do help us remember who we are, why we are here, where we come from, and how it all works together. That's some task! No wonder we are required to have an abundant sense of humor in order to survive that kind of cosmic joke!

Many things come to closure in the fourth path when we least expect them to appear. I had healed my abuse at the hands of my mother who was an alcoholic and who died in a tragic accident when I was sixteen. I had forgiven her and moved on with life and had not spiritually experienced her presence since the year after her death. I was experiencing the final parts of fourth-path skills and some of the early fifth-path lessons when my mother came to me in a dream. In the dream I had the body of a tiny infant, and she was flowing such love to me that

I felt like my body could not hold any more. All the motherly love I felt had been lacking in childhood returned to me in that moment.

My mother apologized for the horrible acts of violence against me and spoke of her love for me. She told me that she had volunteered to be a stumbling block of abuse in my path so that I would learn compassion for the pain humanity suffers. Her actions gave me the opportunity to know firsthand the lessons of healing that were required to overcome pain and misfortunes. In the dream she bent and kissed my forearm on the scar where she once had forcibly stubbed out a cigarette. She looked at me with tear-filled eyes and said she was grateful that I had survived to heal my life and to assist others in healing themselves. In that instant I fully understood. Everything I had experienced in life suddenly became clear. I gained an overview I hadn't had before. The value of the wisdom I had gained through enduring my life's passage had returned me to a place of authentic love.

Everyone on the fourth path learns to see that personal pain can equal personal joy. This initiation is a tough one to accomplish successfully, but it does become a way of seeing all experiences as having equal value when we count the wisdom that we have gained through every experience.

Many people tell me that even after they have learned this lesson, they turn around and whine continually when they are going through rough times instead of applying the wisdom they had thought they carried. Of course we are allowed to feel what we feel as we encounter hard times. But we must *feel and release* all emotions that surface when we are confronted with stressful situations before we can return to being centered and present. When we are fully present we do not whine; we are present because we have taken the steps necessary to come back to center instead of wasting energy on complaining. When our viewpoint is balanced, we are given the energy we need to go through a time of challenge. We have added wisdom to the experience because we have faced the issues and have successfully endured.

Coyote teaches us the wisdom in surfing the waves of feeling as the level of intensity of our personal challenges increases, honing our mastery through our ability to move with the ebb and the flow of life. These lessons regarding emotion are the prerequisites for accessing a level of the Dream Weave that is composed of all of the feelings of humankind on this planet. Mastery in contacting the universal collective layers of energy and consciousness comes on the sixth path, but if we have not done our homework on the fourth path, our lack of personal emotional boundaries and our inability to discern what belongs to us and what belongs to the masses can cause mental or emotional breakdowns on the following paths of initiation.

FINDING WHOLENESS THROUGH EMBRACING OPPOSITES

Women usually must work hard to keep themselves from slipping into empathetic roles in which they take on the pain of others or the pain of the Earth Mother. By contrast, men usually must work to open the pathways of emotion, which may frighten them but which are the only paths of intuitive consciousness that allow them access to the part of the Dream Weave made of feelings. Women need to learn to embrace the thought world that exists within the Dream Weave in order to balance the tendency to be swept away by overwhelming emotions. They can learn to hone proper use of reasoning and intellect in order to balance their feelings. Men learn to break through the tendency to operate strictly out of the intellect by feeling from their hearts and trusting their own emotions. Through learning to trust their own feelings, men can then extend their feelings to include the emotions of others in order to become more aware of the role of intuition in their lives.

Two-spirited people are the third sex acknowledged by Native traditions. Unlike single-spirited people, who carry either a female or a male orientation, two-spirited people have both male and female orientations and dual Sacred Points of View in one body when they are born. Two-spirited people face an extra lesson of relating to both thought and feeling in the Dream Weave from both viewpoints, without allowing one spirit to languish in favor of the other. These unique individuals are usually bisexual, asexual, gay, or lesbian and must learn to balance all the lessons of both genders, finding inner peace by owning both sides of their natures equally without prejudice or judgment.

Single-spirited people learn balance and wholeness through embracing the gifts represented by the opposite sex and developing those gifts within themselves to balance their Sacred Points of View. This balancing act is a fourth-path lesson that allows the male and the female parts of human nature to meld so that the harmony between the two supports unity within the individual. Without this balance, we cannot tap into the mystery of the unseen layers of thought and emotion in the Dream Weave. Coyote can give us a multitude of unrequested lessons showing us that using intellect without heart is just as deadly as using passion or unbridled emotion without reason.

Somewhere along the third and fourth paths, Coyote notices that some of us are feeling quite balanced, and therefore another uncomfortable review of our lessons may be on its way. We may encounter a friend who has learned a few lessons on earlier paths and who will act as a distorted carnival mirror for us. That person may be thrilled to see us and might smugly tell us about the successful lessons that he or she has completed and how wonderful life has become. Here comes the gotcha! The friend might listen to how we are doing and then begin to list what she or he believes we need to be working on in order to make our lives better. This authoritative monologue can act as a horror house mirror that does not reflect where we are at the moment but rather where another thinks we are, based upon silly judgments that apply only to his or her own latest life lessons.

The distorted reflection can send us scurrying to hide under the first bush if we do not know how to disengage from the conversation. We must use skill and artistry to correct the friend kindly or to change the subject, refusing take on the projected list of what is wrong with our lives. If we are unable to shake off other-determined impressions of what we need to fix, we may have an enlightenment trap at hand. Doubting our inner knowing is a precursor to doubts of all kinds, which will continually show up to knock us off balance. One remedy for doubt is to review what we are doubting based upon what we know we have learned and how we have implemented that wisdom in our lives. Then we must reclaim our personal authority over self-defeating thoughts that we have adopted through giving our authority to misguided words of advice.

The fourth path can present us with moments when we think we are losing our grip on what is real in our daily lives. There will be times in all of these initiation paths when we may think we are going crazy from the amount of issues we are asked to handle. At other times we may feel that no one understands the changes we are undergoing and would label us loony if we ever revealed the content of our perceptions, visions, dreams, or feelings. The wild experiences that are associated with these paths of initiation can threaten others because they have no reference points in these areas. In indigenous cultures, the changes that occur in the body, mind, and spirit are readily accepted parts of spiritual initiation. In first-world cultures however, the lack of acceptance of these changes can lead to being attacked by those with whom we share our process. Keeping our own counsel and sharing with others on a level that they can understand is a safety net of discernment that keeps Coyote at bay.

AM 1 GOING CRAZY OR JUST AWAKENING TO MY POTENTIAL?

Every time we complete a set of lessons that shifts the way we see and the manner in which we live our lives, those changes actually shift our Sacred Points of View, reconstructing our impressions of physical reality. When the viewpoint shifts radically, certain physiological changes occur. Sometimes we find that our bodies won't work and that we become temporarily unable to judge distances correctly, bumping into doorjambs or knocking our shins on furniture even when we are not in a hurry or being inattentive. We may develop second sight and suddenly be able to see energy or colors around physical objects. Some people begin to develop accurate psychic gifts above and beyond the personal instances found in their own spiritual processes. These gifts can include, but are not limited to, hearing, feeling, or seeing spirits and precognition of future events.

As these types of changes occur, we may feel the tendency to defend our perceptions by stating, "I'm not crazy!" I have received hundreds of letters where these words preceded a description of a dream or an experience that the writer could not explain. These experiences are all a part of the initiation paths. Humankind is experiencing an awakening process on a massive level, and the understanding of that process has been fairly limited or held as secret for thousands of years.

There have been times I thought I was going crazy when sudden bursts of psychic energy felt uncontrollable. There were other times that I traveled out of body too far, into events I was viewing, and wished that I was crazy and that the situation was not real. Beginning in my early twenties, I was asked to use my psychic gifts to describe murderers and to find the lost bodies of victims, but when I turned twenty-seven, the violence I encountered became too much for my body to handle and I stopped. I had assisted in police work that required locating missing children or planes downed in storms, but those activities took a lot of time and energy, and since I never charged

for those services, I still had to pay the rent by working forty hours a
week. I had come to an impasse and was unsure whether I should offer
my talents in those areas, when I had a dream that pointed the way.

Spirit showed me how I could use my gifts to bring insight to some
hidden and unrecorded parts of human history. In my dream I was on
a seashore in Baja California looking over a cliff. Below me a group of
Spanish-speaking archaeologists were digging in the sand. They were
working diligently, and finally one man turned and yelled up at me,
"Están borrados!" When I woke up I was confused, because although I
speak enough Spanish to get along, I did not understand the word *borrados*. I looked it up in my Spanish dictionary and was shocked to find it
meant "vanished" or "erased." The archaeologist was telling me that
some of the history of ancient cultures containing spiritual practices
that were needed today had been erased from human memory.

Within forty-eight hours after the dream, a man called and asked me
to participate in a project that used psychic information to locate the
ruins of ancient cultures. The target of his first project was the lost library
of Alexandria in Egypt, which burned during the time of Cleopatra and
was said to contain the greatest stores of ancient wisdom ever held in
one place. Some scholars believe that some of the scrolls were removed
from the library while it was burning and hidden in another location.
This was the beginning of my many experiences working with archaeologists in ancient sacred sites.

Though people who have fourth-path dreams are not crazy, there
are people in the world who are unstable and who believe the illusions
or delusions presented by their mental or emotional disorders. These
people are not on the fourth path; they may not yet be on the first
path. People who have completed the lessons of the earlier paths have
healed any psychological or emotional imbalances. People on the
fourth path are functioning, stable human beings who are capable, self-
reliant, and trustworthy. They can expect to undergo changes that will
open new avenues of energy within the body and can expect to feel the
resulting changes in a myriad of ways.

WHERE'S THE CIRCUIT BREAKER?

One of my teachers called these physical changes "the rewiring
process." All the sensory receptors inside the human body are being

activated to accommodate the level of awareness that one is now ready and able to handle confidently. This is not to say that some people on the fourth path are not frightened when the rewiring affects their bodies in ways that cannot be explained by medical professionals. Often during the rewiring process people will have strange symptoms for which they will seek medical advice, but the doctors find nothing amiss.

These sensations are energetic changes that signal the final parts of the fourth path and the beginning of fifth-path lessons. They can take the form of internally felt bursts of energy. Sometimes the bursts of inspirational energy and the feminine intuitive aspect of spirit can manifest as physical shaking. Vibrating or pulsating limbs, insomnia, and muscle spasms are common. Unusual headaches or feeling like someone has unzipped your forehead and there is air blowing on your exposed brain can also accompany the rewiring process. Or people might see thousands of tiny bursts of light, whether the eyes are opened or closed. A tingling of energy, like tiny needles in the head, often accompanies the opening of neurological pathways that have been activated as the energy increase is felt in the body.

These and many other symptoms can begin to appear after the turning point on the fourth path. They are different for each individual and can continue in various forms through the end of the sixth path, while on the seventh path these energy surges appear with less and less frequency. As the Dream Weave energy is integrated into daily life, we may feel these symptoms intermittently, usually at times when we have spiritual breakthroughs or when we gain new levels of awareness. The more we open to this universal energy, the more that creative fire of life funnels through our physical bodies.

The Coyote part of this rewiring process can get expensive. I learned the hard way when I was finishing some fourth-path lesson and beginning some fifth-path challenges. I burned up the electrical system in my car by touching the radio dial. I blew out all the lights on two aisles of a department store before I ran from the building in horror with fluorescent bulbs popping directly over my head in every direction I turned.

For the next seven years I had no other "accidents," until one day I shorted out all the breakers in the house when I reached over to turn on a lamp. The light bulb exploded into hundreds of pieces, and the electric fan, which was fifteen feet away, went up in smoke even though it was not turned on. Ten years later the symptoms started again, and in the space of two months I blew up a television set when I touched the remote control, a computer when I touched the keyboard, and my car's electrical system when it was already running and I had touched the cigarette lighter. Oops! The question is, Do you laugh or do you cry? The expense of replacing something you inadvertently fried with excess electromagnetic energy can be a real drag. This phenomenon is common among healers, psychics, Dreamers, Medicine People, and mystics with monastic lifestyles. Luckily, this does not happen to everyone, and when we become fully grounded the shocks and disruptions stop altogether.

BALANCING THE ENERGY

On the fourth path we begin to adjust our Sacred Point of View to include the point-zero rest place. At the point of rest we detach from polarizing everything into either-or categories. We release the need to mentally label or develop categories to pigeonhole our life's experiences. This ability to hold the neutral zone of nonjudgmental witnesses allows us to become unbiased observers who honor every aspect of human life as a classroom and every human being and part of nature as having something to teach us. The rare quality of being a neutral, unbiased witness is difficult to maintain at all times, because we live in a world that is based upon learning through opposites. From the viewpoint of neutrality, all aspects of duality or polarized thinking can be released. We no longer see the world through the lens of oppositions, but we can see all aspects of any situation without having to choose a side or make a judgment. We accept *what is* without trying to change people or alter life to fit our viewpoints.

For instance, several years ago I saw exactly how energy will manifest the content of the thoughts and feelings it encounters. I was praying with several women in a sweat lodge ceremony at a tribal gathering in the Pacific Northwest. One of the women was grieving the death of her sister. She wailed and released her grief, crying and mourning her loss. In total darkness, the woman next to me began fidgeting and fanning the air around her in order not to take on the "negative" energy that she felt was flying around the lodge. I saw this woman's fear balloon around her like a luminous cloud, and it actually magnetized other energy to it. The cloud of fear was so thick that it was becoming nearly impossible to breathe inside the lodge. Prior to this woman's fear rising, the grieving woman's tears and wails were running like a river into the earth below the hot stones at the center of the lodge, being returned to the Earth Mother. The direction of the grief energy changed when it encountered the fear of the woman beside me, and it began to direct itself to the luminous cloud surrounding the frightened woman. The ceremonial leader had not poured additional water onto the hot stones, but the heat inside the lodge suddenly became too much for three eighty-year-old grandmothers to bear. The door was opened, and the grandmothers chose to leave the ceremony.

That night I was shown that all energy in the universe is neutral. We are the human conductors that direct energy through our thoughts. If we use words to label emotion, or energy-in-motion, the energy begins to transform, becoming the embodiment of our judgments. If we think and direct our opinions toward anything we feel energetically, the form of the energy will change into the thought that was sent. Our thoughts, opinions, and judgments direct energy, which responds by manifesting the exact changes that our thoughts contain. Suddenly I was in the middle of a big AH HA. I had actually seen it happen. I had intellectually understood the process in principle, but I had never before seen the actual energetic flows and magnetism that are transformed by thoughts.

To see how thoughts change energy, we can choose to review every situation we have encountered in the past, realizing that the wisdom we gain allows us to see the overview of what occurred from an unbiased perspective. We learn how to acknowledge the validity of all of the individual roles played out, as well as how to respect the diverse perspectives of all parties involved. The crowning lesson of the fourth path teaches us that *all energy in the universe is neutral* and can be accessed if we hold the proper alignment found in the unbiased perspective. The human consciousness is able to use that universal, neutral energy when it refrains from taking on the mental judgments of being seen as good or bad. Prior to this transformation we experience life from a Sacred Point of View that contains our positive or negative judgment of life's events. The human observer is the sole determining factor of how events are viewed mentally through the brain's duality.

For this same reason, physicists are discovering that subatomic particles will group together in a manner that duplicates the researcher's thoughts or expectations. This variable makes most experiments totally unrepeatable by other scientists because of the various preconceived concepts or expected outcomes held by different researchers. Thought precedes form: as we think, so we will experience. Thoughts begin taking form when emotion is added to the equation, becoming *thought-forms*, which can clutter any path of endeavor until we return to neutral position by recalling our energy from ideas or emotions that create opposing forces within us.

THE MAJESTIC SILENCE AT THE DOOR BETWEEN WORLDS

On a spiritual level, if we do not polarize our thinking and are able to hold a neutral, unbiased view, we are allowed to view all possibilities, probabilities, and potential outcomes held within the Dream Weave. That is why many people on the fourth path who have begun to develop this skill can suddenly become gifted Seers or Dreamers, healers, psychics, or visionaries. These individuals have found the center point within themselves and have embraced the neutral zone without preconceived notions. My Elders call this state of awareness or place within human consciousness "the crack in the universe." The door that leads to every nonphysical level of consciousness in our universe is opened when we can consistently arrive at the neutral state of being with open hearts, loving life and others unconditionally.

The accuracy of our observations and our impressions of what we explore in the unseen worlds of consciousness totally depends upon our ability to maintain the centered state of unbiased neutrality and an inner stillness devoid of chatter. That state of being is the doorjamb that keeps the portal open to the Dream Weave whether we are awake or asleep. The lessons of the fifth path are where we hone the skills of focus and intent that are required in these realms of consciousness.

Some people do experience such frightening paranormal events and unexplainable physical symptoms that they revert to the safety zones they found on the third path. They can allow their fear of the unknown to keep them on a treadmill where they use the processing or healing techniques of the third path to continually fix what is wrong with them, imaginary or not. This refusal to become healed healers and to move forward is a form of spiritual denial created by fear. In some cases we could apply the term *enlightenment junkie* to those who dabble at healing the same issues they have already dealt with for years and years, using the process as a form of avoidance so that they will not have to confront getting on with their lives.

A healed healer is anyone who has become fully present, having released his or her past experiences, issues, feelings, and fears. A healed healer confronts and handles any new issues as they appear and does not allow the wounds of the past to influence the present moment. This individual can then offer loving assistance to others who are also healing their lives. There are many kinds of healers. The act of supporting others in their growth process makes everyone a healer who can listen, offering kindness and encouragement, becoming a living extension of the principle of love.

The fourth path melds with the fifth as we acknowledge the journey of our spirits through time and space while we also maintain grounding and balance in our daily lives. The level of intensity continues as we learn how to live our physical lives with ease and in harmony, while also experiencing the unseen worlds of the Dream Weave.

The metaphorical trials by fire of the fourth path continue as we up the ante in this poker game of spiritual evolution. Coyote is the card dealer who deals from the top and from the bottom of the deck in order to remind us of our former lessons and how they apply to the poker hand of cards that we are presently playing. Stoic poker faces are not required, nor are they allowed if we are to successfully play the game with the humor of authentic masters.

As you look around the table to see the other players, it comes as no surprise that there are none—just reflections of the many faces you personally have worn from time to time. Coyote smiles knowingly as he motions to the walls surrounding the poker table, and you notice that the walls are mirrors reflecting room after room of poker tables filled with players out into infinity. The human beings playing at those tables, reflected in all of the mirrors, are focused on one thought. They all think that their poker game is the only game in town. Gotcha!

CHAPTER 7

Humans have earthly roots, the spirit has wings. By honoring the lineage of being the Earth Mother's children and by finding our spiritual roots in the Dream Weave, our spirits embrace our bodies and together both are allowed to take flight.

—Cisi Laughing Crow

▲▲▲

THE UNION OF WORLDS

I listen to the whispers of
The small, still voice within,
I feel the awesome power of
The sacred mystery therein.

And there within the mystery,
Of the material and the unseen,
I discover my own true essence,
Where the two worlds convene.

I connect with the essence of
My spirit's state of grace,
While I learn to embody
The sacred lessons I embrace.

I stand between the two worlds,
Holding both Sacred Points of View,
By knowing that the two are one,
My sacred journey begins anew.

—Jamie Sams

The Fifth Path of Initiation
The Above Direction on the Medicine Wheel

THE fifth path is the Above Direction on the Medicine Wheel, which represents the part of human nature that seeks the sky, the stars, the other galaxies, the spiritual, the formless, the unseen, the intangible, or the unknown. On this level of initiation we encounter all that exists beyond our natural world, as well as the parts of our spiritual natures that contain the urges of the soul. As spiritual warriors on the fifth path, we become fully connected to our own inner guidance and gain an intimate knowledge of our authentic self, the Spiritual Essence.

After the completion of this path, former doubts of how we are connected to all life and to the Creator simply vanish. This path offers a schematic overview of how things work in the universe and how our Spiritual Essences are interrelated parts of the Great Mystery. We also learn how all life in our universe is interrelated energetically and spiritually. As we embrace the lessons of the fifth path, all remaining veils of separation are dismantled layer by layer. The destruction of the foundations holding old belief systems in place catapults us into states of new awareness that allow us to see life from two undivided, harmonious Sacred Points of View simultaneously, one in the Dream Weave and one in the physical world. This radical departure from our former tunnel vision collapses our preconceptions of time and space, and we must learn how to hold anchor points of awareness in both worlds.

CHANGING OUR CITIZENSHIP

Those who have not already done so, at the end of the fourth path must now adopt the identity and the behavior of a universal citizen before they can continue to explore the levels of awareness in this universe. The universal citizen is a human being who has compassion and cares for all of humankind, no matter what religion, political viewpoint, nationality, race, gender, creed, or color of skin. A universal citizen relates to all religions and all spiritual practices with respect and judges none as being the only way. The universal citizen acknowledges the beauty found in truth and knows that all spiritual practices contain spiritual truths. The universal citizen does not argue semantics or dogma, does not seek to demean the beliefs of others or to belittle the sacred practices of others. The universal citizen honors the paths of every human being and allows all others to explore life in their way without hindrance or criticism. The universal citizen abides by the creed of *life, unity, and equality for eternity* for all human beings.

To live by these principles, as universal citizens we must be connected to our Spiritual Essence and the Creator moment by moment. To maintain this connection, we must be constantly vigilant of all energy, thoughts, and feelings passing through our Sacred Spaces. Self-reliance takes on a whole new meaning at this level of the dance. We come to realize that we are solely responsible for finding and maintaining our divine connections and for using personal impeccability when dealing with all other humans, employing dignity and respect.

Exploration of the spiritual nature of human beings is coupled with finding the authentic voice of our own soul or Spiritual Essence—not the voice we have used in the material world or the intellect's voice, but the inner voice of serene knowing. This voice expresses the soul's authentic intent to evolve. This desire is the first step of any creation. The second step is the conscious decision to act upon this desire. At the beginning of the fifth path a mechanism is triggered within us that is vastly different from anything we have consciously felt or thought before. My teachers called it "the echo." When the voice of the Spiritual Essence moves through the body, the mind, and the emotions and does not encounter resistance, it echoes to the core of our being. That echo of truth is recognized as the urge of the Spiritual Essence. Those who respond to that call echo their conscious desire to enter the fifth path's lessons through making the decision to continue. By desiring or consciously choosing to explore the unseen levels of awareness that exist beyond our physical reality, we are showing our willingness to go beyond the known and into the unknown. Walking this path requires a deep faith and trust in our own process and personal connection to the Great Mystery, God, the Maker of All Things.

On all of the earlier paths we learned various ways to sort through our emotions, our thoughts, and our habit patterns, and we learned how to heal our past. In the process, we made changes in our life. We were basically clearing the decks for the unbiased emergence of the soul's true intent. On the fifth path, the soul's desire is to evolve by bringing heaven and earth together without separation and with full awareness. Our conscious acceptance of our soul's intent is required before the fifth path can begin in earnest. That is to say, we must consciously agree that we choose to move forward into *term infirma*. We echo our agreement to explore the physical and nonphysical parts of human life when we feel excited about the possibilities awaiting us, instead of feeling dread or fear. We are willing to allow ourselves to operate in both worlds, the seen and the unseen. The two worlds become one. The union of the two worlds teaches us not to separate ourselves from being aware of and actively participating in the Dream Weave, continuing also to maintain our daily lives through integrating our perceptions of both worlds.

THE MARRIAGES FOUND IN ONENESS

Several unions of heart, body, mind, and spirit begin to occur the moment we decide to embrace both worlds simultaneously. We gain a certainty of what is right for us personally and what is not appropriate for us. We understand our spiritual growth process without denying the unexplainable aspects that formerly created hesitation. Our new understanding can bring forth many feelings that demand that we honor ourselves. Some people feel a longing to "go home." The deep, unexplainable longing is not for a place but is rather a longing to go home to the authentic self, the Spiritual Essence, and to honor all that the self needs in order to thrive. This certainty comes because we have done our inner work and we know exactly who we are, our strengths and our weaknesses. Our hard-earned wisdom comes from successful rites of passage and the inner knowing created by self-exploration and purification. The voice of certainty that we use in daily life begins to echo the voice of our Spiritual Essences.

Everyone has wondered from time to time, "Where did that statement come from?" or "Why did I say that?" On prior paths we may have spoken before we thought. Often the words we uttered were directed by some unhealed part of ourselves containing emotions that were triggered again because we had not released them. Beginning on the third and fourth paths, we may have been stunned by the words of wisdom that slipped from our lips. In these instances, the voice of the Spiritual Essence uses powerful intent, overriding other conflicting thoughts or feelings in order to be heard. As we enter the fifth path, we develop the certainty of one unified voice of personal authority coming when the mind, heart, will, body, and spirit are in alignment. This union creates a marriage between our physical selves and our spiritual selves. As those two viewpoints become one voice, we stand in our personal power and authority, using our certainty as we embrace both the seen and the unseen worlds.

On earlier paths many initiates may have used the spiritual tools of their particular paths to address imbalances in behavior or old pain or wounds and to correct or heal the body, mind, emotions, or spirit. On the fifth path it becomes necessary to step off those wheels of experience and to adopt self-reliance. For instance, on the fourth path, we have healed our lives, found our purpose for living, and learned how to be effective in the world. With that foundation completed, we no longer need to rely on external direction from others. The authentic divine guidance of our Spiritual Essences instills spiritual authority in our lives on all levels of awareness.

On the fifth path, many of the truths that applied to former lessons begin to be eroded. This destruction of what we found to be true for us on former paths is a good thing. We must relinquish our hold on the past in order to experience the new truths presented on the fifth path. If we hold on to the old truths, we begin to stagnate, and we will create a situation where we are stripped of our comfort zones. Solutions that worked for us before will become ineffective, and we must let go in order to embrace an echoing viewpoint coming from the Spiritual Essence. This second point of view, held by the Spiritual Essence, contains an overview of the unseen and physical worlds and includes new understandings that eradicate some of our false preconceptions about how life works. We are reminded that we are still required to maintain the basic spiritual foundations that keep us in balance.

WELCOME TO TERRA INFIRMA!

On the fifth path we learn the Medicine of Lizard, the Dreamer and Keeper of Dreams, from a different viewpoint. Lizard asks us, "Are you the dreamers, or are you the dreamed?" Are our Spiritual Essences dreaming our physical lives, or are we physical humans who are exploring universal consciousness through the dreams we have while sleeping? We discover that we are both and much more. As we dive deeper into the human potential, we discover that our spiritual consciousness exists on a multitude of levels of awareness and that when we explore those realms we reclaim more life force and energy. We learn how to expand our Sacred Points of View to include other realities that we may have never believed possible.

When I was at this point in my personal development, I experienced a broadening of my Sacred Point of View that changed my opinion about our universe. I was sitting in Tiyoweh, a state of internal silence and stillness, when I began to go out of body and to travel into the heavens with millions of stars streaking by. I passed the other planets in this solar system that orbit closer to our sun. I was suddenly approaching a wall of fire that rimmed Grandfather Sun, and I felt my physical body's fear that it would be destroyed by the flames. I took a slow breath and released the fear as I entered the wall of fire and emerged on the other side. I saw an energetic planet that was hidden behind the wall of fire.

As I touched down, I was greeted by shining beings who told me that they were the Lords and Ladies of the Sun. I was stunned, since I had never heard of these spiritual beings on the paths that my teachers had mapped for me many years earlier. But when a man came up behind me and I turned to face him, it hit me where I had heard about them before. My teachers called these spirits "the hooded ones." The man in front of me was dressed in gossamer robes with a hood resembling those worn by the Christian monks of the twelfth century.

He told me that I was meeting the spiritual beings who held the energetic light for our solar system and that the Lords and Ladies of the Sun were metaphorically hooded because their energetic spiritual forms were not physically perceivable by human beings who believed only in the existence of solid reality. Then he told me that when the human heart was open and the Dream Weave energy flowed effortlessly through the human body, spirit was alive inside of human perceptions. I was instructed by a woman standing next to him that my rite of passage had been completed and that I was now free to move to the next level of the dance, but that I would have to pass through the wall of fire once more as I returned my Spiritual Essence to my physical body.

She told me that when I returned through the second wall of fire, a chain of events would begin that would change my life forever. She called me by a secret name that is known only by the one who bestowed it upon me and indicates the way our spirits are recognized in the Spirit World. Then she blessed me, and I took the courage she offered, descending through the wall of fire the second time. As I was traveling back to my body, past heavenly stars in the night sky, I found a new feeling of excitement and a firm resolve to continue my path through the unknown, no matter what obstacles awaited me in the future.

At this level of initiation we discover that the time has come for the eaglets to leave the nest and to use the wings they were given to fly. Our new self-reliance allows us to become more responsible for the past, present, and future. We no longer need to process every event in our lives or to figure out why something occurred. The successful healing methods of the past do not apply to the uncharted territory that we are approaching. We come to a place of being fully present with whatever we have experienced, and we have the ability to handle new issues in the moment, to let them go, and to move on. The former need to label life's events with certain significance or to address the psychological, emotional, or spiritual importance of life's experiences simply begins to disappear. If this does not occur naturally, we are confronted with enlightenment traps that make it happen.

LETTING GO AGAIN? DO I HAVE TO?

In many instances I have watched people get stuck in the role of being spiritual advisers or oracles for others to avoid doing their own inner work and getting grounded enough to apply the same wisdom to their own lives. They may constantly have to be the teacher or the channel, sometimes valuing themselves only to the degree that they can use their special gifts. Other people become perpetual students and fear flying on their own.

I once observed a woman who was approaching the fifth path. She had developed her intuition and inner wisdom to an accurate level, but she denied her own skills by continually using others to ferret out the importance of every little event she encountered. She was stuck in wondering what would happen to her in the future and went to every fortune-teller and psychic that she came across. If any of those folks told her something she did not like about her behavior patterns, she would rant and rave, scream and yell—but never look to herself for the answers she could have found through trusting her own wisdom and counsel. This activity kept her on a treadmill of fourth-path enlightenment traps and fifth-path pop quizzes for years.

Other people who have used therapy to help them sort out how to make sense of life's experiences get stuck in being counseled instead of becoming the authority regarding their own lives and learning through their own efforts. Some people have adopted "habitual ritual" and use spiritual ceremonies for social interaction with others, unable to be alone and pray or return thanks. Some of these folks are sensitive and caring when they are doing ceremony but instantly revert to insensitive behaviors toward others when the prayer circle or ceremony is over.

These are behavior patterns and fears from earlier paths that are resurfacing to be reviewed. On all the earlier paths we learned the lessons of trusting ourselves to try, fail, try again, and develop the skills we needed. A new level of learning appears when we discover the voice of our own spiritual warrior natures confirming our connections to the Great Mystery. It is necessary to find that voice of spiritual authority and implicitly trust the guidance it gives before we can continue. When we cannot leave the nest of an old pattern and fly free of old ways of being, we stagnate. Until we can see how our own inability to embrace change could deliver us from our self-created Coyote lessons, the muddy roads of detours, pop quizzes, and enlightenment traps found on the earlier paths will continue to crop up in our lives.

On earlier paths we may have received guidance that was tinted with our own issues, clouding the clarity of the message. There may still be aspects of our lives that we are working to improve, but we are asked to remember that everything in life is a skill. We begin with paying attention and listening. Then we learn how to tune the radio dial to the proper frequency, where the voice of our individual Spiritual Essence is coming in loud and clear. The discovery of the voice that echoes our Sacred Points of View, in both worlds of tangible and intangible forces, allows us to discover the spiritual content of our universe. When we align with both worlds we may encounter the voices of spiritual guides, angels, nature spirits, the Earth Mother, sacred Ancestors, Kachinas, extraterrestrials, or spiritual masters like Lao Tsu, the Virgin Mary, Buddha, Kwan Yin, or Jesus. These spiritual beings are usually from our individual spiritual backgrounds or past experiences, but there is no rule that keeps us from discovering any part of the spiritual content of the Dream Weave.

There are many ways to develop the skill of holding a divine point of balance in order to receive these voices of guidance. Some people do it through automatic writing, channeling, or other psychic avenues that allow the messages to be received. In any case, the first step is in desiring the messages or communication that we receive. It can take years to develop fledgling abilities into precise skills that keep the voice of the Spiritual Essence from being tainted by ego. Holding a point of balance between the two worlds is an art. It is common to encounter many sidetracks and seductions along the way. For instance, people who have been psychically gifted since childhood and received these forms of spiritual guidance can filter pure information through their own unhealed issues or lack of balance. Some gifted people can see only at the level of their own personal experiences.

THAT POTHOLE IN THE PATH WAS A HOLE IN MY WHOLENESS?

Yes, that pothole in the path could be a hole in your wholeness. For instance, if you are a family counselor and are still working on your issues regarding personal relationships and fear of intimacy, you could easily slip into offering advice that is tainted by your own unhealed viewpoint or fears. Or if you are a spiritual adviser and you become seduced by the power of having an "all-knowing" form of control over others, saying that God or some spirit said that a certain path should be followed, the information is either false or is being filtered through the shadow side of your ego. Even authentic information or messages received from unseen spirits can be tainted easily. If you have a personal agenda or are unable to set aside the challenges present in your own life, those personal issues will create static, which interferes with the clarity of the information you receive. If you cannot discern who is speaking at all times, the information you receive could be coming from an unsavory spirit who has agendas of its own. Just because people have some fifth-path abilities does not mean that they necessarily have healed the issues addressed on earlier paths.

Another seduction also occurs when the person receiving the messages creates an organization or group where he or she is the sole authority. At any time during this integration process of accessing both worlds, if the person sharing the messages forgets to do his or her own inner work, the ensuing enlightenment traps can be very dangerous. In this instance where sloppiness or lack of integrity creates imbalance, the person may not be aware that he or she has opened to shadow entities who can spiritually possess anyone who is not vigilant and/or impeccable.

Many people at this level of development attain such a high degree of spiritual certainty they often get trapped into becoming "the enlightened one." On the fourth path "enlightened ones" usually feel intellectual superiority, while on the fifth path they display spiritual arrogance. The astonishing results of the wisdom being shared through the messages they receive can lead to an enlightenment trap that slams shut on them when they are so excited that they begin to think that there are no others who have had the same experiences. The fact of the matter is that one day they will encounter another person who has moved into levels far beyond their own. The more developed person can compassionately recognize the pattern of being "the enlightened one," possibly having demonstrated the same behavior at an earlier time.

"Enlightened ones" usually do not want to hear that the level they are encountering leads to other levels of spiritual development, because in their minds they have already arrived! Sometimes it is humorous to the more evolved person observing this behavior; at other times, it is pitiful or maddening, depending on the level of arrogance, unrequested spiritual advice, or the unspoken judgments employed by "the enlightened one." The impeccable course of action in either case is to respond with silent compassion and to bless "the enlightened one" on his or her path.

On the fourth and fifth paths, we are asked to confront *spiritual arrogance* in ourselves or in another to learn how it works. Spiritual arrogance is a state of unawareness or tunnel vision that occurs when we forget some of our basic lessons in wisdom. One form of spiritual arrogance can be seen in healers who are so busy helping others that they do not take care of handling their own issues. These healers are serving the needs of others as a diversion to avoid confronting their own life situations. Others believe that they are beyond needing to look at their behaviors because they have all the answers intellectually; these folks usually have not walked the principles that they espouse. Another example of spiritual arrogance is the condescending behavior in the one who believes that he or she is "the enlightened one." We see this behavior again in the overt or covert competitive comments of people who have come to a place of supposed certainty in their spiritual development and must falsely reinforce their authority by demeaning the beliefs or actions of others.

Many people on the early fourth through midfifth paths, who have life-changing spiritual awakenings, mistake the process and adopt the idea that their souls stepped aside to allow more evolved beings to take over their bodies. As these folks begin to receive and share spiritual information, they begin to integrate their own Spiritual Essences. They sometimes believe that their souls are merging with angelic beings or that they are being "walked into" by extraterrestrial entities. These perceptions may be very true for them at the time, but later on the sixth and seventh paths it becomes evident that every human being is an angelic being. The forgetter mechanism that is encountered when taking a human body teaches us that we must "hide our wings" in order to survive in the brutal physical world of human experiences. The integration process of reintroducing our magnificent Spiritual Essences requires that we drop the veils of denial and own our authentic eternal identities.

Everyone is chosen, but few respond by volunteering to serve. It is a trap to believe that we are chosen above and beyond other human beings or that we have volunteered to allow our souls to be replaced because some extraterrestrial is more able to handle the mission we personally agreed to accomplish while in human form. The desire to immediately give away our spiritual authority plagues the early parts of the fifth path. By the end of the sixth path, these misconceptions regarding personal spiritual authority will have been cleared, and we will be willing to be fully responsible for integrating our highest potential, the Spiritual Essence, bringing that divine potential into our physical bodies and living it without separation.

CLAIMING THE SPIRITUAL AUTHORITY WE HAVE EARNED

Eventually, we can stand inside the crack between worlds comfortably, at all times, moving beyond the ideas of separation. In this state of being, we no longer need to receive spiritual guidance from outside sources. The statement "*They* told me that . . . ," referring to guides,

angels, or other spiritual entities, vanishes from the vocabulary, and
there is no separation between external spiritual guidance and our Sacred Points of View. We stand firmly connected to the Creative Source of
the universe, the Great Mystery, God, without needing our connection
to be relayed through another identity's point of awareness in the spiritual realms of the Dream Weave. We learn to acknowledge that we are
fully plugged in and operating efficiently in the physical and nonphysical worlds. We have earned our place as an activated point of awareness
in the universe. Now we learn how to use that spiritual authority with
impeccable grace.

The fifth path's lessons give us the skills that allow the warrior nature of the Spiritual Essence to be in charge at all times and in all situations. This wise, essential voice knows how to be loving and respectful,
how to listen, and how to be encouraging. This innermost voice has
discipline and authority over renegade emotions and thoughts that can
throw a person off balance or cut the anchor ropes that keep us firmly
centered on our individual paths.

Some people call this voice the higher self's voice. It comes from
the place within us that is always communicating with the Higher
Power or God. In the tradition of the Southern Seers this voice is called
"the clear lake." When we speak, feel, and think like a clear lake, we
simply allow all our thoughts, all our feelings, and all the words of
others to be heard, to be felt, and to pass through us with ease. We also
have the ability to interact without reacting, viewing any situation as an
unbiased observer who can see the obvious, feel all of the emotions
with ease, keep the mind clear of chatter, and still maintain a neutral
point of view.

LOOK IN COYOTE'S BAG OF TRICKS
AND FIND YOUR TOOLS

The art of deflecting unwanted energy is also found on this path. We
learn how to take the sting out of hurtful words by coming from a
place of compassionate understanding, having been there ourselves,
and by returning loving behavior. We continue to use humor or irreverence properly to deflect the stranglehold of seriousness or high drama.
There are several deflection techniques that become second nature
when used appropriately. We develop these skills when we see the need

for maintaining balance moment by moment. When we are present enough to accomplish the art of deflection and the balancing act required and not to take on negative energy, we demonstrate a new level of respecting our Sacred Spaces. This respect and personal responsibility for all that we experience in the unseen and the physical worlds allows us to stand effectively in both worlds simultaneously. We have the ability to perceive both worlds without judging one or the other as being more important because both exist equally within our perceptions.

My teachers taught me many of the tools to maintain balance while deflecting negative energy. These are methods used to maintain healthy boundaries in difficult situations. Here is a story that illustrates a few of those tools. A man I knew was constantly projecting his own issues onto others, blaming other people for all that he felt was going wrong in his life. One day he was busy listing the faults of various friends. When I spoke, he turned to me and accused me of trying to interrupt his tirade of negative chatter. I responded by laughing really hard and saying, "Well, pack my bags and send me on a guilt trip!" He still did not miss a beat and continued criticizing another friend of ours. I interrupted again and said, "And he speaks so highly of you." This time he became furious, and I laughed till my sides ached. He still did not get what I was trying to reflect to him, and he started in again. I gently took his hand and looked into his eyes and said, "It sounds like you have a lot of inner work to do in order to resolve these places inside of you where you feel hurt." It was if I had slapped him: his head snapped back three inches and he got it. Each one of these maneuvers was a tactic that can assist another person's Spiritual Essence to gain control over the voices of blame or seriousness, high drama or lack of personal responsibility.

The fifth path offers us an opportunity to use the voice of balance and to employ every method we have learned to offer others a glimpse of the impeccability they can obtain. We reflect the clear lake's potential serenity into situations that are chaotic or potentially harmful. In one instance, when a man who'd had too much to drink was verbally demeaning others and using ridicule and intimidation as his equalizer, to cut others down to his size, I walked up to him and gently placed my hand on his chest, gathering all the love I could and sending it into his heart. Then I whispered, "Please don't do this, it hurts." I had only met him half an hour before, and so he had no bone to pick with me. The loving energy and my hand on his heart blew through him, and his body jolted into attention. He became silent and shamefully removed himself from the party.

Other people at that same party suggested that they would have verbally humiliated the offender. One of the other men was ready to slug the guy for cruelly insulting one of the women, and everyone was stunned that I chose to handle it by sending love and speaking genuinely tender words. These friends agreed that I handled the situation in the right way, because in his state of drunkenness, this man could have become violent. The ability to correctly assess a situation and to respond accordingly is a gift. The sensitivity of compassion and unbiased observation, coupled with the wisdom of experience, allows us to respond properly, using the power of personal choice at all times. If we react impulsively we cannot defuse the potential chaos; we merely add to it. The fifth path teaches us how to use the authentic voice of our Spiritual Essences in order to bring healing to life. In some cases where a situation has eroded into violence or screaming matches, silently removing ourselves from the situation can be the most prudent move. Knowing when and how to speak is the art we are asked to master.

We have learned how to claim our personal authority and to be spiritual warriors who have impeccable personal boundaries. Now those lessons are expanded to include gentle but firm resolve in maintaining energetic boundaries. If someone is putting degrading verbal venom into a loving environment, we learn how to change gears and to stop the flow of negativity. In a conversation where someone is dishing dirt about another, we can change subjects or use humor, or we can respectfully say something kind about the person being demeaned.

How we handle situations can determine the outcome. If we use anger or threats to stop someone from making a fool of themselves, we have to become responsible for the response we enlist. However, this is not to say that anger cannot be used in an appropriate way. I have acted like I was angry at someone who was coming from a victim viewpoint by saying, "How dare you! You have more strength, talent, and ability to overcome that challenge than most people I know. How dare you demean your personal Medicine by whining like you don't have a single internal resource! You are a magnificent part of Creation!" My anger certainly got the person's attention. The defensiveness that came forth with the first "How dare you!" changed into shock, then to wonder, then to a smile, and finally to a firm resolve to go beyond being a victim. Why? Because someone was angry enough to force that person to see their own beauty and inner strength.

In the instance of one person's misbehavior within a group gathering, we can also use energetic boundaries. Unseen positive energy is a potent weapon against negativity and is most powerful when it is loving or humorous. Coming from the heart is mastered on the fourth path. Effectively using heartfelt compassion with healed personal intent and authority is a fifth-path art. When we master these skills we can achieve results that astound the casual observer. When we use compassion coupled with the intent to *do no harm*, a boundary is formed be-

Energy Boundaries

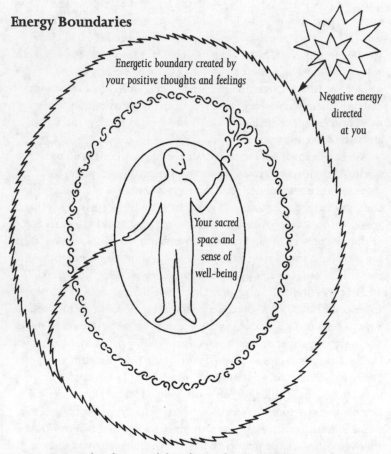

Energetic boundary created by your positive thoughts and feelings

Negative energy directed at you

Your sacred space and sense of well-being

Energetic boundary created through using discernment, intuitive sensing of hidden agendas, and the personal choice of non-interaction

cause the person misbehaving is not being forced to defend himself or herself. The observer must also make a personal choice: whether to enter the arena where conflict is present or to walk away. We can ignore misbehavior, let it go, shrug it off, or deflect the energy by engaging the person through actions or words. The decision is merely a choice of which dance we want to dance with the offender.

YOU DON'T HAVE TO CARRY THAT PERSON'S EXCESS BAGGAGE

Energy that does not come from us but is directed toward us is considered outside or *other-determined* energy. Other-determined energy is energy from another person who is targeting us through focus or intent. The flow being directed our way can be emotional energy, psychic energy, healing energy, desire or lust, compassion, ugly thoughts, the intent to harm, or genuine admiration. In the Dream Weave these unseen flows of energy can effortlessly enter our Sacred Spaces if we are not aware that we must also have and use energetic boundaries.

Energetic boundaries are set in two ways. The first is in the everyday world, where we use our intent to alter a potentially dangerous or negative situation by changing its focus. We do this by accurately observing and by diverting attention from the negative to the positive through our words or actions. The second way we set energetic boundaries is by using our intuition and keen observation to set a boundary in the Dream Weave. To accomplish the latter, we must be fully present and totally attentive to the energy we feel coming into our Sacred Spaces, as well as being mindful of the energy we put out into the world. The mastery of this ability is determined by how much we allow ourselves to feel without being influenced by any issues or present situations that remain unresolved within ourselves. Accuracy depends completely upon one's ability to hold the viewpoint of a neutral witness, deflecting the unwanted energy from entering our Sacred Spaces.

Feeling or sensing energy being directed toward us is a necessary skill if we are to learn how to interact with the unseen worlds inside the Dream Weave. Some boundaries are determined through the power of personal choice. When we choose not to entertain the abusive or mischievous behaviors of the shadow side of human nature, we have created a boundary of certainty in the Dream Weave. We also form a boundary by choosing to protect ourselves, holding a firm intent about what we are willing to experience. These choices include what forms of abuse, negativity, or imbalanced behaviors we will not allow in our daily lives.

Learning how to develop these boundaries is a fifth-path art that can continue throughout all the following paths. The intuitive skills of knowing how to use vigilance and energetic boundaries in the Dream Weave can be learned in a variety of ways. We master proper boundaries in the seen and unseen worlds when we integrate both viewpoints and own our physicality and our spiritual natures in wholeness. We must develop the skills of holding both viewpoints simultaneously, knowing that we are perceiving both worlds, and honoring those senses of the physical and the invisible as a unified and accurate overview of the many levels existing in our universe.

POP! GOES THE BOUNDARY

It is essential for the fifth path initiate to develop the ability to detect hidden or personal agendas among the energies sent to us. I have had many hard lessons in that area. Seventeen years ago, some of my students accused me of being unwilling to receive, saying that I was willing only to give to others. This was not the case, but there was a problem with what some of them wanted to give. I was unwilling to receive gifts that contained hidden agendas. My boundaries were appropriate, and I learned how to sense the unspoken expectations such as "If I give you this massage as a gift, I want you to give me a free healing session."

On another occasion I allowed a stranger who was a reader of my books to give me some bodywork as a gift and paid dearly for the results when I was asked during the session to interpret every dream he'd had in two years. One time a bodyworker, who was also a student, talked and asked questions during the entire session, and I was never allowed to relax. Another time, I received the unwanted gift of being "dumped on" when a masseuse discussed her divorce the first fifteen minutes, refusing to be quiet, forcing me to stop the session. I had to clear my energy field of all of the issues and judgments she was hammering into my body while she was berating her exhusband. Such a mess, and what a valuable lesson for me. By setting proper energetic and personal boundaries I subsequently avoided having to spend valuable time cleaning up my own energy field. I learned a lot about the importance of proper boundaries, and I learned to genuinely thank those concerned for being magnificent teachers.

The inventor and scientist Nikola Tesla never shook any other person's hand because he did not want to absorb anything from another person's energy field that would alter his own awareness or life force. The more sensitive we become to energy and life force, intuition, and spiritual abilities, the more discernment we need. Particularly in the beginning of the fifth path's lessons, we go through periods of ultra-sensitivity and sensory overload. Our energy fields are open to the worlds of feeling, thought, and spirit in the Dream Weave. At these times, we are learning how to be vigilant and how to develop energetic boundaries so that we can properly discern what kind of energy is passing through our Sacred Spaces.

The protective boundaries that we create in the unseen world of the Dream Weave are determined partly by our personal impeccability. If we walk through life with integrity and walk gently on the Earth Mother, respecting all life, we also keep our energetic boundaries clear and in force. If we are leaking life force and our impeccability is at risk, we are weakened so that other people's negative energy can enter our lives.

We can restore our personal honor and the energetic boundaries protecting us from other-determined agendas by catching any imbalances within ourselves and correcting the problem. Those restored boundaries offer protection from the negative energy sent by others unless we then break the rules of our personal creeds and do not call the energy back from that unbecoming conduct. When we find the balance point between genuine humility and owning our personal authority and inner knowing, we learn that *the more we think we know, the more we find out that we know nothing.* The vastness of the Great Mystery cannot be fully understood; the mystery is constantly expanding and is not intended to be solved.

Vigilance, discipline, focus, and the willingness to forgive ourselves and others will allow our boundaries to strengthen once more. Everyone goes through periods of imbalance. This out-of-balance behavior is simply a part of the human condition and growth process. We are tested and rattled by pop quizzes, and we go out of balance. We right ourselves and find new points of balance as we grow. Our center point changes with every rite of passage that we encounter on every path of initiation. It is reasonable to assume that when we are out of balance or on edge, that is exactly when we feel targeted by negativity. The bumps in life seem to occur when we are feeling the most vulnerable. However, if we look at our thoughts, feelings, and actions just prior to the onset of attacks from others, we discover that we leaked vital life force on some kind of unproductive behavior, creating an imbalance. In turn, because we entertained our shadow selves, we were swept up in a chain of events that allowed Coyote to create scenarios of chaos in our lives.

THAT DEAD END WAS A MENTALLY CREATED WORLD OF ILLUSION?

On the fifth path, energetic boundaries can be destroyed also by enlightenment traps that are quite seductive. It is fairly common for some people on the fifth path to believe that they have discovered the way the universe works and that the path they follow is the best way to reach spiritual awareness. This is an enlightenment trap. The mind constructs a foundation of ideas, allowing those people to evolve to a certain level of mastery but no further. The false ideas, which create an inability to move forward, are based upon all that they have experienced on that path. The misconceptions, rigid rules, fixed ideas, or expectations of what will follow are the stumbling blocks along the way. The mind's formulations and misconceptions have created side roads that can dead-end or become so convoluted that these people get tangled in a self-created web of illusion or deceit.

I observed a group of seven people who believed that their system of spirituality was so unique that others should train with them for years and pay them big bucks. This group of people fell into third-path traps of defending their teachings by attacking others who seemed to have the same information. These other teachers were unwanted competition. The group used cheap hexes and shamanic sorcery to intimidate and send harm to the other teachers. This group also fell into a fifth-path enlightenment trap of exaggerating their powers and their experiences. They lied to others of goodwill who were sponsoring their workshops, and while in this imbalanced condition, they continued to explore the Dream Weave with out-of-body techniques.

The mentally created worlds that they encountered and experienced as being truth were no more than their mind's machinations, which were created by their own lack of impeccability. Then they taught others the principles of these mental dead-end states of awareness. Calamity followed with one Coyote lesson after another. The enlightenment trap was sprung because they used deceit to appear superior or all-knowing, which allowed the minions of the shadow and harmful elemental entities to gain access to the energy of the group's thoughts. The dark energy that they called forth is still connected to them, creating massive chaos and fears that they do not yet understand. This type of convoluted path is one way that we learn from our mistakes. The backdoor path cannot be judged as bad but should be seen as if it were one way that a group of people chose to learn how to get tangled up on the path that they followed. The untangling is also a part of learning: backdoor lessons always show us why something does not work. At this level of the dance, we get to see how people reap what they have sown.

ENTER THE TWILIGHT MASTER, WHO IS BETTING AGAINST ALL ODDS THAT EVERYONE ELSE WILL LOSE

Joaquin, Berta, and Cisi, my teachers, taught me that the fifth path can be treacherous when people use shadow behavior to gain acclaim or to become the sole authorities in any area. By enlisting the assistance of dark elemental entities and by demonstrating dark behavior, people can become Twilight Masters. This term is the closest English translation I can find to the Indian word my teachers used. Twilight Masters are individuals who use both the light and the dark of human nature to control or manipulate others. Bending the will of another to your own is what the Southern Seers call BAD Medicine. The paybacks are hell, and at the fifth-path level, the boomerang of negative energy comes back to the sender far more quickly than on earlier paths. The force of the payback depends on the personal intent of the sender and on the amount of energy he or she used to fling it into the Dream Weave and then to send it into the physical world.

In most instances, the Twilight Masters exhibiting this behavior were born with certain paranormal abilities and later learned how to use these gifts to control others. They might have noticed during childhood that certain behaviors forced others to give them what they wanted. Later in life, they might not even be aware of the energy they expend while using the same tactics to gain control over others. Unwittingly, these individuals use energy and focused personal intent to exact the desired outcome from others. Using this form of invasive psychic energy is a breach of trust and a rape of the Sacred Spaces of others. The violation of others and their thoughts or feelings is abusive on any level, but when a person knowingly and intentionally manipulates another person's thought process, or "listens in" simply because he or she can, the offender is asking for some heavy consequences.

For centuries, our adept Native American Dreamers and Seers have transited the energetic web of the Dream Weave discovering pathways to and through energetic worlds. These worlds are levels of awareness where spirit or life force is encountered as a matter of course. The fifth path of initiation adds an extra element of how to appropriately use that invisible energy or life force. Twilight Masters are usually not clever or gifted enough to successfully track their own patterns of energy through the Dream Weave and can become tangled in their own deceit or webs of conflicting intent. The intent to control another, when not dismantled or recalled, will eventually trap the person who originally sent that intent into the universe.

Inattentive Twilight Masters have usually forgotten what they created in the unseen worlds. These energy webs were self-created through their own fixed ideas, lies, or manipulative desires. When Twilight Masters encounter these webs at a later date, they may have forgotten that they created the false pathway through one level of consciousness or another, becoming trapped in that self-created false awareness while out of body. This enlightenment trap is very dangerous and can cause madness or catatonia if these people cannot break the trap they originally created to confound others. For this reason alone, we are reminded that when we invest our life force into negative shadow behavior, we must work hard to reinstate our personal impeccability. If we are foolish enough not to recall that negative energy, forgive ourselves, and then make amends by changing our behavior patterns, we will encounter those same energetic traps at a later date. Twilight Masters tend to lose former extrasensory abilities at some point, and their accurate perceptions of the Dream Weave become convoluted or vanish entirely.

MAPPING THE PATH: DOING IT YOUR WAY

The fifth path has been transited by scores of Medicine people, Christian saints and mystics, indigenous shamans, visionaries, Spiritualists,

Buddhist and Hindu holy people, Islamic dervishes, and pagan Earth-centered oracles throughout time. The energetic worlds seen or experienced in the Dream Weave can be encountered and explored through out-of-body experiences, dream encounters, visions, meditation, prayer, and sacred dances, and during ritual or ceremony. These illuminating moments can occur on any path depending upon the discipline applied by a person actively seeking connection to the Great Mystery or the universe. However, it is on the fifth path that we begin to master these skills and to hone them to a level of excellence that allows us to proceed with certainty in a safe manner.

On the fifth path we are required to address the illusions that we encounter in the invisible worlds of the Dream Weave that we transit while in altered states of consciousness. An altered state of consciousness is a shift in our normal physical perceptions that allows us to perceive energetic worlds. This state of awareness occurs when the reality that we consider to be the physical, everyday world is altered and we are able to see, feel, or sense alternate levels of awareness. We might feel that we are in another time period (the future or the past), in places other than where our bodies are located, or in levels of consciousness made of energy. There are entire worlds made up of feelings, thoughts, concepts, and collected life force.

On the fourth and fifth paths, we can also experience visitations in our physical lives. Visitations can be the appearance of Ancestor spirits, angels, spirit guides, relatives who passed over, power animals, divas, or nature spirits that are not in physical form. In some spiritual traditions, these visitations are looked upon as visions. Visitations also occur on earlier paths if a person is gifted with extrasensory talents or abilities. In every one of these instances, whether we encounter visions, visitations, altered states, or moments of divine intervention, we must integrate the information and the experience from our Sacred Points of View. To determine whether we are being presented with an illusion or not, we must use our developed skills of discernment.

One easy way to discern the intent of the spirits seen in visions or visitations is to check how we feel. If we feel love and have a sense of well-being, there is no illusion or trickery involved. If we feel that the messages contain control or manipulation, we need to banish the spirit by using our will and personal spiritual authority. If we feel fear, or if the messages belittle us or make us feel guilty for not being perfect, these are the tools of a Twilight Master. Command the spirit to get out of your Sacred Space at once, and continue to do so until it vanishes.

In this instance, it is also proper to call on any spiritual help that you feel you need from angels, Ancestor spirits, guides, or the spiritual masters of your particular faith.

GETTING LOST IN THE GREAT BEYOND

I would like to stress that these fifth-path experiences are not the delusions of mentally imbalanced people whose madness has propelled them into convoluted realms of insanity. A person on the fifth path has eliminated those imbalances and is mentally healthy. There is a risk, however, if a person on the fifth path has not developed the authentic skills of intent, focus, discernment, proper use of will, discipline, and the refined ability to travel safely out of body. For these individuals it is more appropriate to gain access to spiritual growth through dreaming while they sleep, in meditation and visions, or through prayer and ceremony. If journeying out of body is attempted without proper training and preparation, it is possible to get stuck in an alternate reality or level of consciousness, which can lead to insanity.

Unprepared people on earlier paths can easily slip into a level of despair or hopelessness. The more they dwell on pain and suffering or upon helpless or hopeless thoughts and feelings, the easier it becomes to slip into the collective abyss of human despair. These uninitiated people obviously do not have the tools needed to separate their minds and feelings from the collective layer of destructive thoughts and emotions, and they believe that the doom and gloom they are experiencing belong uniquely to them. This misconception can lead to chronic depression or suicidal tendencies. A fifth-path person has gained a multitude of balancing tools and has learned to approach these levels with ultimate respect and discernment.

WHAT IF MY EXPERIENCE IS DIFFERENT?

Bringing this esoteric understanding into a more earthy viewpoint is important. Every person has different talents and gifts. Not everyone will experience the paths of initiation in the same way. There is no one way that it is supposed to look. Some people discover different levels of awareness through meditation and transit layers of the Dream Weave through viewing everything with detachment. Certain spiritual disciplines allow people to safely map the layers of consciousness that they encounter. After much practice, these initiates reach a state of serenity where they encounter their own Spiritual Essence and connection to God, receiving the Creator's messages.

The Hindu and Buddhist traditions consider all physical life and other levels of awareness to be illusion, called *maya*. In the tradition of the Southern Seers, all levels of awareness are real because they exist energetically within the universe. Our physical reality is also real, but no more real than the invisible, energetic worlds of the Dream Weave. As human beings, we spiritually embody all ideas and levels of awareness, and we can encounter any thought, idea, feeling, place, or time that has ever been created. Anything that has ever happened in a place is still there. During the fifth and sixth paths we also learn how to move through the energetic membrane that divides past, present, and future. There is no delineation of time in the Dream Weave; we learn to use our will and intent to reach any place or time period in its energetic form.

Our consciousness is a part of all consciousness within the Great Mystery's creation. The universe is constantly evolving in physical form and in the energetic web of the Dream Weave. Every thought or feeling that human beings have adds energy and material mass to the universe, creating new levels of awareness. The illusions, delusions, loving feelings, and thoughts as well as the flows of destructive and creative energy exist in layers. Like a stack of pancakes, these layers of various human thoughts and emotions are encountered as energy during altered states of consciousness. These altered states can be experienced through meditation, sleep dreams, or out-of-body experiences, and at any moment when a person has a vision or mystical experience.

Dreamers and Seers of my tradition learn to select which realities we wish to explore and how to view the existence of other levels of awareness as neutral observers. In this selection process we are required to experience or view all types of energetically constructed levels of awareness without judgment. Those who have developed the tools needed to hold a neutral viewpoint can perceive or experience these layers of energy and move through the collective thoughts and emotions without losing focus. However, before people on the fifth path have the skills of energetic boundaries, focus, and certainty, they can also fall prey to collective fears of the unknown or collective pain and suffering without understanding why those thoughts and feelings are bleeding into their Sacred Space. These bleed-throughs are a part of the lessons of the fifth path and teach us through trial and error how to

make our spiritual, energetic boundaries strong. When we hold an unbiased, neutral viewpoint and are fully aware of the energy that moves
through us, we can learn how to move effortlessly through the various
levels of thought and feeling, ideas and belief systems, without being
drawn into the weave of positive or negative consciousness created on
those levels.

Some people have lucid dreams and then interpret the messages
given to them in visual image form. Other people receive psychic impressions or hear the voices of their angels or spiritual guides as well as
the voice of their own Spiritual Essence. Other people simply feel inspired and know what to do and when to do it because they have integrated their inner voice with the impeccability of a clear mind and
healed feelings. Others find their spiritual connections through vows of
silence, sacred ceremonies, fasting and praying, or a monastic life.
These examples are a few of the multitude of ways that people enter
the fifth path and learn from the lessons presented.

HOW COME IT FEELS LIKE MY BODY IS FILLED WITH MEXICAN JUMPING BEANS?

Unexplained physical symptoms are often experienced on the fifth
path. Sometimes they can be medically diagnosed, but they are usually
the result of new synapses being created within the brain to accommodate the new levels of awareness being encountered. These new
synapses are found in the 90 percent of the brain that science says
human beings do not use. This part of the brain is used to correctly intuit the unseen worlds of energy that exist beyond the physical senses.
When the fifth-path initiate is standing with one foot in each world
and has not developed the skills to accomplish this balancing act with
ease, the discharging of energy in the developing synapses connected
to the Dream Weave can short-circuit the synapses in the brain that
have been connected to the physical body since birth. This phenomenon is electromagnetic in nature and can create sharp pains and other
uncomfortable physical symptoms.

The physical symptoms that often occur at this level can be very dis-
turbing. The body is being rewired energetically, and if we do not hold
the neutral viewpoint, fears coming from the mind and from the cellular consciousness of our own bodies can throw us off balance. Some

people experience muscle spasms and muscle aches that do not go away, which are diagnosed by doctors as fibromyalgia. Others experience forms of vertigo, dizziness, nausea, or headaches that usually appear when trying to return from too long of a sojourn in the unseen worlds. These symptoms can occur when a loud noise disrupts a deep meditation, a sleeping dream state, or an out-of-body experience. The same forms of disorientation can occur during regular daily activity when we drift into what an observer may consider a daydream but is actually a shift of perceptions that opens the Dream Weave's energy to our physical reality, creating dual perceptions of both worlds.

When messages are being sent to us from the Dream Weave, some people experience a recurring physical ache or sharp tingle in one spot in the body. Others see a glow of color in front of them or experience some other phenomenon that calls attention to the need to focus on the message, allowing the signal to be received. Recurring needlelike tingling in some areas of the body or in the head drives some fifth-path people to distraction and in some cases lasts for years.

High-frequency ringing in the ears, usually one ear or the other, is another phenomenon that begins appearing on the third, fourth, and fifth paths. This ringing is called the universal om sound by some Hindu and Buddhist traditions and is considered to represent a state of harmony with all life. In our Southern Seer tradition, the high-frequency sound is considered to be the call of Eagle, signaling that the door between worlds or the crack in the universe is opening to the physical plane. The Eagle soars closest to the Great Mystery and calls us to connect with spirit when we stand between worlds.

From time to time we may experience bursts of energy that keep us from being able to sleep. At other times, we may experience deep fatigue, needing to sleep constantly while our bodies are adapting to the rewiring process. These conditions usually occur when our existing brain synapses short-circuit. As the new synapses are adapting to the previously unencountered energy and levels of awareness that we can perceive on this path, we are affected by the waves of consciousness that ebb and flow through our bodies. In some cases, when we ignore the body's signals, we are forced to pay attention by illnesses that make us stay still. Chronic fatigue syndrome, environmental sickness, cluster headaches, or migraines are common illnesses that can affect people who still refuse to slow down and take care of themselves during the rewiring processes of the fourth, fifth, and sixth paths.

BEYOND THE KNOWN LAWS OF PHYSICS

One paranormal event that often accompanies the rewiring process is disorientation accompanied by altered perceptions of time and space. For instance, some fifth-path people notice when driving their car that they are miles from where they intended to go, and they cannot remember how to get back home until they pull over and try to focus on being present and grounded. Others report going to a business lunch appointment, getting into their cars to return to the office, and then discovering that it is two hours earlier than when they were due for the luncheon meeting that they already attended. These events can be very frightening and make people question their sanity, but they happen every time we move in and out of the Dream Weave, where time does not exist. These experiences are the beginning of developing the skills that allow the known laws of physics to bend and time to alter.

I had once placed a journal that I was writing in on my dining room table. It disappeared when I turned to answer the phone. The journal reappeared three weeks later, in the afternoon, after I took a nap. I had experienced a profound Medicine dream during my nap and was very disoriented when I stumbled into the dining room on the way to splash my face with cold water. I saw the book, picked it up, and carried it with me into the bathroom. When I returned to the dining room, all of the other pens and papers that had been on the table with the book were gone, but I still had the book in hand. I had physically reached the book, which was in another time-space, by returning to that altered state while I was dreaming. The cold water on my face shifted my attention back to regular reality, while the other papers remained in the alternate reality.

These days, many people on all paths are experiencing these same unexplainable events, but they do not know how or why they are happening. This is because so many people have encountered the crack between worlds that the points of access to the parallel world of physicality are now more available. The parallel world of physicality is identical to the one we experience in daily life; however, the time is slightly altered. That duplicate world is less than one second of time different from what we consider to be the correct time. This duplicate world or parallel reality was called the Rainbow Dream by my teachers. This unified or collective prophecy from many tribes is a vision that foretells the coming together of all races and nations. The common symbol accompanying such visions and dreams for centuries was a Whirling Rainbow, and the recurring theme was one of unity, harmony, and peace. The Whirling Rainbow was originally encountered by secret societies of Native American Seers and Dreamers. Visions of this future world's potential gathered energy over the years as more gifted and healed human beings discovered those ideas within the Dream Weave.

That dream of world peace exists in energetic form and is a reality that has been nurtured by visionaries around the world for centuries. That energetic world has taken form and is physically merging with our own. Those who are feeling or sensing themselves being drawn into that duplicate world, where discord is only a forgotten memory, may experience a flutter or flip-flop in the stomach, goose bumps of energy, or the slight shaking of muscles when entering or leaving that layer of consciousness. Enough positive energy, thoughts, and feelings have been invested into this concept over the centuries to allow the dream to take form, creating an alternate world of physicality and consciousness. As people merge with the Dream Weave on the fifth path, they are given the opportunity to explore this second physical world. Sometimes the experiences can include the unexplainable aspects of altered time, place, or space, or mixtures of sensations that confound or scare those who do not understand what is occurring.

People on all paths may experience a rapid heartbeat or flip-flop feeling in the pit of the stomach when they are drifting off to sleep. This is particularly common from the third path onward. It occurs when the body is letting go of being awake and brain waves are slowing into deep relaxation. The actual pounding of the heart and the flutter in the stomach signal that the door that stands at the crack between worlds is opening and that the Dreaming Body of the sleeping individual is being awakened to the other worlds of consciousness.

Although we have discussed the Dreaming Body in earlier chapters, more explanation appropriate to the fifth path is needed here. My teachers defined the Dreaming Body as the energetic or spiritual form that contains the unlimited human consciousness. The Dreaming Body can separate from the physical body and is the vehicle used to travel out of body, in waking or sleeping states, in order to explore other levels of awareness. The dreamer finds the ability to direct the dreaming body when his or her Spiritual Essences provide the warrior's intent and the focused will needed to be aware consciously of things that are happening in dream states and to change those events or encounters through personal choice. Seers use the same ability while awake, using the Dreaming Body to go out of body and to track energy pathways through the Dream Weave in order to find needed information. Both abilities are merely states of awareness that allow the Seer or the Dreamer to discover the same information using different methods.

SYMBOLS AND CONCEPTS EVOLVE INTO KNOWING

The events and metaphorical symbols contained in dreams allow Dreamers to explore the vast worlds of consciousness they have encountered in the Dream Weave while the physical body is sleeping. This ability to accurately interpret dream symbols is the first step in developing the advanced skills of lucid dreaming, selective dreaming, and prophetic dreaming. When Dreamers have developed these advanced dreaming skills, their Spiritual Essence connects with the Dreaming Body when it enters the Dream Weave, providing the needed direction, focus, and intent required to remain consciously aware of all that happens and to remember everything upon awakening. Having authority over the dream states encountered in the Dream Weave and using that impeccable intent to select which dream images one needs to focus upon is a part of the fifth- and sixth-path advanced lessons.

The Spiritual Essence's voice of authority, intent, and focus is also required for Seers to accurately perceive the difference between possible or probable future events. All concepts, feelings, and identities exist within the Dream Weave, yet the ability to accurately discern where a lost child can be found is honed only through discipline. My teachers worked me for eight to twelve hours a day for three and a half years in order to develop the skills I needed. I was twenty-two years old, and although I was learning to hone advanced fifth- and sixth-path skills, many of my third- and fourth-path lessons were not addressed until much later. The reason for this seemingly topsy-turvy, out-of-sequence set of lessons was that I had been experiencing renegade paranormal abilities since early childhood. I say that these abilities were renegade because they could not be controlled. I could not shut the door between worlds and stop the flows of information and energy at will. I needed to learn how to gain control over those abilities so that I could remain in charge of my life and well-being. The example of my life is very unusual, but it does happen. Unfortunately, in the past, most people in this situation did not have access to sixth- and seventh-path teachers. I was very lucky in that regard.

Today there are many fifth-, sixth-, and seventh-path teachers in the world. When the student is ready, those teachers will cross their path. In many cases, the actual teaching is coming from one's own Spiritual Essence. The valiant explorer of these last three paths usually finds what he or she needs within the Self. The completion of fifth-path lessons and the beginning of sixth-path lessons require self-reliance and individual exploration, which leads to personal understanding of the truths one encounters. Peers on these paths share experiences and thereby gain clarity. Further illumination can also be received through books like this one, which I trust will make the events that are individually encountered more understandable. The map of consciousness this book presents is a Western, indigenous model that includes the right of each person to incorporate the disciplines that fit his or her individual needs.

When we gather information regarding the uncharted territories of consciousness that are being encountered, we find deeper levels of acceptance of intangible truths, which dispel our doubts and fears of what was once unexplainable. A form of camaraderie and unity occurs on these last three paths among human beings who are actively confronting the lessons on these levels. When a person goes into the crack in the universe and becomes stable in that state of awareness, an unseen bond forges a unified energy field in the Dream Weave and feeds the Whirling Rainbow Dream of world peace. During the fifth path, that same energy field, created by others who have preceded us, is an unseen force of strength in our lives. From that energy field of goodwill and intention, we are fed the encouragement and assistance we need to become stable, comfortable, and fully aware of being in both the seen and the unseen worlds simultaneously.

SEEING THE SIMILARITIES AND AVOIDING SEPARATION

We must be willing to leave behind any perceptions of duality before we can complete the fifth path and fully embrace the sixth. For example, we can easily slip into the judgments of the past when we are confronted with difficult people or situations. Sidestepping the urge to polarize, refusing to choose one side or the other, is a developed skill. We can avoid causing a separation in our Sacred Spaces by holding a neutral position, stating that we do not take sides. We can also recognize any behaviors of the people concerned with compassion, seeing any similarities between what is being demonstrated and our own past behaviors. To see another in oneself and to acknowledge that we also have been there will disarm any forthcoming judgment. The Mayans understand this principle when they say, "I am another one of yourself." Many similar skills defuse explosive situations that could disrupt our forward progress by requiring wake-up calls, pop quizzes, or enlightenment traps.

The fifth path contains levels within levels of the skills needed to stand with one foot in both the physical and the nonphysical worlds. Although we have been required on earlier paths to balance our earthly responsibilities with our spiritual development, the added weight of the disorienting phenomena on this path can knock us to our knees. The thoughts and emotions that we formerly encountered in the Dream Weave were child's play by comparison to the paranormal activity that can occur at the fifth-path level.

After the fifth-path lessons encountered in my early twenties, I completed most of the third- and fourth-path lessons, which then shifted my focus mainly to the other fifth-path lessons. I was twenty-nine years old when enough of my attention and energy was present to focus on the fifth-path lessons. That is when my roller-coaster ride began in earnest. Without warning, I would feel like I was zooming down a roller coaster while I was trying to simply stand up at work. The nausea that ensued was terrifying because I never knew when or if it would stop. I would go outside, lie on the grass, and try to feel the Earth so I would not throw up. Even with the tools of all my earlier training, I was unable to control the new altered states and visitations that followed these experiences. I finally sold the restaurant I owned because it was too much to handle in the face of the upsurge of uncontrollable paranormal phenomena. These energy surges and paranormal events, along with distressing physical symptoms, continued for another nine years as I embraced sixth- and seventh-path lessons.

HOW DO YOU EXPECT ME TO FLY LIKE AN EAGLE WHEN 1 DANCE WITH TURKEYS ALL DAY LONG?

This balancing act is what my teachers call entering the initiation of the Temple of the City. In ancient times, all of the Toltec and Mayan priesthoods had temples that protected the initiates from the conflict of the outside world. The initiates experienced seclusion and quiet while on the fifth path and onward. In modern times we are asked to experience the same spiritual awakenings without the protection of quiet lifestyles. Joaquin was very specific when he told me that I would have to maintain the integrity of all that I had learned while in the hustle and bustle of daily life. He called this set of lessons the initiation of the Temple of the City because I would be required to use profound discipline to balance the sensitivity required to integrate the energy of the Dream Weave and roll with the punches of daily life in an unprotected environment. Learning to master these lessons usually continues through the seventh path.

As we move into the sixth path we are still learning the lessons of other paths and finishing the last of the fifth-path lessons. The tailormade individuality of these experiences and the random sequence of events is determined through our unique needs. We encounter many different issues on many different paths simultaneously; hence we become multilayered and multifaceted individuals. On the fifth path, it becomes obvious that nothing in any of these paths of initiations is linear. The enlightenment trap that is set in motion through trying to figure out where we are on our path is a mental machination, a Coyote tactic that leads nowhere.

The fifth path teaches us that we cannot count on applying linear thinking to the unseen worlds. There is more to our universe that the laws of physics teach us. Matter, energy, space, and time may be the elements of our physical world, but the truths applicable to physicality do not apply to the Dream Weave. We make up our own rules as we discover how to approach and to transit the unseen worlds. Our rules for how to maintain our personal balance in those energetic realms are individual. The only safeguard against utter chaos and instability is that we continue to use our personal integrity and impeccability. When we can relate to physical life and to others with harmony and loving intent, and when we are present enough to successfully handle any issue or situation that comes up in daily life, we have a firm foundation from which to operate. The added responsibility of encountering the Dream Weave and integrating our paranormal experiences becomes part of the fifth, sixth, and seventh paths of initiation.

HOLD YOUR HORSES, I'M NOT READY!

The decision to keep moving forward is an individual choice. From the midpoint of the fifth path, where the door to the Dream Weave is fully open and massive energy is flooding into the human body, things can really get hairy. Some people choose to stop the resulting transformation from happening. It does not matter how these shutdowns occur. Embracing any of these seven paths is a matter of personal choice. These last three paths are not for the faint of heart. There is no shame in never approaching any of these paths of initiation. There is no blame in choosing to remain in a comfort zone on any path or in not taking any initiation at all. Human beings have lived full lives from their Sacred Points of View throughout time. No person should ever be coerced into moving any faster than he or she can safely experience the process of changes. Knowing what we can and cannot endure is a safeguard that is not to be violated by ourselves or another. As I stated earlier, some human beings choose to explore this path only after their human bodies die. Their souls view the Dream Weave from the nonphysical viewpoint, reviewing how the unseen worlds reflected their physical actions in life.

Time is an illusion that exists in the eternal present, but timing is everything. Some human beings need to experience many lifetimes of development before they are ready to approach any path of initiation. Those who have walked some of the paths of initiation may choose to integrate what they have learned before continuing. One's sense of internal timing is a discernment skill that is begun on the third path and is reviewed at every new level of experience. This ability to honor our internal timing is called forbearance and allows us to move forward synchronistically without waiting or pushing.

We must also hold no judgments regarding the changes that are occurring in our lives. We may lose our desire to be with other people, attend social gatherings, or be in crowds. At times we may find we have no sexual desire or may even recoil from being touched or held by another, just as on the earlier paths we might have been so sensitive that we could not tolerate any type of violence on television, in movies, or in printed material. We may also feel like running from any type of yelling matches or upsets between other people. All of these points of sensitivity are normal waves of initiation experiences and will come and go. Honoring our personal needs and feelings as we are undergoing these changes is of paramount importance.

This is also the path where we learn to remove "I should" from our vocabularies. The physical body is undergoing such intense changes that we can no longer allow the mind to override the body's needs. Everything is being rewired within the brain, the body, the emotions, and the Spiritual Essence. To have the amount of energy needed to accomplish this rewiring process successfully, we must consciously conserve our energy. When the door between worlds is open, a third of our life force begins to operate in the intangible realms, a third is used to develop new brain synapses, and the remaining third is what we feel as physical energy. We cannot allow our life force to be diverted by pushing the physical body beyond its endurance level, which is much lower than when we had the door to the Dream Weave closed. If we push too hard, trying to ignore the various physical, emotional, and spiritual shifts, illness will surely follow.

When the tide of life force returns to balance, we enter uncharted territory and begin to conquer our fears of moving forward and our fears about the unexplainable symptoms and sensations. Other Dream Weave explorers may have gone before us, mapping those parts of the Dream Weave, but the experience is new to us. We feel unusual kinds of energy in our physical bodies, and suddenly the sensations that we formerly experienced infrequently can become a constant fact of life. The formerly uncontrollable ebb and flow of energy changes. At one balancing point, we feel energy streaming through our bodies constantly, and we are forced to deal moment to moment with the new sensations of the resulting trials by fire. We begin to understand, at a deep core level, that we are required to change our perceptions of how things work in our universe every time we encounter the life force contained in every new level of awareness that we explore.

IS IT YOURS, MINE, OR OURS?

One of the final lessons of the fifth path that dovetails into the sixth-path lessons is the ability to distinguish between cleared personal will and emotions and the collective emotions found in layers of the Dream Weave. The task at hand is distinguishing what we personally are feeling and what belongs to humanity, close friends, or groups that we interact with. On the second and third paths we cleared our wounds that once created reactive emotions, but this is a different lesson. As we transit the energetic worlds and continue to interact with other people in the physical world, we tend to absorb the energy contained in what we perceive. The human tendency to absorb energy creates a magnetic vacuum operating through our thoughts. If we develop the skills needed to travel successfully through the energetic worlds, we learn not to grab onto any layers of energy by projecting our evaluations or opinions.

Most of the remaining lessons on the fifth path involve personal spiritual explorations of the universe. We learn how to use our Dreaming Body to transit levels of consciousness within the Dream Weave, and we learn how to expand our Sacred Points of View to include other layers of awareness. Many people allow their spirits to journey into the star-filled heavens. They experience beams of colored light connected to various parts of the galaxy, formless layers of feeling that contain color or sound, and spiritual beings who fill us with loving feelings and blessings. These experiences can be achieved through meditation, dreaming, out-of-body journeys, and altered states induced by other spiritual disciplines. Yes, we have experienced things like this on earlier paths, but on the latter part of the fifth path we begin to hone our skills to the point of accuracy. Using personal intent allows us to gain conscious access to parts of the Dream Weave that we want to revisit.

On the fifth path the two worlds of intangible spiritual consciousness and tangible physicality are no longer separate, and they exist inside of our bodies as well as in our consciousness. Therefore, we can use personal intent to propel our Dreaming Body anywhere we have the energy to go. Available energy is gathered and used only to the degree that we have freed ourselves from the lessons found on earlier paths.

The fifth path dovetails into the sixth, and we actually become conscious of *dancing the dream*: bringing the energy of conscious awareness, found in the unseen worlds, into daily experience and balancing the two. There is no longer any separation between what we experience spiritually or energetically and what we experience in physical reality. Some people call this process the union of heaven and Earth. In the tradition of the Southern Seers, a door at the crack between worlds is permanently opened. On the sixth path, which is the Below Direction, we learn to bring these unseen energies and new states of awareness into a grounded form that funds our physical bodies with the life force needed. The new levels of awareness we learn to tap into in the Dream Weave are danced alive by applying those principles with ultimate vigilance in our daily lives. When we succeed in applying these principles, *walking our talk* goes one giant step forward and becomes *dancing the dream.*

CHAPTER 8

Beyond the threshold of consciousness lies the infinite heart of the awaiting dream. To touch that sacred part of the mystery is to know the eternal aspects of BEING.

—Joaquin Muriel Espinosa

▲▲

PATH OF EMBODYING THE INFINITE

With the lifting of the final veil,
I embrace the wonders that can BE,
The weave of divine Creation,
Expands the universe inside of me.

Transiting layers of consciousness,
I journey far beyond the stars.
Touching every facet of Oneness,
That I once imagined from afar.

I learn to embody the Oneness,
Bringing spirit into earthly form,
Dancing the dream-energy of heaven,
In the safety of Earth Mother's arms.

Within the heart of the universe,
Lies the void of eternal space,
The sacred infinite viewpoint,
My warrior spirit will embrace.

Then far beyond the other side,
I touch all that can eternally BE,
Restructuring my sacred viewpoints,
Embracing infinity inside of me.

—Jamie Sams

The Sixth Path of Initiation
The Below Direction on the Medicine Wheel

THE Below Direction on the Medicine Wheel represents our connection to the Earth. Here we learn how to take the proficient knowledge we've gained, including the proper use of Dream Weave energy, and use that wisdom in daily life. One of the first goals of the Below Direction is to stay grounded and to function efficiently while our bodies are feeling surges of unexplainable energy. The lessons of the sixth path teach us to perceive the nonphysical realities connected to the Dream Weave, discerning the intent and correctly identifying the source before we apply the symbols, metaphors, and other information to our lives.

The marriage of the tangible and intangible worlds on the fifth path was great! The honeymoon is over. Now, do I sink, swim, or float? It is time to lift the final vestiges of that last veil, to connect with the Earth, and to continue to explore the universe's vast realms of consciousness. On the sixth path we learn to discern the differences in the unified energy of all parts of the universe, to embrace the center of Creation, to move through the void, to actualize the neutral viewpoint from the divine, infinite perspective, and master the skills of using universal energy to create healing opportunities in the material world. These challenging tasks can take many years to accomplish. At times we will wonder how we can function with all the various tasks staring us in the face, but in every case, we are required to connect our body to the Earth.

DID MY BODY COME WITH GROUNDING WIRES?

The Below Direction, explored on the sixth path, earths or grounds all the new information we gathered through exploring the fifth path and

204 ▼▼▼ DANCING THE DREAM

teaches us to ground continually as we move forward on the journey. Everything that we have learned by trial and error as we ventured into the invisible realms of universal energy is brought clearly into focus. We are able to view consciously both the physical and nonphysical realms and to successfully operate within both. Once this ability is firmly in place, the body becomes accustomed to the universal energy flowing through it. Another array of perceptions becomes available because the energy is traveling through the body *and* being grounded to the Earth. Prior to this grounding we may have had brief glimpses of the infinite viewpoint, but it was not a perpetual state of being that we could own and maintain.

Prior to the fifth path, we often succeeded in staying grounded during the paranormal events that occurred on earlier paths. However, the power surges found on the fifth path forced us to go to a much higher level of mastery. We can learn to maintain a balance between the regular duties of daily life and the constant surges of energy rocking our body, throwing us into unexpected altered states, only when we allow the rewiring process in the physical body to be completed. I want to review the fifth-path process because the sixth-path lessons begin amid the final throes of fifth-path rewiring, when the energy is assimilated by the physical body, reconnecting with the Earth instead of short-circuiting in the head and upper torso. When we fully ground the energy, mishaps like blowing out electrical appliances will no longer occur.

The fifth path can last as long as it takes for the individual to become accustomed to the energy and to acclimate the body to the shifts in perception that are created by that energy. If we try to speed up the process, our physical body can run a fever or develop other health problems. If we try to slow down the process or avoid resting while our body is adjusting to the energy flowing through it, we can suffer symptomatic electrical shocks that manifest as twinges of pain. When we suppress the flow of energy, our own energy fields can short-circuit and we can become ill as the Dream Weave energy backs up into the physical form, unable to flow through.

Before we began any of the paths of initiation, we were blind to the unseen parts of physical life. Then we learned how to perceive energy. We learned to have one eye open to the material world, then one eye open to the intangible worlds of the Dream Weave. Now we have melded those two viewpoints and can see with both eyes open. This new third viewpoint, which begins to emerge at the beginning of the sixth path, occurs simultaneously with the last of the fifth-path lessons. As we move forward, we develop the ability to work with the energy streaming through our bodies. This is not to imply that when we approach new levels of consciousness the symptoms of disorientation will not be present; they usually return briefly just prior to a breakthrough. These turning points or illuminating breakthroughs usually occur when we find the third viewpoint, which is an authentically neutral point of balance containing the absence of duality or the need to personalize our experiences.

THE THIRD INFINITE VIEWPOINT

Many people have asked me how we find the third viewpoint, which my teachers called "three eyes." I have replied, "Accurately and consciously." Hundreds of techniques are used in the advanced levels of initiation found in various traditions, but naturally I can share only the ones that I have experienced myself. If you have walked the path, you can share it through the examples of your personal experiences and what you personally have observed happening to others as they embrace these initiations. My teachers stressed that if you are only guessing or using another person's hearsay as your source, misinformation can create harm. The highest level of personal impeccability and integrity is required in order to appropriately share the steps of any initiation path.

A mental shutdown is one of the safeguards provided by the human brain. When the mind cannot compute the information given, because the necessary brain synapses are not yet developed, the normal brain synapse will overload, creating a shutdown and the need to sleep. This occurrence forces the person to assimilate the information while the body is sleeping, when the conscious mind is turned off. The data is sorted through and the information stored in the dreaming body's consciousness, and it will not be released into conscious memory until the person has reached the level where he or she can use it. This "forgetter mechanism" assures that the person will be actively walking the path of initiation where the data can be applied through personal experience *before* becoming fully conscious of the information.

At the end of each of the rewiring processes on the fifth path, and again on the sixth path, the new brain synapses become fully connected to the preexisting brain synapses. At this point the body experiences a series of symptomatic shutdowns, which signal the startup of the combined synapse systems. When both sets of brain synapses begin to work in union, we experience a total destruction of former thought structures and learned responses; the third viewpoint begins to emerge when the former thought structures and belief systems crumble. It is only on the sixth path that the ability to successfully hold all three viewpoints is found. By the end of the fifth path the two worlds have become one through the marriage of the tangible and intangible perspectives, the ability to accurately perceive matter and energy without separation.

Even though we are now seeing with both eyes open, we are still viewing all that we have learned, felt, and thought through *a biased veil of personal human experience.* During the development of the third viewpoint, while sixth-path lessons are being activated, we begin a purification process that requires that we remove the veil of personal human experience and replace it with a nondualistic view stemming from an infinite point of view. When we have the third viewpoint we see from the eternal perception, a viewpoint that comes from the Spiritual Essence. From this perspective, the life we are living is a tiny thread within the continuous ribbon containing our life force throughout infinity. My teachers called this ability to see from the eternal perspective "banishing time."

When we are willing to surrender the personal viewpoint, by incorporating it into the universal eternal viewpoints contained in all awareness within the Great Mystery, the veil is lifted. Some traditions call this the lifting of the seventh veil. Now our work begins in earnest: we must be grounded and present enough to monitor all of the energy we funnel through us and observe. Our bodies, minds, and emotions must be connected to our Spiritual Essences. We are becoming the connective tissues that link the seen, the unseen, and the infinite.

When this veil lifted in my life, I had a vision that was like a strip of old celluloid film. Each frame contained a different human face. Some were haughty and vain, others were beautiful and enchanting, while others were filled with poverty and despair. I saw some faces that were disfigured from disease and others that bore scars from injuries. Some faces were filthy, and others were harrowed with expressions of worry, burdened by brutal living conditions. I saw people from all time periods in our Earth's history who came from hundreds of different back-

207 ▾▾▾ The Sixth Path of Initiation

grounds and cultures. The races were all represented, and I watched with fascination as the unique facets of individuality rolled by one at a time.

I was suddenly startled by feelings of fear when I saw an intermingling of faces that were alien to our planet. The Earth Mother's voice whispered to me, saying that beauty rests in the eye of the beholder and that in those alien cultures there was also beauty. I relaxed, and then Earth Mother asked me if I could love all of the people in my vision. I hesitated and went deep into my heart before I replied, "Yes, Earth Mother, I can." I felt a smile and a gentle loving flow of energy as she said, "Good, because they were all you. These are the identities your Spiritual Essence has embraced in physical forms." Then I finally understood the infinite viewpoint.

STRUCTURE AMID THE INTANGIBLE

The steps of the sixth path allow us to attain the goal of being clear conduits of neutral energy, becoming the unbiased connective tissue that spans many levels of awareness with ease. The first part occurs with the lifting of the veil of personal experience and the continued purification of anything that keeps us from perceiving clearly. One of the last things we let go of in this purification process is having to have a rigid personal viewpoint that disallows the infinite aspects of our Spiritual Essences. Our personal viewpoints tend to anchor us in one level of experience, keeping us attached to ideas and feelings that disallow expansion. There are millions of valid truths in our world. We will eventually gain the skill needed to recognize and assimilate the validity in all human viewpoints, while maintaining our uniqueness as well as detached neutrality. We learn that our spirits have undergone many changes in identity and form and that all of those masks of human expression were faces used for the spirit to experience physicality.

When the veil is being lifted, it falls away in tattered pieces, and most people go through some crisis in trying to identify what is happening to them. This experience is different in every case, because parts of this particular veil of separation have fallen away on earlier paths, but the last vestiges of removal always concern the release of personalizing the experience itself and seeing from the perspective of owning our eternal spiritual viewpoint. We must remain present and not get caught in other times, specific identities, or lives: we must banish time. If we cannot accomplish bringing eternity into the present and fully banishing our concepts of time, we influence neutral energy and unbiased perceptions. The purification process requires us to release any attitudes, responses, or actions that have veiled the universal, neutral view of infinity. Anything that separates us from the infinite quality of our Spiritual Essences, such as the human fear of death, has to be released.

The purification process also requires that we eliminate earlier labels that we may have adopted while developing our spiritual natures, such as, "I am a being of the light." Although this may be true, and our intent to help humankind may be pure, the statement itself creates polarity. Being solely of the light disallows having confronted, healed, and embraced the shadow side of our nature, and that polarity keeps us from fully reaching the neutral eternal viewpoint held by our Spiritual Essence. Without adopting the divine neutral viewpoint, we will still be biased to some degree. The ability to simply say "I am" includes all that a person embraces and experiences on all levels of awareness. "I am" also embraces all of the soul's experiences of integrity or lack of integrity, multicultural perspectives, male and female identities, past and future roles of existence, and the eternal quality of beingness.

NO BLINDERS ALLOWED

The next part of the sixth path concerns the development of new levels of discernment. From a neutral viewpoint, we develop the skills necessary to observe energy, discovering the intent behind the energy and how that intent is directing energy in the seen and unseen worlds, now merged inside of us.

The ability to discern the intent connected to energy is another set of lessons in and of itself. Our blinders are torn away once more, and we begin to acknowledge that polarity and duality exist not only inside our material world but also inside spiritual beings who inhabit the nonphysical realms of the Dream Weave. We are no longer allowed to blindly accept that just because we have tapped into the unseen worlds of energy, we can then blithely go about our business, forgetting to monitor the energy coming through our bodies or the intent of the spirits we encounter in the nonphysical realms.

This process of discernment differs vastly from the third- and fourth-path lessons, when we were having to confront shadow-side behaviors in ourselves and in wandering spirits. We are not judging whether our spirit guides are good or evil. We are now adopting a neutral viewpoint that allows us to discern the intent and energy connected to any information we are receiving from spirit and to claim the personal spiritual authority that we have earned. We learn to use that spiritual authority to determine our own course through these final levels of initiation. If a spirit has never had a physical body, it has not mastered the levels that we have completed by bringing spiritual content into a physical body and walking it on the physical plane.

WHAT DO YOU MEAN, ABSOLUTE EQUALITY?

Another realization emerges on the sixth path when we acknowledge that there are no greater or lesser roles among the various life forces that inhabit our universe. Everything contains spirit, and all parts of Creation have equally important roles within the whole when viewed from the infinite perspective of our Spiritual Essences. Human beings are no greater or lesser than archangels. The roles of sages, avatars, and spiritual masters are equal to the spiritual roles of the forces in nature. Everything within the Great Mystery is interrelated and interdependent. Did human beings create personas and identities in order to impersonate the Creator? Or did the Creator use all of the identities in humanity as impersonations, veiling the infinite presence? The answers to these questions depend upon one's viewpoint but do not really matter because all individual facets of Creation melt into One with the touch of infinity.

After we have this realization, we let go of the last vestiges of needing to have go-betweens in order to assimilate the divine will of the Great Mystery or God. We have taken our places within the universe and have assimilated the infinite viewpoint, destroying the human need for spiritual hierarchies or pecking orders. We have ultimate respect for every role within the whole and begin the journey to the Hunab K'u, the Mayan word for the center of the universe, the zero/rest/balance point, the void of divine neutrality. This can be the most frightening part of the sixth path because we start becoming the neutral, eternal viewpoint, duplicating and actualizing it. Suddenly personal will and sense of identity are subjugated to the degree that we must learn to maintain a grounded focus on having any identity in the material world. A static condition occurs that can resemble a fifth-path experience where the domino effect has stripped the gears of the mental mechanisms that formed the way we structured our thinking or thought processes. Don't be fooled; this sixth-path initiation contains major differences.

We will face and enter the center of the universe and be shocked that inside the void, time does not exist and space is infinite. There are no emotions, inside of us or outside of us, because the void exists simultaneously in all realms of awareness. In this state of ultimate, absolute nothingness, which lasts for a time, we could be confronted with the most traumatic situations imaginable, and we would not respond emotionally, spiritually, or mentally. The slate is wiped clean. This state could resemble catatonia if it were not for the fact that we continue to physically handle our daily lives while this process is in motion. All that we have experienced, all that we believe we are, all of our connections to the material and to the invisible worlds of spirit are gone. There is a vast nothingness that continues to expand into more immeasurable nothingness. At the end of this initiation, feelings and life force begin to return, and we learn how to use the two melded viewpoints of the seen and unseen worlds in unison with the third viewpoint of divine, infinite neutrality; hence the term three eyes.

On the sixth path we also continue to develop the skills of telepathy, shape-shifting, bilocation, levitation, dreaming, energetic healing, and other abilities that can defy and shatter the known laws of physics. Not everyone has the same skills, and all roles are equal to all others. If it is not our role to demonstrate these skills on the material plane, we don't need to kill ourselves trying to adopt someone else's role in the divine plan. Some people use their gifts to show humankind that it is possible to manifest miracles on the material plane, while others work in the intangible realms, using energy to assist humankind. The successful completion of this part of the sixth path requires that we use these talents consciously and at will. We have experienced brief flashes of these abilities from time to time on the earlier paths, but now we choose to master those skills.

Now that we have discussed an overview of sixth-path lessons, let us look in more detail at how each of those lessons unfolds.

SHREDDING THE REMNANTS OF THE FINAL VEIL OF SEPARATION

The lifting of the veil at the beginning of the sixth path is brought about by reconnecting the Spiritual Essence's energy to the human body and to the Earth Mother. Through the marriage of the seen and unseen worlds on the fifth path, and by using the knowledge we have gained through embracing that union, we have stopped separating matter and energy or spirit and form. The two worlds are One inside of us, not outside of us. We continue to encounter life from the perspective of our personal human experiences until the veil begins to lift. Then it becomes necessary to adopt the neutral viewpoint of the unbiased witness, who has had many roles through infinity that should no longer carry any significance or importance in our minds. If any identity that we have embodied in other times throughout eternity still affects our perception of being greater or lesser than others, it is time to let it go. We must also purify any remaining desire to label anything that we experience as pertaining solely to our present human identity and learn to see all events rather as part of the continuous infinite experience of one spark of life within the infinite fire of Creation.

Just as a blind person develops the heightened awareness of tactile senses, smell, and hearing, a person on the sixth path also develops the perceptions of distinguishing the subtle differences in universal energy and how those flows of energy are directed. Feeling energy flows directed by human intent is far different from feeling energy directed by other life forms or pure consciousness in the universe. By the end of the fifth path, most people have developed keen abilities of discernment regarding human thought, intent, and emotion. The discernment skills we have learned to use to detect the difference between collective human thought or emotion and our personal thoughts or feelings are usually firmly in place. When the veil is lifted, we are tested on these abilities to not only determine the differences between our personal energy and the collective energies, but also how to use those skills when we are developing the ability to hold the unbiased, infinite viewpoint and to run all of the energy found in daily life and in the unseen worlds through the body and into the Earth Mother and then back into the body without having anything stick.

When the veil is lifted and we successfully assimilate the third neutral, eternal viewpoint, we see ourselves, other humans, and all forms

of consciousness within the universe as cells within the body of the
Great Mystery. Formerly, we have processed all of our physical and spiritual experiences by viewing them in terms of our personal progress
and by integrating our new states of awareness into daily human life.
Now, in order to move forward, we have to let go of the same tools
that brought us safely to the lifting of this veil. The decision we need to
make in order to assimilate the immortal view of the Spiritual Essence
is that we simply observe and allow everything to BE from the infinite
perspective, which contains the timeless overview.

From this point forward in our lives we take on the balancing act of
successfully relating to others at their levels of experience, identifying
their viewpoints, discerning the intent present, perceiving the energy
connected to that viewpoint, maintaining a neutral position, and allowing everything to BE, exactly the way it is, without being drawn
into another's energy field, opinions, or judgments. This feat of neutrality requires that we discern duality when it is present without giving it
any of our emotional energy or thought energy by trying to figure out
why it is happening. This is the first essential goal of the Below Direction on the sixth path after the veil has been lifted.

Universal life force flows through our consciousness and our physical body *only to the degree* that we are able to maintain our grounding
along with mental and emotional detachment. In this process of reconnecting with the Earth Mother, some people may not notice when they
are not grounded and will have to develop certain earthing skills to
maintain balance. It will help tremendously to visualize the circular
flow of energy down the front of the body, into the earth, returning up
the back of the legs and spine, over the head, and returning down the
front to the earth. Exercises that flex and tone muscles also help. I
highly recommend the Pilates method, tai chi, walking, and stretching
exercises. I have found that strenuous exercise is too hard on the body
and the spirit at this stage of development.

It is very easy to slip unwittingly into the energy fields of others
when we are bringing the third neutral, infinite viewpoint into focus
in our lives. The second we think we are past physical symptoms or
have a bit of breathing space, we often let down our guards. We learn
to use the skills of being fully aware of what is energetically connected
to our daily lives and of maintaining the integrity of our Sacred Spaces
without collecting energy as it moves through us and into the Earth
Mother. Oops! Here come the pop quizzes that set off a whole new set

of discernment skills or activate a review of the energetic boundary lessons we learned on the fifth path.

When the veil is lifted, there is a resistance to being in contact with others. Often we feel that we are being beaten up by the energy contained in daily activity. We tend to want to become hermits from time to time on many of the paths of initiation because we are developing new sensitivities that are not understood by those who have not explored the same levels of consciousness. When we begin holding the neutral, infinite viewpoint, every particle of feeling, thought, and intention in our surroundings begins to gush through our physical bodies as flows of energy. The overwhelming gush of sensory perceptions is unbelievable and affects our emotions, our state of mind, our health, and our stamina. We are caught in a riptide of universal energy that leaves us feeling like a wet dishrag most of the time. After the body begins to adjust to these phenomena, things level out and we begin finding anchor points that ground the energy flowing through us.

I'VE GOT TO PAY ATTENTION WHILE GOING WITH THE FLOW?

When we get to the second part of the sixth path, the skills of perception are again honed to razor sharpness as we learn how to sense universal streams of energy, which are those not directed by or connected to human intent. We begin the sixth path by harnessing one stream of that universal energy and successfully directing it through our bodies, into the earth, and back into the universe, maintaining the constant circular flow. Mastering this flow is the way we maintain a fluid, flexible viewpoint and our personal balance while remaining acutely aware of the energy of the Dream Weave and how that energy melds and flows through the physical reality of daily life.

In my early twenties, my teachers insisted that I learn how to track energy. This means that I had to be intimately in tune with the various feelings that accompanied streams of energy found in the Dream Weave. These lessons continued as I began the sixth path, and the degree of difficulty increased. To accomplish the next degree of difficulty, I had to learn how to distinguish the difference between the energies connected to animals, plants, stones, and human beings within the Dream Weave and to relate those energies to what I observed in the

214 ᵥᵥᵥ DANCING THE DREAM

physical, natural world. Then I learned to distinguish those energies from the energy contained in the collective layers of human emotion, collective human thoughts and belief systems, human beings whose spirits who had crossed over, and the energy of spirits who had attained various levels of spiritual mastery. These lessons in the discernment of energy and how energy operates at different levels form the foundation for allowing energy to be neutral but also recognizable as it moves through our perceptions.

At the beginning of the sixth path, if we are blinded by the light shining throughout infinity, we will be shown that we must acknowledge equally the continued presence of dark energy in the seen and unseen worlds. We learn not to align ourselves with one or the other. In order to be clear and to be able to view energy from an infinite viewpoint, it becomes necessary to discern without holding an opinion. What the heck does that mean? We not only learn how to view what exists in the physical world and in the energetic worlds, we also learn how to allow all that we perceive to simply BE what it is, without holding an opinion for or against it. This is one tricky set of lessons, because we cannot accurately observe the universal forms of energy moving through our bodies if we unwittingly label it through some careless judgment we have made from our human viewpoints.

In any type of altered state or spiritual experience, it is necessary to allow ourselves to simply BE in the experience, for any form of thought will act like glue and slow down the process. For example, we can feel the intensity and the various textures of the energy flowing through our bodies, but to label it as being something that we have to personalize or unravel by subjectively discovering the cause will make the energy freeze in motion. If we notice the energy getting stuck because we are experiencing bodily sensations or discomfort, and we ask "why is this happening to me?" the sensations of discomfort or confusion will stick. We can remove our opinion that the feelings are personally related to us, and the energy usually will begin to flow again. Another example of this can be seen when our hearts are filled to the point of overflowing and the incredible joy of life is filling our senses. In those moments, the energy is moving. If we try to analyze, asking "what does this mean?" or "what is making me feel so good?" the loving flow of pleasure or happiness will stop cold.

About twelve years ago, when I touched on this lesson for the first time, I finally understood that by holding the neutral viewpoint, my energy field had become like the free space on a bingo card. I was working with addicts, people going through recovery who were working on healing their childhood abuse issues. I was staying at a motel nearby, and I went to the recovery center daily. On the second night, I became depressed for no apparent reason, and I started crying uncontrollably. I started having visions of people committing suicide, of ritual abuse, and of other horrors involving faceless people. None of these events had ever been discussed with me by any of the participants of the workshop. It took me quite a while to disentangle myself and to restore my proper boundaries. I had unwittingly grounded the Dream Weave energy of the participants, running it through my body in order to transform the imbalance to neutral, healed energy.

Good-bye, lie! I had to let go of one of the basic precepts that I had used in my healing practice years before. Although I had not been taking clients for years, I unwittingly was applying the false idea that unhealed energy must be transmuted through the body of the healer. By eliminating this idea, a whole new perspective opened to me, and I realized that neutral energy facilitates and provides the extra fuel that is needed by those who seek healing. The person choosing to change can actualize his or her healing because more usable energy is present.

This example shows one of the pop quizzes of the sixth path. There are no vacations. We cannot let go of our discernment skills at any time. We must be vigilant moment by moment, noticing the energy contained in any place that we are not familiar with. While we sleep, the natural boundaries that we are aware of using while awake can unwittingly be set aside. This is particularly true when we adopt the neutral viewpoint of the sixth path, having cleared our own energy fields of duality. At this level of initiation, we have become open conduits for universal energy. The warning signal occurs when we feel unusual feelings that do not seem to be natural or belonging to us. When this occurs, we are being put on notice that we must track the energy we are feeling and view it from a external neutral position while maintaining our boundaries on every level of awareness. This type of vigilance keeps us from taking on thoughts or feelings that belong to others.

I got another sixth-path review pop quiz regarding energy and our emotions and thoughts just a couple of years ago. I was getting ready to go to sleep one night and was lying in my bed before I turned off the lamp, when I began to hear a faint melody. It was winter, all the windows were closed, and I decided to close my eyes and listen. The moment I decided to listen, the music expanded to add other instruments and sounded like an amazing symphony. I became so enthralled in the beauty of this majestic music that it took a while for me to notice that it was changing with my feelings. Every time I felt my heart soar, the music crested with a crescendo of magnificent sound, and as my feelings moved to contentment and joy, the haunting melody shifted. Then I realized that I was hearing the music of my spirit, body, emotions, and heart. I had a fleeting thought, "How am I doing this?", and the music stopped. I instantly got back into my feelings, and the music began again.

I had heard the universal "music of the spheres" in my early twenties, during a time when I had entered the stillness, Tiyoweh. I knew then that the music of the spheres was the sound connected to all energies and reflected their individual dances in the Dream Weave. Years later, I understood that I was being given another view of how my own eternal being danced in the universe and the music that my Spiritual Essence was directing in conjunction with my body. I could perceive it only when my mind's thoughts were not in the way. My spark of life was the conductor of that symphony, and the music reflected the patterns of life force flowing through my spark of life, moment by moment. The divine music of my infinite spirit had always been there; I just did not heard it until I rediscovered that layer of awareness from the infinite, neutral viewpoint.

THE UNBIASED WITNESS

Once again we are reminded of the Native American saying that anything that has ever happened in a location is still there. When we bring the energy of the unseen into the physical realm, we are required to identify correctly the energy contained in any given situation or locale. That can be tricky because we cannot judge it as being bad or good; we simply must observe the obvious without engaging in thought. By becoming the unbiased witness, holding a neutral viewpoint, we are able to experience accurately the flows of energy that are present. In the material world, the energy present in any given situation contains all thoughts and emotions, intentions and agendas, as well as the basic life force energy and the behaviors of every person involved.

If we wish to continue on the sixth path, we will need to learn to perceive all of these energies without adopting any of them. We cannot become attached to our perceptions, nor can we reject any part of what we perceive. By reacting to the situation in any way, we destroy the un-biased neutrality of our observations. It becomes necessary to allow en-ergy to flow through us effortlessly as we are continually observing, discerning, and understanding the viewpoints of all life forms and con-sciousness within the universe. We must be careful not to absorb or un-wittingly actualize anything that we encounter either in the energy worlds or through physical contact.

At this second stage of development we also begin to ascertain the texture and the quality of the energy connected to various spirits who exist within the nonphysical realms of the Dream Weave. Many of our former discernment systems must be upgraded or destroyed. Many times on earlier paths of initiation we were given instruction in the form of messages, inspiration, and spiritual advice. Those beautiful gifts stood us in good stead when we needed them and helped us reach our next level in the dance. A turning point comes after we have developed the gifts of accurate discernment from the neutral, infinite viewpoint and have applied that ability to the Below Direction by correctly using it in our physical reality. Most of what we have accomplished at this stage on the sixth path has not been attempted, yet alone mastered, by spirits who have never taken physical bodies. When the level of mastery of the student exceeds the level of mastery of the teacher, new methods are needed. New levels of discernment are now necessary, because we can once again be blinded by the light.

IF I OWN WHAT I PERCEIVE, AM I ACCOUNTABLE?

On the sixth path, we must let go of the need to give away our spiritual authority. We have the authority we need when we can hold the neutral viewpoint, tapping into both the tangible and intangible worlds simul-taneously. Then we experience the infinite connection that allows our bodies to become living conduits of universal energy. Becoming the connective tissue between the physical and nonphysical worlds gives a person certain levels of adeptship, mastery, and spiritual authority. We can receive hard lessons in discernment if we immediately try to give that hard-earned spiritual authority to any spirit guide that happens to appear or to some angelic presence who perhaps never experienced the physical realms.

If we do not question the information we are receiving, we can be led directly into an enlightenment trap. Any spirit who has not faced the treachery of slugging it out in the trenches of the material world or any angelic presence who has not had a physical body cannot accurately guide or teach a human being who has attained this level of mastery. This is not to say that some angels who have never had bodies or other evolved spirits do not have magnificent levels of mastery of their own. They do. They have evolved in different ways—ways that do not include the slow maneuverability of the material world—and therefore they have no idea what we go through to get to this level of initiation. Nonphysical beings operate at the speed of thought, without the hindrances of matter, and we must follow the process of using a body as the vehicle to win the same results.

We can choose to use discernment every time we encounter a spiritual presence. Even if we experience the appearance of Jesus, Buddha, the Virgin Mary, Kwan Yin, or an archangel, we must question them about the levels of consciousness we are embracing and how best to use that energy in physical life. Such pertinent questions will weed out the pretenders. Any spirit who cannot answer truthfully and specifically will vanish. Those spirits who have mastered the physical realms can answer with ease and will give accurate, applicable information that directly applies to what we are experiencing. In keeping a sense of humor, we come to realize that not all spiritual advice is user friendly: it has to stand the test of application to a physical body and experiences on planet Earth.

Some people learn the forerunner to this lesson of discernment when they are on the third and fourth paths. A spirit guide of some channel or psychic tells them not to worry about their house being foreclosed on and that all they need to do is meditate more, eliminating the "get a job and figure out how you can work with the bank" advice. If they lose their home because of lack of discernment, blindly taking foolish advice, they may come to realize that they must take action in the physical world to solve the problems encountered in physical life. What if the channel is off balance or is having a chaotic day in his or her personal life? Who knows? That spirit guide could have been the channel's Uncle Harry who lived on welfare and was a hopeless, mentally confused person before he died. The bottom line is that at this stage of the game, we begin to realize that no oracle or psychic who has not experienced the sixth or seventh paths can see our state of being clearly because he or she has not yet gone around the corner to see the road that we are presently walking.

On the sixth path we begin to realize that as humans we are unique. We explore the universes of consciousness, we bring them into our bodies, and we walk the wisdom in the material world. We continue to explore the nether regions of the Dream Weave that we began discovering on the fifth path by expanding our awareness of what exists within those realms. Along the way we encounter many types of consciousness and diverse energies reflecting a multitude of worlds that contain thought, life force, consciousness, and emotion vastly different from our own. If we can successfully hold the neutral viewpoint while we acknowledge the other types of awareness within the universe, we expand our understanding without adopting or taking on any of the identifying traits of the energies we encounter.

Soon we come to realize that as human beings, we are being given an opportunity to evolve in a way that is experimental and unusual. Some parts of Creation chose to evolve without matter, as pure spirit or consciousness. As human beings, we have been given the opportunity to explore as many levels of consciousness as we have the energy and the skills to do so. By eliminating the ideas of spiritual inequality that are contained in hierarchy, the infinite viewpoint becomes real in our experience. We can attain a heavenly state of grace that is unconditionally compassionate and loving while our Spiritual Essences are fully connected to physical bodies. We handle the physical realm daily, until we can master every part of the energy connected to being human in the tangible and intangible realms of consciousness. We are constantly gathering more skills to maintain balance, which requires that we become more and more present as vast amounts of universal consciousness and energy flood through our human bodies. Just when we think we are beginning to handle being the connective tissue between the material world and hundreds of layers of energy and awareness, we begin to be drawn into the void at the center of the universe.

HOLY COW! WHAT'S THAT PLACE UP AHEAD THAT I CAN'T SEE?

In the Below Direction we discover and explore the energy that animates life in the natural world and how that energy connects to other layers of life force in the universe as a whole. As we continue to explore the levels of consciousness, lines of energy, and layers of spirit within the Dream Weave, we also discover the same energy in earth-connections spanning our natural world. We feel the same universal energy and perceptions inside the physical body as we become secure in our ability to BE in the experience and to ground the energy into the Earth Mother. By following those flows of energy into the center of the Earth, we continue to discover the life forms and life force in our planet. Experiencing the energies of planetary consciousness and all levels of awareness in the cosmos creates larger and larger circles of awareness that grow within us. Eventually we end up in the center of the void of the unknown and the unknowable.

In life we all have spaced out from time to time, experiencing points of bewilderment or blankness when we have been daydreaming or when we have become ungrounded. When our minds or emotions drift away from being fully present and attentive, we usually feel like we got lost in our thoughts or skipped a step. Or recall earlier paths, where we experienced the complete destruction of belief structures or we encountered the domino effect, when all of our mental processes, emotional responses, or behavioral gears were stripped. These types of experiences gave us a tiny inkling of what it means to face the void. On the sixth path we are more present than we have ever been in our lives. We observe the obvious, discern the intent, and funnel the neutral energies of many realms of consciousness through our bodies while remaining fully aware of everything material and intangible. Yet, when we consciously encounter the center of this universe, we can unexpectedly be swallowed by the lack of movement, light, sound, color, energy, emotion, thought, and intent.

The Mayans call the center of our universe the Hunab K'u. The Southern Seers call this place the heart of the Great Mystery. That heart of all contains the pregnant void of Creation and exists beyond the enormous bright light that people see in near-death experiences. Beyond chaos and beyond order, the heart of the universe contains such a vast nothingness that Dream Weave explorers can become lost or consumed by the void. The heart of the Great Mystery is the original Sacred Point of View, which created this universe. The void is unknown and unknowable because it contains all that has not taken on energy or developed form.

This experience is not like encountering a black hole in space while journeying out of body, dreaming, or meditating, because those areas contain vortexes of energy that can be felt and movement that can be perceived. When we approach the void of the Hunab K'u, we can feel like we are succumbing to being devoured by nothingness or like we are having a near-death experience without the blinding light to welcome us to our next level of experience.

For a few years prior to actually entering the void, we vaguely feel something happening that we cannot understand, and we are confronted with our own resistance to moving beyond a comfort zone that has given us wonderful insight and a multitude of spiritual bursts of information and energy. On a subconscious level there is a feeling that we have the right to stay in this place of inner knowing because we have earned it. We forget the universal law that *everything evolves* and that movement is required in order to go to the next level of the dance. The closer we get to the void, the more precise we think we are becoming in using our integrity and impeccability. In fact, we usually have developed a whole new set of spiritual belief systems and judgments, which keep us from seeing the truths presented in daily life because we think we know exactly what the authentic, universal spiritual truths are. The illusion is created by the mind's tendency to neatly package and label our own discoveries, which usually blinds us to other possibilities. Because we have adopted certain behaviors and ideas that have stood us in good stead on our paths, we tend to stay close to what works for us, and we inappropriately let others know that their choices are not as appropriate as ours are. Nothing could be further from the truth.

As we move through the layers of universal consciousness, closer and closer to the void at the center of the universe, we usually have no idea that we have developed an attitude and are bantering our spiritual opinions or holding our hard-earned states of understanding as medals of honor. Since we are fully in touch with heightened states of awareness a lot of the time, we do not notice that we have become opinionated regarding the less-than-perfect behaviors of others and are possibly inflicting on them our own spiritual truths or the adopted beliefs found on our paths or the moralistic rules that once gave us the discipline we needed. In one way or another, the Great Smoking Mirror will allow life situations to reflect back to us examples of how our newly created judgments or unconscious opinions are keeping us from maintaining the neutral or unbiased view moment to moment.

On some level, the mind senses the approach of the void and triggers behaviors that prevent having to fully let go and enter the nothingness. The mind's last-ditch effort to remain in control floods our consciousness with all of our former decisions, opinions, beliefs, and determinations in order to keep us from consciously noticing the void that we are approaching. The mind uses our self-righteous attitudes and our beliefs about what is spiritually impeccable to make us feel self-assured and to keep us from banishing the last vestiges of old brain circuitry, which sometimes is our only anchor to a sense of well-being or balance. The mind's unconscious fear of surrendering to the void that it perceives but does not understand is a natural phenomenon. It occurs because we are in a spiritual comfort zone that supports our certainty. However, the mind's expanding understanding of consciousness within our universe can also feed our spiritual arrogance. Every time we find fault with another person at this point in our process, we are being given the gift of being shown where the mind still holds fixed determinations and judgments. Unfortunately, because the sixth path contains so much paranormal activity, often we are not grounded enough to acknowledge what is actually occurring and to see ourselves as the source of the imbalance.

DISCERNING WHERE WE STILL HOLD JUDGMENTS

Because our ultrasensitive focus is on exploring the intangible, the authenticity of what happens in our physical lives while we are in heightened states of awareness can become distorted. The mind's tendency to resist the impending surrender of *all* the self-created rules about what has worked for us can manifest as finding fault with others, being certain that others do not understand our superior viewpoint, labeling where some people are on their paths, as well as condescending or competing with anyone who has another viewpoint. Every single judgment, opinion, and belief we still hold tends to come up during the few years after the lifting of the seventh veil while we approach the void.

These lessons are preparation for entering the void and can become very uncomfortable because the impeccability we thought we had attained is being challenged in a way that we never expected. We are asked to look at what we have defined as impeccability and to determine if any of our beliefs stem from moral rigidity and outdated dogma. Our refusal to purify ourselves of rigidly adhered-to beliefs can create delay or avoidance only for a short while. Behaviors and events that we have forgiven and let go of long ago can be recreated by the mind's fear of letting go, which speeds up the process of surrendering to the void. We can deny our mind's influence, or we can buy into the notion that we have no further judgments and are not directly influenced by our own opinions regarding spiritually impeccable behavior. We may go kicking and screaming, but we will eventually go into the void.

When we enter the void, we feel changes within us that seem to neutralize all thought, emotion, and movement. The void exists inside of us as well as in the universe. The void begins expanding, mushrooming inside of us at an alarming rate and consuming everything that we place our attention on mentally or emotionally. Every technique that we have ever used to reconnect with our own light, with spirit, and/or with the Creator refuses to work. We can begin to sense that we will never feel energy or find the light again. The tiny anchor that holds a part of our conscious awareness in daily life can question all that we are experiencing and can fear the outcome until those ideas are also consumed by the void. The places inside of us that always held the light and the dark have evaporated. The stars and formless colors of the Dream Weave that we began experiencing on the fifth path's Above Direction have vanished.

If we try to use the intent or focused will that we once mastered in order to transit various realms of consciousness, it fails us. If we initiate the techniques we used to direct our awareness during lucid dreaming, those systems and abilities become nonexistent and the silence is deafening. Static space containing nothingness rambles on forever, and there are no blueprints or lines of energy to follow. There are no anchors or points of perspective that might indicate which direction is up, down, or sideways. We cannot rely on our intuitive feelings or tracking systems to indicate how to pass through the void, because they also have vanished, along with objects, time, emotions, and all senses of perception, into an all-pervading absolute nothingness.

This experience is internal and external. We feel the void in the universe and inside our body. How long it continues depends on the individual's ability to embrace the void and to have it fully present during this sixth-path process. It is unlike any death process that we have ever experienced. In earlier instances of death and rebirth, we could feel the changes as the old melted away and emotions surfaced. Embracing the void brings up none of those symptoms; in fact, there are no symptoms other than eternal nothingness. There is no way to alter the experience. The absence of life force within the nothingness does not include any concept of simply BEING that we ever could have imagined. Serenity of beingness contains feeling without thought and anything that has energy or content is also nonexistent. Eventually we move all the way through the void and come out on the other side.

While this experience is in process it is possible, although difficult, to operate in daily life; the process becomes safer and more comfortable if a person can retreat from chaotic daily activity. Rest and the lack of strenuous physical activity is helpful in the beginning, while later in the process, as the emergence begins, we need to engage in light exercise to restore a sense of life force to the muscles and cells of our bodies. For the most part, when we are inside the void and are aware of it being inside our bodies, we have no sense of energy present that needs to be grounded. Any sense of timing has long since evaporated, and we lose the former ability to apply forbearance.

We are required to be fully aware of the void and the material world simultaneously. That is one reason why the sixth-path tests of discernment just prior to this event are so important. Without those discernment skills fully operating, it is easy for people who have not done their homework to slip into a comatose state or to lose touch with the material world altogether. If a person has authentically owned his or her spiritual authority, he or she will not lose focus or collapse into the nothingness when the former guides, angels, spirit helpers, or the light of God or Great Mystery fails to appear.

THE OTHER WORLDS AND REALMS OF CONSCIOUSNESS

On the other side of this experience, many parallel levels of consciousness that we are operating in while silmultaneously living in the material world become crystal clear, and we have conscious access to those alternate realities *at will*. Yes, many people have had the experience of seeing what they were doing or being on different levels of awareness throughout the former paths of initiation, but those experiences came to them in a random fashion. Mastery as it is developed in the sixth path, is the ability to hone our skills of perception to the degree that we can identify one level of consciousness or one specific reality within the universe and hold that focus and intention accurately and precisely in order to observe all that it contains. These abilities are possible after we have emerged from the void and have passed through the Hunab K'u, the center of this universe. That is not to say that these talents simply emerge; on the contrary, we are required to continue to develop our abilities and the skills to maintain any state of awareness simultaneously and to keep our Earth connection strong.

One of the drawbacks of having experienced these levels of initiation is that it becomes very hard to find others to talk to who understand firsthand the process that has been completed. How can anyone who has not been there understand this step or the next one? The path seems to get lonelier and lonelier when the person who has emerged from the initiation hardly knows how to communicate and must define the undefinable in order to find a common frame of reference.

The person at this level of mastery who sets up court and takes students or devotees, surrounding himself or herself with adoring people, is no more or less enlightened than the lone wolf who chooses to maintain a solitary existence, quietly embracing his or her path, seeing friends and family infrequently. How people choose to interact with other human beings does not determine the level of mastery they have attained or the spiritual authority they have earned the right to use.

At this point in the initiation process, it becomes very easy to let go of any desire to do anything that requires energy or effort. The difficulty at this point, just emerging from the void, is that we detach. It becomes ultimately difficult after embracing nothingness to remain interested in anything that happened earlier on our paths. It can take concerted effort even to recall viewpoints that we once held as true after we have assimilated the infinite perspective's neutrality. We can experience vast distances even between our present understanding and the viewpoints we held when the veil lifted at the beginning of the sixth path. Common ground with others becomes harder to find; if we try to relate what we have experienced, we can feel like babbling idiots. Sometimes it also becomes difficult to relate to other people who don't have a clue what any of the intangible viewpoints contain, and those who think they understand can drain the life force energy that is finally returning to us by asking us to interact with them in ways that we cannot.

RESTRUCTURING "HOW TO FUNCTION"

After all wars and natural disasters, every part of life has to be reconstructed, from the buildings to the economy, from the value systems to the sense of community. Everything that disappeared has to be rebuilt from the ground up. When we emerge from the void, everything must also be reconstructed from the center outward and must contain a continuity that allows all viewpoints of awareness to have equal bearing in our lives and to be equally funded with life force from within our Sacred Spaces. This includes the restructuring of time and timing, solidity and matter, feelings and emotions, boundaries and discernment, the body's cellular consciousness and motor skills, as well as our connections to the Earth and gravity.

Sometimes there is a bizarre feeling that if we become any more different from other human beings, we might just as well have disappeared into the void. Once again, we must reacquaint ourselves with the reason we began the first path of initiation. Being of service to humanity is the core commitment that grounds us to the Earth and to human interaction on the material plane. After we emerge from the void, we can spend quite some time adjusting our multiple perspectives before we begin again, continuing to follow our individual paths. The first lesson of the seventh path occurs when we successfully emerge from the nothingness of the void. At that point, where the sixth- and seventh-path lessons dovetail, we reevaluate what our Spiritual Essences are is asking us to accomplish. We begin to reestablish our purpose, our joy, and our roles in life from a totally new perspective and point of balance.

DON'T GET BENT OUT OF SHAPE IF IT'S NOT YOUR JOB!

The restructuring phase of the sixth path continues into the seventh path and requires discipline, multiple levels of focus, and the return of a new form of desire. We have to wish to move forward instead of attaching ourselves to the static point of nonmovement that we encountered in the void. We can choose to develop one or more of the skills that bend the known laws of physics as long as we realize why we want to do that. If we have chosen to develop these skills, strenuous discipline may be required before we can master these abilities at will. These abilities can include, but are not limited to, telepathy, bilocation, shapeshifting, instantaneous manifestation of matter, levitation, consciously altering time, or complete control over all bodily functions, including the heartbeat. Many people have experienced certain uncontrollable or instantaneous instances of one or more of these talents during the latter parts of the initiation paths. Being able to perform these feats *at will* is another matter altogether, and is NOT required in order to continue onto the seventh path.

When on the third path, some people have made attaining these skills their goal, inadvertently assuming that all "real" spiritual adepts or enlightened masters must demonstrate these skills. Desiring to be held in esteem by others, and in order to show spiritual prowess, some people have claimed to have these abilities when they in fact do not. Those who have worked diligently and have accomplished these skills would never think to comment on their attainment. Those who possess these abilities do not need to talk about them. Everyone who passes through the void and returns does not necessarily develop the same skills. No one is required to focus solely on attaining mastery of these types of gravity-defying talents before experiencing the full force of the seventh path's lessons. Say good-bye to that lie!

No single model reflects "how it is supposed to be" or "what abilities everyone is supposed to have" on any level of initiation. Some people are soul-level healers and tap into layers of awareness within the collective consciousness of humankind, accurately working with those energies. Other people may focus on assisting humankind through bringing forth needed information that will elevate human consciousness. Some teach what they have learned, and others quietly hold the doors of awareness open through prayer or energetic transfers of life force. Other humans pass through these levels of initiation and live quiet lifestyles where no one ever suspects the level of mastery they have attained.

Everyone at this point in the initiation process uses his or her gifts in different ways, and all are individually guided by an inner knowing that assures a uniqueness of purpose within the Great Mystery's divine plan. The only purpose of being able to levitate or to physically manifest wondrous miracles for the masses is to teach humankind that those things are possible in the material world, and that role does not belong to everyone. The intent is to show through example, not to show off or lord one's abilities over others. Spiritual actualization or enlightenment is not determined by the power or prowess connected to the attainment of these extraordinary abilities.

An enlightenment trap can show up for some sixth-path people at this stage of development if they have not gone through the void and they still believe that they must reach their self-determined goals of psychic prowess. Often people who have been gifted since childhood are so invested in their extrasensory antennae that they feel the continued development of their personal psychic prowess is necessary to attain the next levels of transformation. This trap manifests when people are unaware that they are limiting their perceptions by constantly having to verbalize or state them in regard to the paths that others are following, creating a view of another person's reality that can be misguided if the person they are trying to read has already gone beyond the lessons of the sixth path. A sixth-path person may verbalize his or her psychic assessment of another person who has passed through the void. In such an evaluation, thought forms are produced that must be diffused if the recipient has already gone beyond that level of experience, so the former condition presented by another's judgment is not recreated in the present moment.

Another enlightenment trap can occur when anyone strictly adheres to a schematic of the layers of consciousness in the universe that was created by people who lived in past decades. This use of ancient systems can create tunnel vision if the systems are too specific with regard to what is possible. The evolving levels of awareness in Creation cannot be viewed properly if thought forms and labels have limited the divine potential and the constant evolution of consciousness within the Great Mystery. Since 1987 the massive expansion in spiritual, human consciousness has destroyed many former spiritual belief systems that were held as truths at the beginning of the twentieth century. If we hold onto our former identities and beliefs in the inability of others to see for themselves, we can stand suspended at the edge of the void for a long time. After experiencing the void, we can become ill if we continue to hold onto any mechanisms or beliefs that limit our expanding consciousness or the potential of the collective by pigeonholing every possibility or by not allowing others to know what is true for them.

Each individual path will continue to change and will develop new opportunities for growth. Human beings who have made it through the void and have returned from the heart of the universe have become flexible enough to bend the known laws of physics simply by holding the infinite, neutral viewpoint. They can accurately identify points of consciousness and tap into the life force within the universe without having to verbalize it or label the processes of others. That ability alone makes individuals stand with the personal spiritual authority that comes from authentically BEING.

In reviewing the sixth path I would like to address some of the symptoms that can appear when the remnants of the final veil are lifted. We can encounter physical symptoms including temporary blindness, flashes of color that alter our ability to perceive the material world, the loss of solidity within physical objects, and the transference of energetic patterns onto anything we see in the material world. The effort it takes to hold the viewpoint of solidity while we operate in daily life can create unbelievable exhaustion until the skill is mastered. It becomes a balancing act to correctly use the life force we have available to hold the material world in place and still feed our bodies with enough energy to maintain health. We master another level in the lesson of appropriating life force when we use part of our personal life force to discern all that we encounter and another flow of life force to stabilize the neutral, unbiased viewpoint, the infinite viewpoint of the overview, and the human, Earth-connected viewpoint.

COYOTE SIDETRACKS AND POTHOLES

I have already given some examples of pop quizzes we encounter when we begin to hold the neutral, unbiased viewpoint while continuing to explore intangible universal consciousness. Some seductions or dead ends can appear also during the third and fourth parts of the sixth path. I have personally encountered certain enlightenment traps and coyote lessons that appear after emerging from the void of Hunab K'u or the heart of our universe. One, which I have mentioned already, is the lack of desire to do anything. Sometimes we can remain in a rather suspended state where any type of structure or routine becomes threatening. It can seem as if we are in neutral and the body we are trying to operate will not get into gear even if the throttle is fully open. With the lack of desire still present, it can become necessary to jump-start our lives so we can find something that excites us enough to shift gears and move forward.

Another pop quiz that can be encountered after emerging from the void is the tendency to align with the life processes of others whom we care about. When you have an affinity for someone, it becomes easy to slip into that person's energy field without noticing. You understand what that person is experiencing, because you have been there at one time, so it is crucial to be aware of what belongs to you and what belongs to another. By the end of the sixth path, we have become so used to holding multiple points of view simultaneously that we can inadvertently add another viewpoint belonging to someone else. When we begin to reprocess life using a perspective that we embodied long ago, it's time to watch out and to redefine our emotional and energetic boundaries and use acute discernment to keep from collapsing time. We must avoid combining the experiences that belong to someone else's present situation with our past experiences in order to maintain an accurate assessment of where we are personally at this time in our own process.

Another coyote snare is the failure to recognize when we have actually cleared the void and are once again encountering the movement of energy contained in the universe and the material world. If we have fully assimilated the nothingness of the Hunab K'u and do not begin to define the energy we encounter in life, we can take it on or become it instead of simply viewing it. If we have not reconstructed our discernment and boundaries, we take on a world of dissimilar viewpoints, intentions, energy, and identities by collapsing them into our Sacred Spaces. If this occurs, we are in trouble, for our bodies can lose the ability to digest life force. If we have unwittingly assimilated energetic life force that belongs to another species, spiritual being, and/or person we feel close to, we often experience a loss of appetite or difficulty in breathing.

We may find also that we can unwittingly assimilate the consciousness of other life forms. If those life forms are red-blooded animals, which contain the same elements as the human body, we may not have too much of a problem, but if we energetically assimilate energy from trees, rocks, other planets, stars, and other life forms that do not work in harmony with the systems of the human body, we put our health at risk. We are ultimately responsible for untangling those webs of energy that belong to other life forms in order to regain our sense of individuation. When we individuate, we still remain connected to all energy and consciousness, but we are able to differentiate between the various kinds of life force and to prevent the ones that operate in opposing fashions from entering our physical bodies. It is kind of like saying that we cannot run a Ford truck with a Toyota engine. The skill of differentiating illustrates another aspect of the wisdom contained in the ancient Native American saying, "Walk gently on the Earth."

For example, at this level of initiation it is possible to exchange the atoms or particles of energy contained in stone with the atoms of the human body. We can experience the intangible life force of any object by remote viewing and by using energetic perceptions while simultaneously seeing it physically. If we were to become ungrounded and could not hold both the material and the intangible perspectives from a detached or neutral viewpoint, we could inadvertently assimilate the inert energy contained in solid stone, and our bodies could suffer tremendously. It is necessary to be fully present and to use acute discernment in order not to assimilate or actualize the energy and consciousness that do not belong inside of our physical bodies.

The seventh-path lessons begin to unfold when we return from the heart of our universe, the void of nothingness, and can reenter the world with all of our various perceptions altered but fully intact. We function once again on many levels of awareness, but with a new overview that shifts our sense of what is possible and what no longer has any importance or validity. The majority of the work of the seventh path usually cannot be approached until we have reconnected and realigned with our purpose for BEING. That new alignment can be achieved only from the perspective that we choose to embody when we reach the other side of the Hunab K'u and ground ourselves to the Earth Mother once again.

My personal experience on the sixth path took seventeen and a half years. That is not to say that it will take others as long as it has taken me. Many of the initiation experiences come easier today than they did eighteen years ago because of the lowering of the Earth's magnetism and the increased electrical cycles per second, or hertz. The electromagnetic systems of the human body are responding to the shift in the Earth Mother's electromagnetic energy system. We are experiencing 9 to 9.9 hertz in 1997, and it will increase to 13 hertz by the year 2012. Many people have now blazed the trails into the Hunab K'u and have returned, allowing others to find and follow these paths.

THE CRYSTAL SKULLS AND DREAMING THE RAINBOW DREAM

The potential that exists for human beings to become fully conscious and clear is represented by the original thirteen crystal skulls that were given to the people of Earth by another culture that came from beyond the stars. The Mayans called these people the "Sky Gods." The thirteen crystal skulls contain a metaphoric message that reflects the thirteen hertz that will be experienced by everyone on Earth in the year 2012. Along with the lowering of the magnetic field of the planet, the higher electrical waves of the thirteen hertz will shift the collective consciousness of humankind to a new level of awareness, which will contain all the understandings acquired by experiencing every lesson on all seven paths of initiation. The assimilation of these understandings will create the actual manifestation of the Whirling Rainbow Dream of world peace.

CHAPTER 9

*To become fully conscious we must outwit deception and sur-
mount every veil of separation, destroying all illusions of inequality. When that is achieved, every spark of life within
Creation awakens inside the human body, and we literally
dance the dream alive.*

—Joaquin Muriel Espinosa

▲▲

THE EVER-PRESENT PATH

There within the starry heavens,
Lies the potential of all that can BE,
Hidden from view in the natural world,
When our human eyes could not see.

Yet, the ever-present present
Stands in the spirit's Sacred Space,
An infinite gift from the Creator
To the Earth Mother's human race.

When we journey into the NOW,
We dance the dream once more,
Around the heart-fire of Creation
Allowing all sparks of life to soar.

The awakening dream embodies
Our earthly human forms,
And within the sacred pattern,
A conscious universe transforms.

—Jamie Sams

The Seventh Path of Initiation
The Within Direction or the NOW Direction
on the Medicine Wheel

MY Cherokee and Seneca Ancestors called the seventh direction on the Medicine Wheel by two different names. In the Seneca tradition the seventh direction is called the Within Direction, and the Cherokees call it the NOW Direction. Both names are applicable and describe two of the seventh path's characteristic aspects. The Seneca viewpoint is that we must bring all that we have learned into our innermost being and walk the wisdom of all directions in our physical bodies. From the Cherokee viewpoint, the NOW is also bringing wisdom found on all paths into the body and being fully present, walking with that beauty moment by moment. We have the ability to slip into past and future *at* will on the seventh path, and being fully present takes on a whole new level of importance when we embrace the ever-present present of the NOW Direction.

When we are fully present, we become the sum total of all the strengths found in our family trees, and we have surmounted the weaknesses found in the past seven generations. When we are in balance, we become the focal point of all that is possible in the future because we are relating to all that is present in the NOW. We open the paths of consciousness for the next seven generations to follow. Time flows through us, but we are not subject to its passing because we have embraced the infinite aspects of humanity and are living extensions of the Eternal Flame of Love. We respect the life force and sparks of awareness found in everything in Creation, allowing ourselves to BE an integral part of the whole.

The Southern Seers have a slightly different perspective, teaching that on the seventh path we becoming living extensions of the Fire of Creation. Every spark of life inside every atom that exists within the universe is acknowledged as being connected to the human body and living inside the immortal consciousness of our Spiritual Essences. As we come into our seventh-path lessons, we can experience the aliveness of every cell in the body and the consciousness of our Spiritual Essences fully embracing the biological part of our human makeup. The most dense part of the human being is the physical form, the flesh-and-blood body. This sacred vessel holding the human spirit is activated in an astonishing way as we walk our seventh-path lessons.

By the time we reach the seventh path, we are fully aware that these intangible parts of the human makeup contain energy. Those energetic parts of humanity contain sparks of the Great Fire of Creation, which is the creative life force of the Great Mystery. Once activated, those sparks of life become living beacons that send and receive life force energy, connecting to all other life forms and creating a living, breathing web of life. The intangible descends and is omnipresent in the tangible cellular structure inside the human body. When we achieve this new Sacred Point of View, the Medicine Blanket of solid physicality comes alive. The patterns of the Medicine Blanket, which once were seemingly still or solid, begin to move and shift. Every living thing or physical object that we see appears to be floating in layers of patterns and colors, making all that we view seem to move or breathe with aliveness.

Some people begin to glimpse these patterns when they allow their imaginations to see the forms or faces in tree knots or a stone they pulled from a brook. On earlier paths this ability is developed when we slightly change our perception and allow the spirits of nature to bring the spark of life and the patterns within solid objects into our perceptions. Other people have experienced these moving patterns when in altered states and/or meditation. Many cultures have used sacred plants during ceremony to briefly remove the veils between human beings and the Medicine Blanket. The Medicine Blanket covers all life and is composed of the changing patterns or moving particles of energy contained within the solid objects of physical reality. Some people who have had extrasensory gifts since childhood will notice a slight difference in the colors of the energy surrounding objects and a new intensity to the spectrum of colors. The Medicine Blanket of life's energetic patterns forms the solidity of daily life, and at this level of experience, we see not only the translucent patterns of energy but also energy flowing through the molecules in solid matter and interacting with other life forms. Sometimes seventh-path people must also learn how to make things solid again so they do not become accident prone, bumping into objects that they can see through.

YOU CAN'T TAKE IT WITH YOU— EXCEPT IN SYMBOL FORM

When I began my seventh-path lessons, I was presented with a dream that I did not understand fully for years. In the dream I was flying. I looked down at my body, and it had become the body of an owl. I flew through the first of seven Mayan arches covered with symbology in the form of ancient Mayan stele. I could not see the encrypted messages except in symbol form. I cleared the first arch and flew directly into a small sun and through it. The sun exploded into a rainbow of whirling light and, like fireworks, sent rainbow lights raining into the sky. The second arch contained more carved symbols. After clearing that arch I flew through another small sun that exploded into a whirling rainbow. This process continued until I cleared the seventh arch. The last sun I flew into was much larger, and my owl body was set afire, becoming a phoenix. At that moment I became the flames and then ashes. The ashes dissolved and became a glorious rainbow of light, which sent beams of majestic, radiant colors back through the arches I had flown through. The beams of color descended like a liquid rainbow of light, covering the Earth. Our beautiful planet began to shake, and then a Whirling Rainbow emerged at both poles, flooding rainbows of light back into the universe, spreading in all directions as the Earth Mother turned on her axis while orbiting the sun.

Upon reflection, I understood the dream's message that I had moved beyond the veils of separation and was beginning to embrace some of the lessons of the seventh path. I had been required to use Owl's Medicine of discernment and wisdom at each rite of passage along the way in order to pass through the Mayan arches containing the symbols of all that must be understood. I realized that the symbols we take with us through all initiations are encoded molecules found in the double helix of the DNA, which changes when the context of the bio-logical, emotion, intellectual, and spiritual aspects of human potential evolve. The symbols were geometric forms resembling crop circles or petroglyph designs and were the result of the DNA being changed through the rewiring processes at each gate of awareness. I was given a glimpse of the future in that dream, and I was shown that the encoded messages of geometric molecules that are connected to human brain synapses and DNA will one day be discovered by scientists. A map of developing human consciousness will be made available to humankind.

In the dream, I was given further clarity at each sun and was shown one level of wholeness, symbolized by all the colors of the rainbow. When my body became the phoenix and then ashes, all that I had believed myself to be was destroyed and my Spiritual Essence emerged, radiating the multicolored aspects of my awareness back through the Mayan arches and into my own physical body, extending to all life on our beautiful planet. There was no longer a separation between my body, my spirit, other life forms, my consciousness, the universe, the Great Mystery, and the Earth Mother. The dream and that personal rite of passage took place in March of 1989, and the intricate understandings and subtle nuances continue to unfold today as I watch former understandings being reflected back in the beauty of other people's transformational processes.

The seventh path contains many levels and layers, which are revealed step by step as we walk with acute awareness, using the multi-layered perceptions that we have developed and applying them in daily life. There is a point on this path where our former ultrasensitivity must be balanced through reintegration into the cellular consciousness of the body. This process begins when a person has successfully cleared the void, the heart of the Great Mystery, the center of our universe, and is required to return to actively using the human form as the antenna receiving all signals of universal consciousness. This process makes the body equally important to the spiritual aspects of being. I would like to address the steps that I have discovered on my journey, one by one, so that the overview can be seen by each reader, who will experience his or her own steps in a myriad of individual ways.

DEVOID AFTER THE VOID?

After returning from the void, it becomes necessary to restructure our Sacred Points of View once more and to reconnect to desire. For instance, if we have fully assimilated the void, we may need to recreate the desire to live, the desire to have companionship, the desire to create, sexual desire, and the desire to reconnect with our purpose for being. The vast nothingness of the Hunab K'u can eliminate all the mechanisms connected to "doing" and create such a serene state of "being" that it can take great effort to turn and face the challenge of reconnecting to our spiritual purpose for walking the Earth. There is an illusion of being complete, and it becomes very difficult for some people to acknowledge that the work is just now beginning. What is this work? Being fully present and reclaiming all the levels of awareness that one has attained by bringing unlimited consciousness into the cellular structure of the physical body. We begin to reactivate the body's 357 sensory perceptions within the cellular memory, grounding the awareness to the physical form and the body to the Earth. So much energy is flowing through the body that we must continually use movement and exercise to maintain the flows of life force and keep the energy connecting to the Earth and circulating in a fluid manner.

After we restructure our purpose for being, we must develop the skill of shifting the balance of our attention to different layers of our perceptions at will. That is to say, we are required to hold a solid view of daily life in order to remain effective in the physical world. We can also choose to learn how to shift our attention at will to the energetic realms and to the energy connected to thoughts. When we develop these skills we must also use precision to be able to discern instantly the intent and agendas in any situation where many energies and levels of awareness are present. One of the avoidance mechanisms that some seventh-path people encounter is that in the beginning, holding all of these viewpoints can be very tiring, and some people choose to focus on one area and scan others without remaining fully present and vigilant. Every time this occurs, the pop quizzes begin to issue wake-up calls.

For example, we can be tested on all of our former lessons from earlier paths the moment we let our attention wander or become too relaxed. It can come as a huge shock to find that we have been misled by another person when we were focusing on being spiritually compassionate. In not observing the obvious in a given situation, or not speaking up or maintaining proper boundaries, we can become too good-hearted and be drawn unwittingly into unpleasant situations. We must remember to stay fully grounded and walk our talk in daily life, keeping our perceptions of the intangible available but not senior to our attention on being in the NOW physically. The inability to change focus instantly from one to the other can be disastrous if our attention is needed in a life-threatening situation or an actual medical emergency.

Although we attain more of the abilities of being fully present as we undergo our seven levels of transformation, each level requires that we find balance while we are in process. The skill of finding balance is often overlooked by people who have bought into the illusion that they have finally made it to the goal. *The seventh path is not the goal.* Living physical life with boundless grace, heightened awareness, grounded presence, and compassion while continuing to evolve and serve is one choice that is being offered. Individual decisions vary; even at this stage of development there are detours and enlightenment traps, which have seduced many a traveler.

ANCHORING LIFE WITH SIMPLICITY AND WISDOM

Relating to others at their levels of understanding, rather than assuming that all have also done their inner work and have impeccable integrity, will keep Coyote at bay. We must also embrace compassion toward others who are learning their lessons and show mercy when they are insensitive or merely out of touch with the present. My impatience with others and my lack of mercy toward myself has been a major issue for me during the seventh path. A friend who spoke with me about these issues reminded me that compassion and inner peace are found and accumulated over time. Just like our earlier-path lessons, the grace and patience that we choose to embody on the seventh path is learned through experience. Our compassion for ourselves and for others is one way that we learn to invest our life force in order to collect the benefits of unswerving compassion and inner peace. We can see that in order to maintain balance, walking our talk can involve a whole new set of disciplines that require boundless energy, grounding, compassion, focused intent, and mercy toward the self and others.

The amount of exploring that one has achieved in the intangible realms is only as valuable as it can be applied appropriately to daily life. Mastery at this level requires us to hold a certain amount of our attention on any tangible or intangible part of the universe that we want to access. This balancing act holds two major challenges. One is that if we fully surrendered to the nothingness of the void, we have authentically let go of any desire to focus on anything, much less the desire to hold several differing focal points at once. The desire to focus on anything at all must be reconstructed, from our new Sacred Points of View, along with every other part of our lives that still has any meaning, importance, or validity. Finding enough anchor points to continue living on the physical plane can be difficult. Some people remove themselves from daily life and live a hermitlike existence at this stage of transformation because they do not see the rite of passage at hand. To continue to interact with the world and to own the desire to be of service is a tough choice, requiring ultimate courage and commitment.

The second challenge occurs when we begin to feel the massive amount of life force available to us begin to return, thundering through the physical body. The task at hand is how to appropriate this monumental amount of energy and maintain connection to the Earth and to all other levels of awareness simultaneously. We learn how much focus we must appropriate to various areas of our lives and how much of our attention is required in each area in order to achieve harmony. If you remember the earlier example of the circus performer who was successfully spinning many plates on top of sticks, now imagine that the former skills and balancing acts must be completely relearned because those abilities were surrendered with everything else and every other learned response while transiting the journey through the void.

Unlike the ascension process, which led us to the Above direction and then led us to connect the Above with the Below, the third challenge is the descension process. As we descend, we must pass through all former levels of awareness or unconsciousness, along with every issue we have ever faced, without absorbing those behaviors again. Like a mammoth review pop quiz, life reflects all emotions, fixed ideas, and behaviors back to us, mirroring every facet of our journey through the actions of others. As our energy continues to recycle through all layers of consciousness and into the body, through the Earth and back up through the body, we get to experience all of the forces within us that were once at odds with one another. The review pop quizzes begin when we must reestablish our personal inner peace without grabbing onto any layer of former issues in the processes of descending and reconnecting.

Once again we are reminded that everything that has ever existed in any location is still there. What a shock! It applies to us as well because we have authentically banished time; every issue we have ever faced and conquered in life can be present in the NOW. We can learn how to focus on the present moment by acknowledging all that we have surmounted in the past and fully grounding the body so that we do not drift into our own past experiences or personal history. The realization that all of our prior wounds and issues still exist in our consciousness in other layers of time is a real challenge, forcing us to be fully present at every moment unless we want to reexperience unwittingly all that has gone before. Reconstructing a way to view time in the physical realm can help to keep us from duplicating or embodying our past issues when faced with other people who are learning our former lessons.

COYOTE'S PROJECTION GAME

When our energy finally returns after we emerge from the void, if we react when confronted by a situation that pushes our buttons, it will come as a complete shock to find our emotions suddenly resurfacing. Then we need to determine how to feel them and let them go creatively. This is one part of the descension process of walking our personal Medicine in the Temple of the City. Such a challenge reminds us that we are still very human and that none of what we have experienced means a dang thing if we cannot handle life while standing in the direct line of fire. Ouch! This is another instance where mercy toward the self becomes necessary. The seventh path is a process of reaching a state of grace, and if we are hard on ourselves because we are not yet walking on water, the ensuing lessons can humble us until we learn to love ourselves as unconditionally as we love others.

One of the challenges likely will be well-intentioned advice that comes from others who are clueless but who believe they understand what is really happening in our lives. Welcome to Coyote's projection game; it's all done with mirrors, and all reflections are equal. If we haven't been there and done that, we will at some point in time. And if we have been there and don't want to do it again, we had better use our personal authority to stay grounded in the NOW! Using a little humor makes the process easier to deal with; we then can deflect the projections without making judgments.

We could effectively be sucked right back into the dregs of human frailties and confusion if we do not reestablish our balance in a gentle way when we emerge from the void. Things can get pretty hairy if we have totally surrendered to the nothingness of the void and have emerged feeling like we embody a black hole. The black hole of nothingness that we have assimilated vacuums up the universe and all consciousness while we are sorting out how to funnel it into our human body and to then restructure everything from the center outward, rediscovering some kind of new multifaceted personal identity. When we are clueless about how to BE and how to still be able to create the desire to continue in our life's process, the restructuring process can confound us totally.

EXPLORING THE COSMIC ASPECTS OF THE BODY

By refunneling life force through our bodies and by using that energy on the physical plane, we activate the sparks of life within the cellular structure of the physical form. The map of the universe emerges inside the body, and all consciousness on all levels of awareness begins to respond the moment we place our attention on any given thing. The catch is that we must focus on the NOW, tapping into the present moment, not the past or future. The ability to find anything that we choose in the universe, instantly locating it within our consciousness and connecting that awareness inside the physical body's cellular structure, is the culmination of the earthing or grounding process. Being fully grounded and authentically present takes on a whole new meaning at this stage. We can, for instance, perceive the strands of muscle tissue breaking and retwining while we exercise, and we feel every current of energy moving through or getting stuck in various areas of our bodies. When we can do this, we have become fully grounded and acutely aware of the cellular structure of the body and the vast spiritual consciousness that is taking hold within. Every cell within the skin appears to move and form patterns, like symbols or maps, showing various layers of the universe or parts of the Earth Mother where the doorways are physically open to other dimensions. Surprising as it may seem, these paranormal abilities can be accessed easily when we are fully grounded.

In time, we realize that the universes of consciousness within every cell of the body can be as fun to discover as all the layers of awareness contained in the universe. Then we learn to monitor the energy flows

in the organs and cells, and we begin to understand certain regenera-
tion processes that are not yet acknowledged by science. We can perceive the radiant patterns of energy coming into the body and see how
they are recycled through the Earth. Those connected points of awareness offer us a totally new spectrum of colors. We notice that the light
spectrum in the physical world ranges in color range from magenta to
chartreuse green, while the new spectrum begins with an apricot yel-
low and flows through a vivid turquoise that is unlike any blue-green
that we have ever experienced visually. By following the patterns, colors, and feelings, we can monitor energy within the Earth and see how
it affects the human heart. We can watch how the body responds to energy, noticing how molecular energy gets stuck in our cells when we
lose focus or balance or when we do not move it through exercise. We
can become acutely aware of how negative thoughts and judgments
impinge on the cellular structure of our bodies, to the point of creating
renegade or degenerative cells if we allow the negativity to affect us.
When we develop the skill of fully using the cellular consciousness and
antennae of awareness inside the body, we have reintegrated our Spiritual Essences into the physical form.

At this point in development, the various shifts in the Earth's energy
can be felt as easily as our own emotions, but we must develop the
skills of individuation to keep a clear overview. When there is a volcanic eruption in the Caribbean, we may experience a disruption in the
life force flowing through our body. We may perceive it as a ripple in
the flow of energy that we feel physically or emotionally. Awareness of
the subtleties of the various energies are developed skills, like anything
else. The seventh-path person may choose to focus on becoming that
physically sensitive or may choose to hold the position of detachment,
remotely viewing the place where the energy is felt but not allowing it
to disrupt the body's harmony. We eventually learn to accept these abilities and bodily sensations because they are merely a part of BEING.
What does BEING mean on the seventh path? BEING is embracing consciousness, all life forms, all sparks of life, all levels of awareness, and
physically feeling it inside of one's own body. There is no separation
because we have intimately embraced BEING an interrelated, fully present point-of-awareness within the whole of Creation.

Although many people have experienced brief glimpses of these
geologically sensitive or physically prophetic abilities on earlier paths,
the passage through the void erases the need to cling to these talents as

part of our spiritual identities. If we wish to use these talents because they apply directly to our spiritual roles, we can choose to reclaim them. When we successfully go through the void and emerge, any former illusions of needing to accomplish certain psychic feats or become the all-knowing oracle completely vanish if these gifts do not contribute to our authentic spiritual purpose. Coyote laughingly reminds us that if our Spiritual Essences did not sign up for the mission of showing humankind that these abilities were possible for all human beings, we learn to personally observe these talents as equal to knowing how to change a flat tire on our car.

NO MORE INEQUALITY!

I was shown how the ideas of inequality can meld into oneness through a dream I had in 1989. I was told that there would be no more red and no more purple. I asked what that meant because I did not understand. I was shown that the rainbow is seen as a flat ribbon in the sky with red at the bottom and purple at the top. Human beings have regarded the physical realm as being red like the blood of life and the spiritual aspects of our nature as being like the lilac or purple at the top of the rainbow. In the first through fourth paths, when the desire to spiritually evolve begins to emerge, some people adopt the judgmental ideas that spirituality is desirable and, therefore, that physicality is not as important as spirituality.

On the seventh path, the culmination of the merging of body and spirit brings us full circle. In this transformational process, we see beyond the two-dimensional view of the rainbow. It is not a flat ribbon at all but a three-dimensional hoop, its bottom red edge connected to the top purple edge in a circle that signifies the whirling rainbow, the symbol of the Native American Whirling Rainbow prophecy of world peace. The red and purple merge and become the color magenta, which is the metaphorical marriage of heaven and earth, the spiritual and the physical as equal parts of BEING. When unity is achieved inside each human being, there is no longer any room for separation in thought, in feeling, in deed, or in actualizing our BEINGNESS. We bring that eternal beingness into our human forms, and we begin to achieve the understandings of the Within Direction. Using our gifts of forbearance, without waiting or pushing, we embrace the path and our personal processes moment by moment. The initiation process, which brought full understanding of the NOW Direction, has allowed us to appreciate the value of the skills we have developed and how those skills serve us when we use them with precision.

THE TRACKS OF TIME
AND BEING HERE NOW

The oneness that becomes a stable state of BEING after we emerge from the void and fully reconnect the body to universal consciousness allows the human body to become an antenna for universal energy. The body becomes an activated point of awareness standing in wholeness, connected to the Earth and funneling universal energy into all other parts of Creation. We also stand at the center of the crossroads, where time, all of life's experiences, and sentient feeling can move through us effortlessly if we pay attention. We can choose to tap into the past and the future from a point of balance that sees time as an illusion. We have learned that time merely allows physical humans to move through experiences and process them in increments. Since we have assimilated the eternal viewpoint, we view the passage of time in a far more expansive manner. From the seventh path's infinite viewpoint, we can see all that our spirits have experienced, and we realize that our present life is no more than a brief flash within eternity. Although we glimpsed this perception on the fourth through sixth paths, we find it actualizing within the body at this level of the dance. We can also choose to experience multiple realities and time periods, honing our grounding skills. These perceptions allow us to have multiple views of historic scenarios and present events simultaneously.

During these seventh-path lessons it is also possible to realize that from certain viewpoints in the future, our spirits are able to look back upon what we are doing in the NOW and to influence us by showing us all the possibilities available in what we consider to be the present moment. These discoveries regarding the absence of time can begin on the fifth and sixth paths, and we are allowed to explore the possibilities for our human evolution. Those future selves, the more evolved aspects of our future identities, can communicate needed information or offer guidance as easily as the angelic presences or spirits that guided us on the earlier paths. We eventually learn how to remain grounded in the

NOW, authentically trusting all potentials that the future may hold. There is no need to swing with time's pendulum into projecting future events or to dig into our past lives, because all of time exists in the NOW. The desire to see around life's next corner probably vanished when we emerged from the void. All that concerns us now is the actuality of the present moment.

RELAX? DON'T COUNT ON IT! IT'S ALL DONE WITH MIRRORS!

For me, one of the toughest parts of the seventh path was learning to become the clear lake once more, from a totally different perspective. We discussed the clear lake earlier, in relation to the fifth path, as the process of learning to allow all our thoughts and feelings and the words of others to pass through us with ease. It is common for fourth-through sixth-path people, who have developed a certainty of their perceptions, to assume they know what others are experiencing. In some cases, the people being labeled or pigeonholed have far surpassed the experiences of the people judging them. Ultimate patience is required every time we are faced with such a situation on the seventh path. In reflecting another person's viewpoint back to them, we must be so fully present that we authentically discern the level that a person is operating on without becoming the reflection itself. At times like this, we test ourselves on our ability to respond with grace. Seventh-path pop quizzes come in many forms and ultimately require the impeccable and appropriate use of all the skills we have mastered.

One form of enlightenment trap occurs when a seventh-path person, who has just emerged from the void, falls into taking on the judgments of someone who needs to be the enlightened authority or the oracle. Unless a person has passed through the void, it is impossible to see inside of it or beyond the nothingness to the other side. A seventh-path person who has recently emerged from the void experiences so much "free space" and uncertainty that other people's projections of what is "really happening" can be unwittingly assimilated, because the grounding stability of the multifaceted Sacred Point of View has not yet actualized.

The seventh-path person who has fully transited the void and has restabilized has experienced the total erasure of attachment to spiritual feats and psychic perceptions as badges of spiritual accomplishment. That person has replaced the lack of boundaries, which were released inside the void, with a strong grounded awareness that is equipped with mirrorlike deflection mechanisms. When we reestablish our certainty, we usually can deflect any misdirected words of wisdom from earlier-path people. Frankly, unless a stabilized seventh-path person's boundaries are being actively stomped on, he or she doesn't give a hoot about someone else's behavior; it is viewed simply as what is happening with another person at the moment. In order to maintain the qualities of grace, inner peace, and balance, we need to apply mercy and compassion to the self and to others.

The unbiased reflection of the clear lake is simply a mirror. The seventh-path lessons required in order to become that illusion-free mirror are tough ones. It is very easy to slip into another person's shoes because we are BEING the mirror that reflects all patterns in the Medicine Blanket of physical life. As with all earlier paths, we must be careful not to assume the attitudes and energy of others around us but rather, maintain our personal clarity, individuation, and a loving attitude.

There are times when we simply reflect back to others the level they are personally involved with so they can feel at home with us. This ability requires that we balance our sensitivity and perceptions of the intangible realms with our astute focus, observing the obvious in any situation. We are reminded to accept others wherever they are in the human maturation process. It is inappropriate to give unrequested advice or to be patronizing when we impart information that was requested. One of the most effective mirrors we can learn to use is listening and asking pertinent questions, which allow others to come up with their own truths. The art of mirroring all that is present takes a great deal of skill and is not possible unless we are fully present. We are asked to be aware of other people's situations or dilemmas, to be compassionately interested, and to remain authentically connected to the Earth.

Turmoil or high drama can throw a seventh-path person off balance and wreak havoc as easily as with a third-path person. It may take more chaos to unseat the balance of a seventh-path person, but everyone must learn how to remain continually balanced in those instances where life plays hardball with our serenity. If we briefly get attached to an emotional situation, our clarity is compromised. If we become ungrounded, even for a moment, the observations we perceive can become tainted. If we lose our sense of individuation, we can unwittingly take on the energy of others or regress into behaviors that were healed long ago. Knowing how to surf the waves that collapse time is an art.

ALLOWING OTHERS TO EXPERIENCE THEIR PROCESS

We are required to use unbelievable forbearance to allow others to go through their own process of discovery and not crush their illusions for them. When others are sure that their present experience is the ultimate disaster in the universe and that no one will understand, watch out! The person going through high drama will be able to see only the cosmic importance of his or her personal needs and immediate desires. Just being near that person can drain the energy from anyone who is unaware of the vacuum mechanisms that are present. High drama experiences can create a whirlpool vacuum that draws the observer's life force into the needy energy field of the person in crisis. For seventh-path people who are not being fully attentive, the results can be devastating, recreating the destabilizing effects we experienced when we emerged from the void.

We may have let our attention slip momentarily because we are acclimating to simply BEING. During this period of time on the seventh path, we experience a lull in the paranormal activity that seemed to hound us through the earlier paths. Just before entering the void and during that process, it seemed that no more "exciting stuff" was happening and no earth-shattering revelations gave us an adrenaline rush. After we return from the void and have finally gotten reacclimated to life, there is a rest period of sorts where we are given review pop quizzes. We are tested on all the earlier skills that we surrendered during the passage through the nothingness in the heart of the universe. It can be a total drag to realize that we must also rehone skills that at one time were second nature. If we are not vigilant, it is easy to get lazy and to slip into the habits, dreamspace, or lessons of others with whom we share our lives simply because we have relinquished most of our personal sense of self.

No matter what we have experienced on the seven paths, the challenge of being compassionate amid the uncertainty of emerging from the void remains the focal point. The doubts that can occur at this stage of the seventh path can be debilitating if we give them the use of our life force. We are reminded that we have come full circle and that we are beginning again with a vast amount of wisdom under our belts. The task we face is in *appropriately applying* all that wisdom moment by moment. By using that ability with precision, we remain fully in the NOW. The key to reemerging with grace lies in maintaining a flexible form of balance in the Temple of the City, or modern life, and being very gentle with ourselves. This is not the time to be surrounded by a three-ring circus of high drama and people who are bouncing off the walls. The balance that comes from increasing our interaction with life and others gradually is highly advisable.

DO YOU REALLY WANT TO DO IT THE HARD WAY?

When I was trying to restructure my life after emerging from the void, I was raw and wide open. I had remained at home without seeing anyone except five close friends for half a year, and still I was not ready to reenter the hustle and bustle of the Temple of the City. Suddenly life screamed, "Lights, camera, action," and the Temple of the City came to me. I was stalked and my life was threatened, and when I regained my balance from that set of events, I was thrown into another situation that knocked me to my knees. An old friend called and asked me to meet with some people I did not know. I was suddenly surrounded with people and situations that mirrored every type of high drama imaginable, complete with the smoke-and-mirrors games.

As usual, I did it the hard way. I tried to emerge from the void in the midst of this chaotic hullabaloo that had found its way to my doorstep. I crashed and burned in a big way. Coyote has laughingly given me worst-case scenarios in most of my life lessons to allow me learn how to surf the *really* big waves. I may wipe out a few times in a row, but I always seem to keep on surfing. At least I can laugh about it. I had to learn to find the humor because Coyote is one of my main power animals. Coyote is the Medicine that determines how I experience life and how I learn and grow. I am finally understanding that I don't have to apologize about how life happens for me, and I don't need to explain the crazy antics of my *shock and flow* dance to anyone.

GEE, DID 1 FORGET THE PUNCH LINE?

It is the ultimate cosmic joke when we realize that we have come full circle and we see our entire journey as equal to the journeys of others who danced it differently, equal even to the lives of people who never embraced these paths at all. I finally realized that my entire journey was equivalent to a cosmic soap opera. Dang it all! Coyote sure can dish out the hilarious lessons that allow us to see our individual dances with the long view, and through the equalizing lens of an infinite spotlight. The realization of coming full circle can make us wonder whether to laugh or cry. From personal experience, I highly recommend laughing till your sides ache!

Yes, the journey was grand, we learned a lot, and we can tap into the energy, life force, and consciousness of rocks, animals, other human beings, stars, planets, other life forms, spirits, angels, duality and oneness, and solidity and intangibility. Is that what BEING means? Can we be fully present and walk it here? Can we honor the spirit housed in the body of a hopeless wino lying in the gutter as equal to our own? Yes, especially when we know from the infinite viewpoint that he or she may one day be a messiah of some world that is yet to be discovered in our universe. This unlimited facet of BEING contains the art of ultimate compassion and the authentic embodiment of timeless equality. The eternal viewpoint is in the ever-present present, and it is the Great Mystery's gift to humans who are in the process of BEING. The beauty is that the process of spiritual evolution is as infinite as the spirit.

When we can authentically banish time and assume the infinite viewpoint on the latter part of the seventh path, we come to realize that nothing we have ever been and nothing we will ever become is more important than the life we are presently living. As human beings, we have been given the common mission of bringing the unlimited potential of the Great Mystery into human forms and walking the marriage of heaven and Earth through the vehicle of a physical body. Millions of spiritual beings who have never taken a human form are watching us to see if we will live up to our humanity and our spiritual potential. Unimaginable numbers of Spiritual Essences are waiting for the unique opportunities that we have been given to BE human, and yet we take these magnificent physical experiences in consciousness for granted. Those angelic presences see the difficulty of our chosen human paths and honor the courage we have shown by enduring the forgetting of our own divine identities. The magnitude of this understanding offers us a challenge that we can choose to reclaim after we emerge from the void and need to redefine our purpose for BEING.

In taking up the challenge once more, we understand that we have housed our infinite spirits inside skin, flesh, and bone. We have endured the joys and sorrows of the human condition, but it no longer has any significance, for we recognize all that we have undergone is equal to the unfettered bliss of a spiritual presence who knows no separation. Having a body that endures heartache, that ages and hurts, sickens and dies, is a privilege that offers us an opportunity to accomplish a feat of ultimate value. Ultimately, we choose to endure the trenches of human pain and suffering by taking physical bodies again and again if necessary, because we honor the oneness in humanity. We understand that all human beings must discover the oneness for themselves, and we are willing to commit ourselves to that eternal quest and to assist all others with ultimate grace and compassion.

THE PARTY NEVER ENDS, SO DANCE ON!

In the final stages of the seventh path, we can see that the melding and merging of all life force and points of awareness whirl into infinity, expressing individual dances that weave together so intricately that only a few courageous souls choose to view each thread of life in the Dream Weave through the microscopic lens of the human Sacred Point of View. Coyote snickers and reminds us that our personal dances within the universe, known as "the evolving consciousness party," never end. Coyote whispers that we just change costumes a few times, but in the interim between dances, we all yank off our masks and try diligently not to be blinded by one another's radiant light. When the music starts up again, we don our masquerade costumes and giggle to one another as we return to the Earth walk of human life, where we instantly forget who we are, why we came, and that we are only playing the infinite enlightenment game. Coyote laughingly calls this form of human forgetting "one huge, spiritual hangover"! The Trickster reminds us that we must have been drunk on the Great Mystery's love potion and were blissed out when we volunteered for human duty on planet Earth!

We can trust that Coyote, the divine Trickster, already knows what it means to see the exquisite joy of oneness and the brief moments of our human despair as being equal. To endure the tragedies of the human condition is why we all volunteer to return, and to offer kindness to the brokenhearted who have forgotten that they too are infinite spiritual beings who are not alone. We return to walk the Earth and to offer a multitude of sacred paths that will help every human being to tap into and embrace the Remembering.

We eventually rediscover that we will continue to evolve beyond this time and space. Since we are eternal beings, our consciousness is ultimately connected to the Great Mystery, and one day we will meld our consciousness with stars, planets, galaxies, and nebulae, assuming those identities as we continue the paths of awareness available in the oneness of this universe. The process is already in motion when we connect to the universe as it exists within us. We are in training for the ever-unfolding adventure of BEING, which evolves beyond matter and time, beyond duality and into absolute oneness.

Human transformation is the many-patterned path that flows throughout time and space, attached to matter, and challenged by the limitations of our human frailty, experiencing life in a human body. Every part of the discovery process can be expanded beyond our wildest imaginations. When we authentically attain all of the skills presented by the lessons on all seven paths, the journey begins again. The eternal viewpoint of the infinite spirit settles within the human form and continues the moment-by-moment process of mastering the challenges of life on planet Earth, accumulating grace and compassion. In the process it is our Earth Mother who sheds a joyous homecoming tear and opens her majestic arms, whispering, "Welcome home."

On the final lessons of the seventh path we see the infinite state of BEING, and we know that the journey is never over. We learn that we are being exactly what we are being at any given moment, and that we are all reflections of the constantly evolving universe, divine expressions of the Great Mystery's love. The physical realms are equal to the nonphysical realms, and each person's path is one part of divine expression that is no greater or lesser than any other. We all wear a series of masks that hide the divine presence and eternal identity of our Spiritual Essence. Life's journey beyond the seventh path contains no final frontiers. For some people, the completion of the paths of initiation can make those former rites of passage seem like faraway dreams, as if everything happened in another lifetime. However, we continue to envision many new horizons as we seek further wholeness. We learn to reaffirm the presence of divine, compassionate grace inside ourselves and stand tall in that presence. The completion of the seventh path simply means that we are awake to the unlimited possibilities that we can choose to embrace within our universe and in other universes of sound, light, movement, and content. We have gone full circle, arrived within, and we choose to walk the wisdom that we have encountered, using a physical body, dancing the dream of infinite oneness in the here and NOW.

Glossary

Above Direction. (1) The fifth direction on the Medicine Wheel, which traditionally teaches us to explore the mysteries of the heavens, the intangible, the Sky Nation, the stars, the heavens, other planets, spiritual consciousness, and the Great Mystery. (2) The fifth path of transformation, where we discover the wonders of the energetic parts of Creation and we explore the vast realms of consciousness available to us in our universe. We go beyond the physical aspects of life and journey into realms of awareness and other realities that exist simultaneously within the universe.

Altered State of Consciousness. (1) A shift in our normal sensory perceptions that allows us to perceive the intangible or energetic counterparts to our everyday world. (2) The ability to use any form of perception that we have personally developed to reach states of heightened awareness.

Banishing Time. An ability to be fully in the NOW with no duality, no judgments, and no internal mental chatter. In this state of awareness we have no need to alter time, no need to possess time, no need to turn time back or to hurry time along, because all time periods are accessible in the present moment. We have authentically banished the linear illusion of time and see the present moment from an infinite viewpoint, which includes all that has been and all that will be.

Below Direction. (1) The sixth direction on the Medicine Wheel, which teaches us to connect to the Earth and the wonders of the natural world and to ground our spirits in our physical bodies. (2) The sixth path of transformation, which teaches us to take the content of our personal empowerment, authentic abilities, and intimate connections to the universe and to bring those aspects of self into alignment with the Earth Mother and the Great Mystery simultaneously, using the physical body as the connecting link between the two.

Dark Night of the Soul. Any period of time in a person's life when chaos and confusion continue without a break. Life will often present challenge after challenge, one heartache after another, or ongoing devastating experiences without any relief in sight. These periods force us to reevaluate what we think, how we feel, what is really important, which values give us strength, and what to let go of that no longer serves us. These Dark Nights create major reality adjustments that force us to reevaluate our priorities.

Divine Intervention. (1) An unexplainable event that changes any course of action and alters the outcome. (2) Miracles or a magical shift in the course of any path that brings a beneficial and totally unexpected outcome. (3) When the divine presence of the Creator, the Great Mystery, God is felt and experienced in a person's life. (4) When spirit removes obstacles from one's path and creates an unseen safety net of loving protection.

The Domino Effect. (1) The leveling mechanism that strips the mind of entire false belief systems and acts like a row of dominos standing on end. When the first false belief is tipped over, the rest fall, down to the last domino. (2) The radical shift in perceptions that occurs when we remove a false idea that unravels mentally constructed belief systems, stripping the mental circuits that once propelled our responses to life through rigidly held views of reality.

Dreamers. In the Native American context, Dreamers are gifted tribal members who can accurately access information while sleeping. Information acquired by Dreamers can be found in the form of prophetic dreams, dreaming the locations of lost people or possessions, dream encounters that contain spiritual instruction, and/or messages from the spirit world.

Dreaming. All forms of dreaming include images that can be found only by shutting off the mental chatter and entering the stillness or silence of Tiyoweh. (1) When people sleep and dream they are shutting off the conscious mind, which allows the intangible realms of consciousness to be accessed with accuracy. (2) The waking forms of dreaming are sometimes considered to be visions, visitations, and/or psychic impressions. (3) Dreaming also includes images internally or externally experienced while in meditation, hypnotic regression, or deep relaxation.

The Dreaming Body. (1) The energetic or spiritual form containing the unlimited human consciousness. The Dreaming Body can separate from the physical body and is the vehicle used to travel out of body and explore other levels of awareness. (2) The Dreaming Body is also the nonphysical duplicate of our physical form, which we use to gain access to the intangible realities created by all others forms of consciousness and layers of awareness existing within our universe.

Dreamspace. All the levels of consciousness one can tap into while sleeping, meditating, or entering an internal place of stillness. In waking states or sleep states one gains access to the Dream Weave, and the dreamspace is held in place by the boundaries of the individual's consciousness. Entering the boundaries of another person's dreamspace without permission can create physical harm or holes in the energy field of the person experiencing the altered state of consciousness.

Dream Weave. The intangible web of life, which is comprised of threads of energy, thought, emotion, intent, ideas, and life force; the connective tissue that exists in our universe as the unseen energetic pathways, forming a web that is connected to all solid matter, all levels of awareness, and all animate and inanimate life forms.

Earth Walk. (1) A physical, human lifetime. (2) The birth-through-death walk upon the Earth Mother that is experienced by human beings. (3) Your life and experiences here on our planet.

The East Direction. (1) The beginning direction on the Medicine Wheel, which represents the dawning of life, the place where the sun rises, our physical and spiritual places of birth. Traditionally, the East is the place in life where we encounter illumination, clarity, and inspirational breakthroughs. The East Direction is also the place of unconditional love and the location of the Golden Door of Illumination opening into the intangible worlds of the Dream Weave. (2) The first path of transformation, where we are suddenly awakened to the realization that we have a purpose in life and that we choose to serve humanity.

Energetic Boundaries. (1) The boundaries set by using our intent in
the everyday world to alter a potentially dangerous or negative situation by changing the focus of the event. We do this by accurately observing and by diverting attention from the negative into the positive
through our words or actions. (2) The boundaries set in the Dream
Weave by using our intuition and keen observation. To accomplish this,
we must be fully present and totally attentive to the energy we feel
coming into our Sacred Spaces. The mastery of this ability is determined by how much we allow ourselves to feel without being influenced by the emotions that remain unhealed within ourselves.
Accuracy depends completely on one's ability to hold the viewpoint of
a neutral witness, deflecting other-determined energy or the intentions
of others from altering our sense of well-being and balance.

Enlightenment Trap. (1) Any behavioral sidetrack or seductive detour
that lessens personal integrity or that blinds a person to his or her inappropriate actions. (2) A test set up by an individual's Spiritual
Essence that allows a person to follow a crooked path, which diffuses
impeccability and personal integrity, until he or she becomes aware of
the dead end created by the decision to ignore the obvious.

The Eternal Flame of Love. (1) The principle of love, which is seen as
a central flame or spark of life force inside the spirit. (2) The divine
essence of the Creator's unconditional love, which abides in the center
of every living thing. (3) The singular essence common to all life in our
universe, which transcends the illusion of separation. (Also see Spark
of Life.)

Fire of Creation. (1) The central creative force within this universe
which appears as blinding light or a blazing fire. (2) The eternal fount
of creative energy that streams from the Maker of All Things, God. (3)
The essential creative principle of the Great Mystery, which directs life
force to all parts of Creation and infuses all living things with the spark
of life or Eternal Flame of Love. We begin our spirit's journey by
emerging from that Fire of Creation, and upon the death of the body,
we return to that same source of light, being absorbed by the fire from
which we came. During the paths of transformation, we encounter that
light while in human form and our spirits are reactivated, remembering our missions and embracing our divine potentials.

Forgetter Mechanisms. (1) Any veil that keeps us from remembering
our purpose, our authentic spiritual identities, our connections to all

life forms, or our divine connection to the Creator. (2) Any activity that numbs us and keeps us from heightened sensory perceptions, such as avoidance, denial, addiction, or the refusal to be still. (3) The mechanism that is triggered when we do not listen or when we are ungrounded, namely, the refusal to be here now and to digest the obvious in the moment. We have no memory of an event when we tuned out what was happening or being said. When we are attentive, emotions accompany our experiences and can be recalled to reinstate full and accurate memory.

Future Selves. (1) The parts of our personal identities that exist in the future; who we will be in a year, ten years, after our body dies, or in some future life. (2) The part of the human spirit that has gone beyond the understanding that we consciously embrace in the present.

Generational Patterns. Ways of feeling, thinking, or being comprised of fixed ideas or learned responses that we adopt in our family environments. These patterns are unwittingly or actively passed from generation to generation because we view life through the lenses of acceptable behaviors, perceptions, or group thinking that we learned while growing into adulthood.

Great Fire of Creation. See Fire of Creation.

Great Mystery. One of the Native American names for the Creator, God, the Maker of All Things, the Great One, the Great Spirit. The Great Mystery embodies this universe. All tangible and intangible parts of Creation are the constantly evolving aspects of the Great Mystery. We are all cells within the divine body of the Creator, as are all other life forms and levels of awareness within this universe. For this reason, Native Americans capitalize *Creation*, as the Sacred Space and/or divine body of the Great Mystery.

Great Smoking Mirror. (1) The Mayan concept of the mirror presented by life, which allows us to see the reflections of ourselves through the behaviors of others. (2) The smoke that wafts in front of life's mirror that forms the illusion of separation, which keeps human beings from recognizing themselves in the faces of others. When we see beyond the illusion, we recognize that we are all one.

Healed Healer. (1) Anyone who has released being victimized by old wounds or personal history, having healed his or her past experiences, issues, feelings, and fears. A healed healer no longer lives his or her life through the lens of past wounds and faces life with the clarity of being in the present moment. If old pain is triggered in a present situation, the healed healer can feel it and release it in the NOW. (2) Any individual who has healed his or her life and offers loving assistance to others in any way that he or she can. The act of supporting others in their growth process makes everyone who can listen, offering kindness and encouragement, a healer.

Initiation. (1) A rite of passage that tests a person's skills and expertise in any given area. (2) A ceremony used in ancient mystery schools to determine the level of accuracy of the initiate's spiritual abilities. (3) In modern terms, life is the initiation, and the challenges we face daily are the tests, showing us our skills and our weaknesses and allowing us to see where we need to grow and how we need to change.

The Invisible World. Also called the unseen or intangible world, the spirit world, the thought universe, the alternate realities, or other dimensions of awareness. All are various terms for the layers of consciousness found in the Dream Weave. The unseen energetic elements of the Dream Weave are comprised of every thought, feeling, and awareness in the universe. The invisible world also contains the life force and spirit that is energetically connected to our physical world. *Dreamtime* is an Aboriginal term interchangeable with our Native terms: unseen world, invisible world, the other side, the spirit world, and Dream Weave.

The Medicine Blanket. A Native American metaphor for the fabric or solidity of everyday human life. The Medicine Blanket is the physical manifestation of the thoughts and emotions, viewpoints and judgments we hold internally. How we perceive the events in our lives is determined by the combination of our actions and everything we think and feel at any given moment. In certain levels of heightened consciousness we can see the moving patterns of energy that create the patterns of the Medicine Blanket as they spiral and shift around the solid objects found in our daily reality.

The Medicine Bowl. (1) A bowl used by Medicine people to grind healing herbs. (2) A blackened bowl filled with water used by Seers to see visions of the future. (3) A Native American metaphor for the human body, the vessel containing the spirit. (4) The symbol for the healing available to humankind.

The Medicine Wheel. (1) The Native American symbol for the wheel of life, which has no beginning or end. The Medicine Wheel contains the four cardinal directions of East, South, West, and North, which represent phases of human growth and transformation that can be accomplished by learning the lessons of each direction. (2) A physical representation of the Medicine Wheel, constructed with thirteen stones placed on the Earth in the twelve directions (like the numbers on the face of a clock) and one stone in the center. The Medicine Wheel's symbol of the circle of life teaches us the lessons of confronting life's challenges and seeing every experience in life as an opportunity for growth. (3) The symbol of the wheel of life, allowing us to count the cycles of growth and change that we undergo during our lives. The Medicine Wheel also teaches us that all life is interrelated and that all living things contain a divine purpose and occupy equal places within the circle of the whole.

The North Direction. (1) The fourth direction on the Medicine Wheel, which represents the place of wisdom, the Elder, the winter of human life, or the emotional and spiritual maturity gained through experience. (2) The fourth path of transformation, which teaches us to be compassionate and to share our wisdom with others, to live our lives with open hearts and to continue to learn. (3) The authentic beginning of the wisdom path, where we acknowledge that every living thing is a messenger and that every life event is an initiation and contains vital steps of transformation.

The NOW Direction. (1) The seventh direction on the Cherokee Medicine Wheel, where we learn to be fully present and aware of everything that is happening at every single moment in life. We learn the mastery of keeping all of our wisdom, integrity, and personal impeccability simultaneously in motion, applying those pieces of wisdom to the present moment without being drawn into the past or the future. (2) The NOW is also the seventh path of transformation, where we have emerged from the void in the center of the universe and must reconstruct our lives to incorporate all that we have experienced, bringing those multidimensional viewpoints into wholeness inside the body and being fully present with all perceptions fully operational. (Also see the Within Direction.)

Past Lives. (1) The concept that our souls have experienced many lifetimes and that we take new bodies and are born again and again in order to gather understanding of the human condition. (2) The spiritual teaching of some, but not all, Native American tribes that human beings have walked the Earth Mother in many different time periods and that our spirits return to partake in the human experience in order to complete the circle of lessons set for us by the Creator. (3) Any former life that one's soul has experienced in physical form.

Pop Quiz. (1) Life's ability to test us unexpectedly on anything we have learned. (2) The reappearance of situations and/or issues that we believed we already handled and learned from. (3) Unwelcome surprise encounters that allow us an instant replay of former uncomfortable situations, giving us the opportunity to step outside the arena of conflict and to handle the situation by refusing to react in the previous manner, which created polarity.

The Remembering. (1) The process of spiritual awakening, where human beings begin to reassemble all fragments of the human potential. (2) The healing process whereby we heal our past wounds and our self-defeating behaviors and feelings, allowing the veils of separation that we once held in our consciousness to be lifted. We begin to remember our roles within Creation, our divine purpose for being human, and our connections to our Spiritual Essences.

Sacred Point of View. (1) The personal viewpoint of reality constructed through the accumulation of all that one believes, feels, knows, and has experienced. (2) The viewpoint sacred to an individual and totally unique because no other human being will have the same database of experiences, thoughts, talents, abilities, and feelings. From this personal Sacred Point of View, human beings can perceive the energy and the solidity within our universe and can choose how to relate to their individual views and experiences in life.

Sacred Space. The energy field surrounding an individual and containing all his or her thoughts, feelings, issues, perceptions, including the person's body, possessions, creations, and dreams. In the Native American definition, this Sacred Space is found in between in the inbreath and the outbreath, in the space between two heartbeats.

Seers. The Native American term for a person gifted with extrasensory perceptions who gains access to the intangible realms while in waking states. The Seer makes accurate information available through the use of heightened senses, which can include, feeling, seeing, healing abilities, prophecy, hearing the voices of spirit, or conceptual perceptions of the intangible energy found in the Dream Weave.

Spark of Life. The divine creative spark placed inside every atom in the universe; the infinite essence or spiritual part of the Creator, the Great Mystery, God residing in every part of Creation within the universe. (Also called the Eternal Flame of Love.) Through this spark of life inside our beings, we are able to become living extensions of the boundless creative force funneling through the Great Mystery. The seven paths of transformation allow humans to rediscover their individual sparks of life and to embody that creative force through personal divine connections.

Spiritual Essence. (1) In the Seneca language the Spiritual Essence is called the *Orenda*. The Spiritual Essence contains the divine essence or spark of life that the Creator placed inside the eternal identity of each soul or spirit. The Spiritual Essence can inhabit a human body, but when that body dies, the Spiritual Essence is infinite and fully conscious with or without a physical form. (2) The infinite, multifaceted identity of a person's spirit, which is a living, eternal extension of the Creator, the Great Mystery, God. (3) The eternal aspect of human beings, called the soul or the spirit by many spiritual traditions.

The South Direction. (1) The second direction on the Medicine Wheel, traditionally the place of childlike wonder, innocence, and humility. (2) The second path of transformation, which teaches us to eliminate any feelings, behaviors, and ego-based activities that keep us from attaining humility. We learn to readopt the magic of childlike innocence, healing any desire for revenge-based behaviors. On the second path we begin to move beyond being controlled by envy, jealousy, or bitterness.

Temple of the City. (1) A term coined by my teacher, Joaquin Muriel Espinosa, to describe the task of maintaining integrity and spirituality while interacting with life in our modern world. (2) Joaquin's concept of the difficult lessons that teach us to deal with all forms of chaos in our lives while we embrace the unseen aspects of the universe, balancing chaotic activity and stillness with grace. He said it was easy for people in monasteries to be spiritual, but the modern initiate who has embraced the paths of transformation is afforded no rest or quiet to assist the process, adding to the degree of difficulty a hundredfold.

Tiyoweh. (1) A Seneca-language word for the stillness or silence that we encounter internally when there is no chatter coming from the mind's thoughts. (2) The activity of Native American spiritual discipline translated literally as "Entering the Silence."

Twilight Masters. Individuals who have mastered the use of the light and the dark sides of human nature in order to control or manipulate others. Instead of integrating the two sides to attain balance, they show their understanding of the light to fool unsuspecting humans, and they employ their mastery of dark forces to harm people they consider to be opponents. Twilight Masters also use the lure of claiming to be spiritually enlightened in order to draw others of goodwill to their way of thinking. By masquerading as a spiritual, caring individual, the Twilight Master influences or bends the resolves of other spiritually committed individuals in order to serve his or her hidden agendas and selfish aims.

Universal Citizen. A human being who has compassion and cares for all of humankind, no matter what religion, political viewpoint, nationality, sexual preference, race, gender, creed, social standing, or color of skin. The universal citizen relates to all religions and spiritual practices with respect and judges none as being the only way to achieve enlightenment.

Veils of Separation. (1) The layers of illusion that require humans to learn through duality or polarity. (2) The seven forgetter mechanisms that keep human beings from remembering the infinite viewpoint of oneness held by the Spiritual Essence. (3) The seven levels of unconsciousness adopted on the physical plane when a spirit takes a human body. (For specific details on each of the Veils of Separation, see chapter 2.)

Visitations. The visual appearance of Ancestor spirits, angels, spirit guides, power animals, relatives who have passed over, or nature spirits that are not in physical form. In some spiritual traditions, these visitations are looked upon as visions and/or divine intervention.

Way of the Weird. (1) The Norse or Viking concept of divine intervention. In ancient times, when the course of events changed in an unexplainable fashion, the sudden shift was attributed to the gods, the hand of divine intervention. (2) Today, we use the word *weird* to denote something out of the ordinary, strange, or undesirable, but in its original form it referred to the divine presence changing the course of one's life in a manner beyond human comprehension.

The West Direction. (1) The third direction on the Medicine Wheel, which is the place where the sun sets, the time of introspection, healing, and listening. (2) The third path of transformation, where we learn to heal our bodies, our judgments, our relationships, our self-esteem, and our unwanted habits. The path where we begin to develop our intuition and our ability to listen, and where we skillfully develop our personal effectiveness in life.

Will. The emotional body, which contains all feelings, emotions, desires, intuition, and heightened senses. In order to reach the heightened parts of awareness, we must clear the will. To eliminate any impediments to authentic personal will, we must heal any reactive emotions, desire for revenge, cruelty, and destructive impulses. When these base emotions are cleared, we begin to gain access to authentic personal will and intuition. Then we can experience any feeling that appears, acknowledge it without judgment, and allow it to move effortlessly through us without having to act upon the destructive impulses that the feelings formerly triggered.

The Within Direction. (1) The seventh direction on the Seneca Medicine Wheel, which teaches us to bring all parts of our experiences and wisdom into the human body and to walk with the beauty and balance of living those high ideals. (2) The seventh path of transformation, where we develop the ability to be awake and aware in all situations and to be in command of our perceptions from the physical perspective as well as from the infinite spiritual perspective of the Orenda, the Spiritual Essence. (Also see the NOW direction.)

Index

Elk Medicine, 103
Emotion; blocking, 73–74; collective
versus personal, 197–98; as energy, 11, 74–75; fear and false beliefs, 80; feeling, importance of,
12–13; fourth veil of separation
and, 33
Energy: all matter contains, 71, 236;
balancing, 159–60; colors of,
236–37; deflecting unwanted,
175–80, 178, 230–31; discerning
kind of, 208–9, 214–17, 230–31,
244; draining, 36, 37, 72, 110;
Dream Weave as, 10–11; Earth's,
244; emotions and, 72–74; exercises to ground, 212; feeling or
sensing energy directed toward us,
179–80; gathering, 11; grounding,
203–4, 212, 220; investing,
74–75, 135; mastering the flow,
213–16; misusing, 11; negative,
11–12, 72, 146; psychic bursts,
156–59; Second path and, 71; Seventh path and, 240–42; thoughts
change, 160–61. See also Fifth path
Enlightenment traps, 95–98, 109,
114–15, 117, 119, 124, 138, 140,
170, 172–74, 182–83, 184, 195,
227–31, 247, 258
Espinosa, Joaquin Muriel, 15, 25, 28,
30, 89, 112, 134, 183, 195, 201,
233
Eternal Flame of Love, 23, 33, 235,
258
Extrasensory perceptions: premoni-
tion, 58; sixth veil of separation
and, 34. See also Intuition; Paranormal experiences

Family, being respectful of, 47–48
Fasting, 29
Fear of abandonment, 105–7
Fifth path or Above Direction, 5, 30,
165–99, 203, 255; belief systems,
erroneous, 182; boundaries, 178,

180–82; collective versus personal
emotions, 197–98; deflecting
unwanted energy, 175–79, 178;
detecting energy of others,
179–80; issues to resolve, 172–74;
letting go, 170–72; oneness,
167–68; physical symptoms,
188–89, 204; spiritual authority,
174–75, 217–18; Temple of the
City, 195–96, 242; timing and
readiness, 196–97; Twilight Masters, 183–84; universal citizen,
165–67, 264; visions and paranormal experiences, 168–70,
184–88, 190–94, 196, 197–99
Final beginning, 55–56
First path or East Direction on the
Medicine Wheel, 5, 45–64, 257;
balance, 62–64; being respectful,
47–49; bending without breaking,
61; choosing to be our personal
best, 50–51; examination of beliefs, 54; expanding tunnel vision,
56–57; final beginning, 55–56;
first veil and, 55–56; as rite of passage into adulthood, 45; serving
others, 51–55; spiritual warrior,
becoming, 59–60; wake-up calls
and, 49–50; weird or paranormal
experiences, 57–59
Ford, Neela, 148, 149
Forgetting/forgetter mechanism, 14,
151–52, 174, 205, 258–59
Forgiveness and release of the past, 76,
83
Fourth path or North Direction on the
Medicine Wheel, 5, 129–62, 261;
balance, 145, 159–60; bliss, pit-
falls of, 142–45; circles of self,
146–47; developing psychic gifts,
156–57; door between worlds,
161–62; dreams, 147–50; embracing opposites, 154–56; energy
bursts and physical changes,
157–59; energy directing,